IMPROBABILITY, CHANCE, AND THE
NINETEENTH-CENTURY REALIST NOVEL

IMPROBABILITY, CHANCE, AND THE NINETEENTH-CENTURY REALIST NOVEL

∽

Adam Grener

THE OHIO STATE UNIVERSITY PRESS
COLUMBUS

Copyright © 2020 by The Ohio State University.
All rights reserved.

Library of Congress Cataloging-in-Publication Data
Names: Grener, Adam, 1981– author.
Title: Improbability, chance, and the nineteenth-century realist novel / Adam Grener.
Description: Columbus : The Ohio State University Press, [2020] | Includes bibliographical references and index. | Summary: "Reading chance as a tension between randomness and order, this book shows how novels by Jane Austen, Sir Walter Scott, Charles Dickens, Anthony Trollope, and Thomas Hardy resist the demands of probabilistic representation to develop strategies for capturing cultural particularity and historical transformation"—Provided by publisher.
Identifiers: LCCN 2020000043 | ISBN 9780814214428 (cloth) | ISBN 0814214428 (cloth) | ISBN 9780814278093 (ebook) | ISBN 0814278094 (ebook)
Subjects: LCSH: English fiction—19th century—History and criticism. | Probability in literature. | Chance in literature. | Realism in literature.
Classification: LCC PR861 .G74 2020 | DDC 823/.80936—dc23
LC record available at https://lccn.loc.gov/2020000043
Other identifiers: ISBN 9780814255933 (paper) | ISBN 0814255930 (paper)

Cover design by Regina Starace
Text design by Juliet Williams
Type set in Adobe Minion Pro

For Meredith

CONTENTS

~

Acknowledgments		ix
INTRODUCTION	Realism and the Improbable	1
PART 1 •	REALISM AND DIFFERENCE	35
CHAPTER 1	Probability, Particularity, and the Uncertain Futures of Austen's Very Minor Characters	41
CHAPTER 2	Reading Chance, Encountering Otherness in Scott	69
PART 2 •	CHANCE AND SCALE	97
CHAPTER 3	Dickensian Coincidence, Cognitive Mapping, and the Victorian Metropolis	101
CHAPTER 4	Odds, Statistics, and Chance: Problems of Causality in the Trollopean Bildungsroman	125
CHAPTER 5	Chance, Historicism, Hardy	149
CODA	The Difference of Scale	175
Works Cited		181
Index		191

ACKNOWLEDGMENTS

∼

ONE DOES NOT spend a decade thinking about probability and chance without also dwelling at length on related ideas of fortune and luck, so it is easy for me to see how this book has found its way into the world only through a considerable amount of good fortune and a healthy dose of luck. In its earliest forms, my thinking on these ideas was supported by a Sage Fellowship at Cornell University, as well as generous encouragement and feedback from James Eli Adams, Harry Shaw, and Laura Brown.

I am grateful for my experiences at Vanderbilt University, which were supported through the generosity of the Barbara and Frederick R. Suits Honor Scholarship. I would particularly like to thank Vereen Bell, Carolyn Dever, Teresa Goddu, and Mark Schoenfield—they provided me with my first and best models of what it means to be a scholar, teacher, and colleague.

This book would not have been possible without the support of a New Faculty Fellowship from the American Council of Learned Societies, which allowed me to spend two productive years at Johns Hopkins University where the final shape of this book began to come into view. I am grateful to Doug Mao, in particular, for his mentorship.

At Victoria University of Wellington, I have found myself among supportive and inspiring colleagues who make day-to-day life at the university a pleasure. I would especially like to thank Nikki Hessell, Dougal McNeill, Sarah

Ross, and Heidi Thomson for helping me to bring this project to completion through active encouragement as well as less tangible forms of support.

My favorite aspect of my time at each of these institutions has been the opportunity to work with bright, curious, and dedicated students. They have shown patience with me as I have worked through my thoughts about some of the novels I discuss in this book, and they continue to provide reminders of why I value the labor of scholarship and teaching.

Helpful comments and suggestions from anonymous peer reviewers enabled me to improve this book. Ana Maria Jimenez-Moreno and the staff at The Ohio State University Press provided valuable support as this book began to take material form. A version of chapter 3 appeared in *Narrative* 20.3 (2012), and a version of chapter 4 appeared in *Genre: Forms of Discourse and Culture* 50.1 (2017). I am grateful to The Ohio State University Press and Duke University Press, respectively, for permission to reproduce that work.

Over the years, my thinking on this project has been aided by friends and colleagues who have engaged with my ideas and helped these ideas to gain the kind of clarity that can come only with dialogue. I want to thank the following individuals who read drafts or contributed to my thinking in some form along the way: Sarah Allison, Nick Bujak, Hamish Clayton, Ben Glaser, Nathan Hensley, Ben Parris, Bryan Rasmussen, Jesse Rosenthal, Philip Steer, and Daniel Williams. I am especially grateful to Anna Gibson and Megan Ward, both of whom provided feedback and encouragement at critical junctures in this book's journey.

I have been very lucky to chance upon some wonderful collaborators in New Zealand. My work in the last few years with Markus Luczak-Roesch, Emma Fenton, and Isabel Parker has helped me to see the central concepts in this book from unexpected and surprising perspectives as I worked to complete it.

I owe a great deal to my family—my parents, Barb and Darwin; my brother Nick; and sister-in-law Kayje—for their love and support through the years. My parents instilled in me the values of curiosity and perseverance which helped this book come into being.

Finally, I dedicate this book to my wife and best friend, Meredith. This book would not exist without the considerable sacrifices she has made, as well as her uncountable, daily gestures of love, humor, and patience. Thank you.

INTRODUCTION

Realism and the Improbable

> But what does probability—a mathematical idea—have
> to do with fiction? The answer is: Everything.
> —AMITAV GHOSH, *THE GREAT DERANGEMENT*

IN HIS 2016 WORK, novelist and critic Amitav Ghosh identifies probability—or rather improbability—as the reason that "serious" literary fiction has yet to integrate climate change into its representation of reality (11). In explaining this claim, Ghosh articulates the basic tenets of "probabilism," a term that Peter Widdowson, in his work on Thomas Hardy, uses to describe "the orthodox critical discourse of realism against which" works have been assessed since the nineteenth century (Widdowson 17–18). Ghosh describes his encounter with a tornado in north Delhi in 1978, an event that was without precedent in the meteorological history of the region and one that he experienced only by chance, as he happened to be traveling that day by a route that he "rarely had occasion to take" (Ghosh 12). Even though the experience has preoccupied his imagination for years, Ghosh explains that he has never been able to "translate" it into fiction (16). The reason, he suggests, is that the event would evoke the "incredulity" of readers, since "only a writer whose imaginative resources were utterly depleted would fall back on a situation of such extreme improbability" (16). Ghosh clarifies that improbability here does not mean the opposite of the probable, but rather "an inflexion of it, a gradient in a continuum" (16). He asserts that the mathematical idea of probability has "everything" to do with fiction because probability theory and the modern novel came into being at the same time, in the same European milieu. Although the modern novel is "built upon a scaffolding of exceptional moments," the concealment of this scaffolding remains "essential to its functioning" (23). The novel's commitment to a vision of the "everyday" (17) generates the "irony of the 'realist' novel" (23): "It conjures up reality" through "a concealment of the real." According to the logic of probabilism, then, even though the effects of climate change now shape the fabric of our lived reality, the extreme weather events by which it is most directly experienced remain at odds with "the grid of literary forms and conventions that came to shape the narrative imagination in precisely that period when the accumulation of carbon in the atmosphere was rewriting the destiny of the earth" (7). Thus, for Ghosh, the realist imagination spurns the improbable because it is constrained by the dictates of both readerly belief and mathematical notions of frequency and likelihood.

By anchoring realism in a conception of the "everyday," the discourse of probabilism overlooks the fact that realist novels represent worlds that are deeply historical and often turn to the improbable to highlight that fact. To take one famous example: The flood that concludes George Eliot's *The Mill on the Floss* (1860) foregrounds the tension between the standard of probability and the imperatives of a realist mode attuned to cultural specificity and historical transformation. Eliot's flood has been critiqued using the language of probability since the novel's publication, revealing the continuities between Ghosh's contemporary discussion and a much longer tradition of associating realism with ideas of probability. Perhaps most notably, Henry James claimed in his 1866 essay on Eliot that *The Mill*'s conclusion was the novel's "chief defect—indeed, the only serious one" (930). Although there is nothing "essentially unnatural" about the flood, James claims this "*dénouement* shocks the reader most painfully" because the "story is told as if it were destined to have, if not a strictly happy termination, at least one within ordinary probabilities." Similarly, an unsigned 1860 piece in the *Westminster Review* begins by asserting that works of art must arrive at "an external probability and an internal harmony" (Carroll 139), which leads its author to conclude that the novel's "*dénouement* is altogether melodramatic" (143). Meanwhile, Edward Bulwer-Lytton, in a letter to publisher John Blackwood, asserted that "the Tragic" should "come step by step as if unavoidable," lamenting that it does not in Eliot's novel (Bulwer-Lytton, qtd. in Carroll 121–22). When Blackwood forwarded the letter to Eliot, she responded by admitting that "the tragedy is not adequately prepared" (Eliot, qtd. in Carroll 123). Yet as careful readers (and rereaders) of the novel know well, Eliot does plenty to prepare us for the flood, most notably through early and persistent associations of Maggie with the river, water, and even the idea of drowning. Moreover, the chapter where the flood arrives extends the novel's repeated references to periodic floods, as locals "talked of sixty years ago, when the same sort of weather, happening about the equinox, brought on the great floods" (473). The problem with the flood is not just its deficient preparation but also what another early reviewer called its "incongruity" (Carroll 228). The shock produced by the flood is linked to the feeling that it does not follow by necessity from preceding events and that it is of a scale too great for the "everyday" lives of Maggie and Tom. However, as many critics have emphasized, the world Maggie and Tom inhabit is far from static; Eliot depicts the lives of characters embedded in a world that is undergoing an epochal "world-historical" rupture into modernity (Hensley 50). The flood thus may be seen to materialize an incongruity between levels of representation: the particularity of the individual lives of the Tullivers and the "*epische Breite*" [epic breadth] of the historical backdrop Eliot claimed she was trying to achieve (Eliot, qtd. in Carroll 123). If the flood seems to fall outside of "ordinary probabilities," this asymmetry draws attention to the fact that Maggie and Tom inhabit a world that is historical rather than a timeless, unspecified everyday.

Improbability, Chance, and the Nineteenth-Century Realist Novel steps outside the framework of probabilism to argue that improbability is central to the representational aims and strategies of the nineteenth-century realist novel. It demonstrates how central figures in the realist canon—Jane Austen, Sir Walter Scott, Charles Dickens, Anthony Trollope, and Thomas Hardy—develop a realist mode that is fundamentally historicist in its commitments, and it shows how improbable events like chance and coincidence are integral to this project. It therefore argues that what is most important and interesting about realism is its capacity to represent a historical and contingent world, rather than its ability to occlude its status as fiction or to conjure a conventional (or convincing) depiction of the ordinary or everyday. Although the following chapters generally focus on more mundane events than Ghosh's tornado and Eliot's flood, these cataclysms highlight how important probability has been to theories of realism despite the fact that realist novels persistently flout our sense of the probable. The narrative strategies that are the focus of this study— Scott's experiments with the supernatural, Dickens's fondness for coincidence, Hardy's seemingly fatalistic use of chance—are the features of their works that have exasperated critics and befuddled students grappling with the concept of realism. This book recuperates chance and coincidence as tools for realist representation by linking questions of narrative representation to historical shifts in the meaning of probability. By relying upon an implicit congruity between ideas of realism, credulity, and quantitative frequency, the paradigm of probabilism overlooks how the meaning of probability has changed profoundly over time. Narratives have been evaluated against the standard of probability since

Aristotle, but what that standard might imply changes with the meaning of probability itself.[1] These shifts in the philosophical foundations of probability are particularly significant in the nineteenth century, as an "avalanche of printed numbers" beginning in the 1820s transformed how probability theory dealt with ideas of causality, order, and randomness (Hacking, *Taming* 2). These changes were driven by the increasing interest in statistical conceptions of probability and were tied inherently to changing dispositions toward chance. A theory of realism based upon improbability allows us to acknowledge that realist novels frequently draw attention to (rather than conceal) their narrative scaffolding by defying our sense of the probable; to analyze the effects produced by novelists' strategic uses of chance; and to explore how the novel form participated in the "probabilistic revolution"[2] that transformed the way nature and society were understood from the nineteenth century onward. This book's central claim is that mathematical and statistical notions of probability are of little use as an evaluative criterion for realism, but that the evolution of these ideas is essential to understanding how the realist novel engaged questions of contingency, difference, and scale that accompanied the massive transformations of British society during the nineteenth century.

By approaching the formal question of narrative probability through historical meanings of probability and chance, this book demonstrates how the shifting foundations of probability raise fundamental issues about how narratives—and particularly realist ones—represent character and event. To discuss a narrative in terms of probability is to draw upon the complex, unstable, and often confusing matrix of ideas associated with the term. In a philosophical context, probability can refer either to our subjective states of belief or to objective frequencies in the world. As historians of probability such as Ian Hacking have argued, the modern concept of probability that emerged in the late seventeenth century is "Janus-faced": "On the one side it is statistical, concerning itself with stochastic laws of chance processes. On the other side it is epistemological, dedicated to assessing reasonable degrees of belief

---

1. Douglas Lane Patey notes that "since the time of Aristotle's *Poetics* it has been understood that 'probability' (or 'verisimilitude') may be a test of literary works, but the notion has seemed transparently commonsensical, so much so as to have no history, only periods of greater or lesser ascendance. But by treating probability as a stable category native wholly to literary criticism, as one that does not change and that can be understood without reference to larger contexts, literary studies cannot grasp or explain the phenomena they discuss" (x).

2. This phrase is the title of a two-volume collection of essays that appeared in 1987, where authors detail the spread of probabilistic thinking across the natural and social sciences. In his contribution, Hacking argues that the emergence of probability theory is not a revolution in the Kuhnian sense, but is nevertheless the "great philosophical success story" of the past two centuries: "Today our vision of the world is permeated by probability, while in 1800 it was not" ("Revolution" 45).

in propositions quite devoid of statistical background" (Hacking, *Emergence* 12). Although the subjective and objective sides of probability are now seen as distinct—and for some philosophers, incommensurable—interpretations of the concept, this distinction is *historical*: it emerges and is codified over the course of the nineteenth century.[3] In a literary context, probability can refer to a narrative's fidelity to the external world or to its internal consistency or patterning. As Harry E. Shaw puts it, "Probability involves our sense of a novel's 'fit,' both the way it fits the world that it imitates and the way its parts fit together to produce a unified whole" (*Forms* 21). Although one could argue that the philosophical and literary discourses of probability have little to do with each other, Ghosh's brief discussion illustrates how deeply they are intertwined in critical discourse. In claiming that the mathematical idea of probability has "everything" to do with fiction, Ghosh brings together ideas of statistical frequency (the rarity of the tornado), degrees of belief (the "incredulity" it would evoke), narrative construction (the "scaffolding" of narrative events), and fidelity to the external world (the necessary "concealment of the real"). These different meanings of probability are held together by commonsense notions of realism that take the world itself as given and assume that some fictional works aim to reflect or reproduce that givenness.

However, by rearticulating Aristotle's conception of narrative probability in the quantitative terms of modern probability theory, discussions of fictional probability have often relied upon an implicit appeal to the universal, thereby evacuating realism of its capacity to represent historical difference and change. In identifying plot—the imitation of action and events—as the most important component of tragedy, Aristotle's *Poetics* enshrined probability as a governing norm of narrative causality. According to Aristotle, "The function of the poet is not to say what *has* happened, but to say the kind of thing that *would* happen, i.e. what is possible in accordance with probability or necessity" (16; translator's emphasis). That this Aristotelian understanding of narrative probability is still operative in the nineteenth century is clear from

---

3. In regard to different interpretations and terminologies of probability, Donald Gillies notes: "Most philosophers of probability agree that the various interpretations of probability can be divided into two broad groups. Unfortunately, there are considerable differences among philosophers about how these two groups should be named. [. . .] Interpretations of probability [can] be divided into (1) *epistemological* (or *epistemic*) and (2) *objective*. The difference is this. Epistemological interpretations of probability take probability to be concerned with the knowledge or belief of human beings. [. . .] Objective interpretations of probability, by contrast, take probability to be a feature of the objective material world, which has nothing to do with human knowledge or belief." Complicating matters is the fact that "some advocates of a particular interpretation of probability regard this interpretation as the only valid one. [. . .] It is, however, possible to argue that one interpretation of probability is valid in one particular context, and another in another" (2; original emphasis).

Bulwer-Lytton's remark that the inadequately prepared tragedy of *The Mill on the Floss* "fails accordingly in the pathos and terror it would otherwise excite" (Bulwer-Lytton, qtd. in Carroll 122). Bulwer-Lytton here rehearses Aristotle's dictum that tragedy succeeds in "evok[ing] fear and pity" when "things come about contrary to expectation but because of one another"—that is, when the plot is organized according to probability and necessity rather than by chance (Aristotle 17). At the same time, it is also clear that by the nineteenth century, discussions of narrative probability were being shaped by the terms and assumptions of the modern, quantitative notion of probability. The reviewer of *The Mill on the Floss* who emphasized the need for both "external probability" and "internal harmony" takes up but extends Aristotelian principles. When Aristotle speaks of the probability of plot, he means the internal probability or harmony of the poetic work. Indeed, the philosophical value of poetry for Aristotle resides precisely in its ability to distance itself from the messy contingencies of history. To couple "external probability" and "internal harmony" is to confuse or even collapse Aristotle's categorical distinction between poetry and history. This development, however, shows how the early critical discourse around realism registers the influence of mathematical ideas of probability by reconceiving narrative probability in quantitative terms. As chapter 1 will show, this quantification of Aristotelian theory occurs explicitly in Richard Whately's 1821 review of Jane Austen. In his review, the logician Whately faithfully repeats the principles of Aristotle's aesthetic theory, but does so by speaking of probability in terms of whether the "*overbalance of chances*" is for or against a particular event ("*Northanger*" 90; original emphasis). Whereas for Aristotle probability was nonquantitative, opposed to chance, and tied to the universal, Whately sees narrative probability as a measurement of chances that reflects the fidelity of a narrative to "real life" (88).

If Aristotelian theory provides one context for understanding how narrative, probability, and notions of "the real" become intertwined, the expansion of finance capital in the eighteenth century offers another. Probability has been seen as a key link between the category of fictionality that defined the emerging novel form and the market economy in which that form circulated. The modern theory of probability that appeared in the late seventeenth century—discussed in more detail shortly—both acknowledged and rationalized uncertainty through a mathematical calculus that managed risk by subordinating individual cases to the stability of aggregate patterns. As Lorraine Daston has shown, the management of risk became institutionalized over the course of the eighteenth century in sectors such as the law, insurance, and lotteries through probability theory's capacity to transform uncertainty into calculable risk (112–87). In *Spectres of the Atlantic,* Ian Baucom has extended the work of Catherine Gallagher and Deidre Lynch to argue that these social practices—particularly that of maritime insurance—were underpinned by a "speculative epistemology" that defined the fictionality of the early novel and the operations of finance capital (59). Baucom characterizes this epistemology as an "actuarial historicism" and suggests that both the early novel and the culture of speculative finance relied upon a logic of typification that produced the real through an abstraction from particulars (43). The credit of finance and the credibility of fiction were mutually constitutive, creating a "new category of reference" (68)—a "'theoretical realism'" (32)—that was at once imaginative and true. As Gallagher argues, the "founding claim" of the novel form that emerged in the mid-eighteenth century was "a nonreferentiality that could be seen as a greater referentiality" (342). This fictiveness was a form of "imaginative play" (346) where the dynamics of belief can be linked to both the Aristotelian poetics of probability and the practices of speculation and credit that "helped even common people to accept paper money" (347).

Ideas of abstraction and aggregation continue to link the novel form to the production of the social domain into the nineteenth century, but, as probability theory acquires an increasingly statistical inflection, emphasis shifts from questions of referentiality and credit to the dynamics of contingency and order. Over the course of the nineteenth century, statistics underpinned a range of practices and modes of knowledge that resulted in the production of what Mary Poovey has called "the social body," and recent work in Victorian Studies has analyzed the form of the novel in light of these processes of abstraction and aggregation. As Poovey argues, the "gradual consolidation of a distinctly 'social' domain was facilitated by efforts to comprehend—to understand, measure, and represent" mass phenomena such as poverty (*Making* 8). The constitution and management of the Victorian social body relied upon an inductive formal logic that enabled the particularities of distinct objects, persons, and events to be stripped through "the imposition of a conceptual grid that enables every phenomena to be compared, differentiated, and measured by the same yardstick" (9). Nathan K. Hensley has shown how these processes were necessary for the projects of the liberal state and empire, illustrating the range of ways this formal logic and political rationality rely upon a "violence associated with the departicularizing processes necessary for inclusion into the democratic state's biopolitical model of care" (90). In a similar vein, Emily Steinlight has demonstrated how the various genres of the Victorian novel—from the urban novels of Charles Dickens and Elizabeth Gaskell to the sensation fiction of Mary Elizabeth Braddon and Wilkie Collins—give form to a "biopolitical imagination" capable of thinking about population and its excesses (3). While Hensley and Steinlight analyze how the nineteenth-century novel addresses notions of population and aggregation, Gage McWeeny has claimed that literature of the period captures the modern experience of living among a world of strangers in the urban milieu, arguing that the realist novel becomes the "engine of the everyday" (17) by remaking the stranger into "the bearer of a representativeness or generality" (18).

Whereas this body of scholarship focuses on the processes of abstraction and departicularization that accompany ideas of the mass or population, the novelists whom I examine in this book turn to chance and the improbable to affirm a commitment to forms of historical and cultural knowing that remain at odds with the "conceptual grid" underpinning statistical thinking. This book is concerned less with how the realist novel explicitly engages the increasing importance of statistics to a diverse array of nineteenth-century disciplines and discourses than with how the form of the realist novel negotiates the "figurational challenges" that accompany a world increasingly comprehended through processes of abstraction and aggregation (McWeeny 3). The realist novel's formal and thematic engagements with ideas of probability reflect an awareness of how probability became defined by the tension between randomness at the level of the particular and lawlike regularity in the statistical aggregate. I argue that probability becomes a problematic ideal for realist novels as it becomes tied to forms of abstraction and aggregation that are at odds with realism's commitment to historical and cultural particularity. This book traces how realist writers, in response to the paradoxical aesthetic standard that probability comes to represent, strategically turn to chance and improbable events like coincidence to render a world that is seen as contingent in its particularity, yet orderly, knowable, and even ordinary in the aggregate. Its attention to the importance of chance, coincidence, and contingency in the realist novel adds to a growing body of scholarship on how the Victorians responded to the experiences of accident, risk, and uncertainty that accompanied the modern metropolis. Work by Tina Young Choi, Elaine Freedgood, and Paul Fyfe has explored how the novel engaged thinking about risk and urban accidents that were both singularly unpredictable yet statistically inevitable across the social body. Fyfe's work on accidents and the Victorian metropolis, in particular, identifies literary challenges to social processes of abstraction and aggregation. As he argues, Victorian writers "counter[ed] empiricist and managerial attitudes" by "accentuat[ing] the randomness or accidentalness of the metropolis to other ends, specifically to challenge positivistic and politicized notions about causation, dis/order, and change" (18). Not only do the following chapters chart a longer history of how the novel reflected developing attitudes toward chance and contingency, but they also link these engagements with chance back to foundational questions of narrative form and construction that have been with us since Aristotle.

By reading the nineteenth-century realist novel in view of both transhistorical narratological concepts and historically specific meanings of probability, my approach privileges realism's capacity to represent cultural specificity, embedded experience, and historical transformation. On the most basic level, these novelists turn to improbability to come to terms with a world of difference, change, and transformation—a world, in short, that is historical. My approach to realism, therefore, challenges the idea that realist narratives are committed to creating a convincing or credible illusion of reality. Ghosh's assertion that the "'realist' novel" must conceal its "scaffolding" of exceptional moments embodies a prevalent position (or assumption) that realist narratives strive to conceal or occlude their status as fiction in order to immerse readers in their worlds. Hilary Dannenberg, for instance, offers a book-length account of the idea that all narratives are built upon a scaffolding of coincidences, but that realist ones can succeed only by hiding that fact. In her view, "realist texts [. . .] attempt to camouflage the ultimate, extradiegetic causal level of the author [. . .] by constructing a narrative world with its own intradiegetic connective systems" that encourage the reader "to believe in the internal logic and autonomy of the narrative world and thus that it is a 're-creation' as opposed to a fictional 'creation'" (25). Narrative theorists like Dannenberg are generally thinking about realism in a broader historical context than its specific nineteenth-century manifestations. Yet the reviewer of Eliot's novel who emphasized the need for both "internal harmony" and "external probability" highlights the origins of this narratological view in the nineteenth century. Henry James and his followers propagated the critical perspective that an author's presence ought not to be felt through (among other things) the exposure of a narrative's scaffolding. We can see, though, how probability provides the foundation upon which this conception of realism is constructed; it is a hinge upon which the Aristotelian principle of internal causal coherence could be extended to the idea of fidelity to the external world. Yet to claim that the degree to which a narrative solicits belief is contingent upon whether its event are statistically likely in the real world is to misunderstand the fact that our subjective beliefs about the world are quite different from the objective frequencies measured by statistics. My aim is neither to determine the validity of probability as an aesthetic standard nor to challenge the usefulness of readerly belief or "immersion" (Dannenberg 5) as a way of analyzing the experience of narrative. Rather, my aim is simply to show how the most important effects produced by these novels—and the dynamic engagements they create with their narrative worlds—are not predicated upon either cultivating belief in their reality or fulfilling the evaluative standard of probability. The manner in which these novelists consciously interrogate the idea of probability or construct improbable plots demonstrates that ideas of plausibility or believability can take us only so far in understanding the imperatives of the realist project.[4]

My effort to extend discussions of fictional probability beyond questions of credulity shows how nineteenth-century discourse around realism shifts from the issues of facticity and fictionality that accompanied the rise of the novel in the eighteenth century. While probabilism presents one conception of realism that associates the novel with the ordinary or everyday, another important line of thinking has argued that the novel form emerged not as an instrument of disenchantment—enforcing the ordinariness of the real—but rather as a vehicle of reenchantment. In particular, Jesse Molesworth and Sarah Tindal Kareem have both argued for the importance of the improbable to the codification of the category of fiction and the emergence of the novel in the eighteenth century.[5] For Molesworth, the irrationality and improbability of plot illustrate how the novel emerged as a form "seeking to heal the rift between the magical and secular worldviews" (2). Working within a psychoanalytic framework that sees novelistic plotting as an instrument of fantasy or desire, Molesworth establishes the connection between the culture of gambling in the mid-eighteenth century and the emergence of narrative forms that imbue the individual or the ordinary with a sense of renewed

---

4. In what is perhaps the most theoretically rigorous and sustained example of the critical discourse of probabilism, Robert Newsom concludes that fictional probability is best conceived as the effort to structure a game of make-believe that both reflects a reader's general beliefs about the world (allowing them to engage the fictional world as if it were real) while also creating a space of play where those beliefs might be revised. Newsom asserts that the question of how novels thematize probability is secondary to the question of readerly belief: "To look at how a narrative thinks about doubt, expectation, chance, likelihood" presupposes that we have already "enter[ed] a particular fictional world" (14–15). I approach the problem the other way around: I argue that the way narratives think about probability and chance must guide our consideration of what it means to "play the game" of fiction (to borrow Newsom's idiom), at least with realist novels. More recently, Karin Kukkonen has made probability central to her cognitive approach to narrative as a way of understanding how our engagements with narrative are a continually evolving set of probabilistic expectations.

5. In a slightly different but no less important vein, Srinivas Aravamudan has decentered the story of the realist novel's teleological rise by restoring the oriental tale to the body of eighteenth-century prose forms that included multiple realisms and generic categories that are overlooked by critical paradigms which privilege forebearers of the "eighteenth- and nineteenth-century high realist novel" (25). As he argues, "To separate novels as realist fictions of the mainline from oriental tales and romances, set aside as deficient precursors or accidental subgenres, ignores how prose fictional genres responded in different ways to questions raised at the same time about the value of fictional and nonfictional narrative" (28).

significance in a secular world Kareem likewise characterizes fiction as a vehicle for the reenchantment of the world, but instead of seeing the improbable as a manifestation of "paranoid fantasy" (Molesworth 9), she links it to the category of wonder—the effort to integrate the marvelous within the real. In linking the question of the willing suspension of disbelief required by fictionality to the philosophical foundations of Humean skepticism, Kareem shows how formal techniques of the early novel—such as defamiliarization and suspenseful plotting—embed uncertainty and provisionality in a manner that "cultivate[s] wonder as a rational response to the ordinary" (22). In stark contrast, then, to a probabilist definition of the novel in terms of the ordinary, these scholars demonstrate the importance of the marvelous and the improbable to the early novel. Yet for both, the realism of the novel is still tied to questions of believability and the reader's immersion in the world of the text: For Kareem, the cultivation of wonder is linked to fiction's "capacity to convince" (4), while for Molesworth the improbability of plot feeds into the psychological desire for a "pseudo-magical remedy for the discovery of one's own ordinariness" (9).

In extending this scholarly attention to improbability into the nineteenth century, this book shows how the function of improbability shifts once the category of fictionality becomes fully codified.[6] In particular, I show how improbability has less to with the dynamics of readerly credulity than with problems of representation. For the novelists I examine, chance and coincidence become instruments for cultivating specific forms of attention to the worlds they represent, supporting theorizations of realism that see it as fundamentally historicist in its aims and commitments. If narrative improbability is a structure of dissonance, it is one that can be reconciled with the historicist endeavor to both recognize and understand otherness, a project that some have identified as the defining feature of realism. Devin Griffiths, for instance, has argued that the formal structure of analogy grounds the invention of "comparative historicism" in the nineteenth century, a mode of thinking that "rejected static schemas, epic narratives, and the stability of earlier typologies of change in favor of comparing and analyzing local patterns *between* individuals, artifacts, epochs, and social systems" (3; original emphasis). Griffiths's work builds upon Harry E. Shaw's influential account of realism in *Narrating Reality* (1999), which argues that "nearly everything important about realism stems from its attempt to come to grips with the fact that we live in a histori-

---

6. In her reading of *Baron Munchausen's Narrative of His Marvellous Travels and Campaigns in Russia* (1785) and its sequels, for instance, Kareem demonstrates not only the continued instability of the category of fictionality in the late eighteenth century but also how, "by 1792, fictionality, the tonic for credulity, is itself taken for granted" (155).

cal world" (6). Realism, for Shaw, "involves, on a fundamental level, structures and relationships, not the 'immediate' presentation of objects or even situations" (94). It fulfills its "claim to tell us what our world is really like" not by creating plots that accurately mirror or mimic events as they unfold in the real world, nor by creating an illusion of reality that occludes its status as fiction. For Shaw, realism instead relies upon metonymical connections to create "a set of 'contingent' (that is, historical) and systematic relationships" (101) that facilitate a dynamic engagement with and "movement between positions in and above a given historical moment" (xii). Realism, that is, approaches the world in its historical specificity, aiming not simply to document its particularities but to leverage metonymy to grasp the underlying structures and forces that organize those particularities. It does not take the world or its meaning as pregiven or transparently accessible, but it does assume that there are structures that make it knowable, if only contingently. "At the most general level," Shaw suggests, "the realist novel attempts to forge connections between the disparate elements of a reality seen as radically historical, and to place the reader in a fruitful relationship with the tentative totalities it creates" (98). My approach to realism through the improbable shows how disrupting the illusion of "everydayness" can be a step—and perhaps a necessary one at that—toward representing the world as "radically historical."

Improbability, Chance, and the Nineteenth-Century Realist Novel thus turns to chance to read the realist novel's engagement with ideas of probability against the critical discourse of probabilism. In exploring how probability theory altered the way in which the world was conceived over the course of the nineteenth century, it shows how realist writers engage these shifting foundations of probability in their efforts to put readers into "fruitful relationship" with a historical world. As they analyze how these novelists leverage the improbable toward realist ends, each of the five chapters identifies how chance and coincidence are linked to core problems of realist representation: the didactic status of literature (Austen); the encounter with historical and cultural otherness (Scott); the experience of the metropolis (Dickens); the reconciliation of individual ambition and social order in the bildungsroman (Trollope); and the impact of evolutionary theory on conceptions of historical change (Hardy). Each of these problems embodies a tension between the particular and its obverse—the universal, the typical, the representative, or the average. This tension also defines nineteenth-century probabilistic thought. By decoupling realism from the probable, this book shows how realism developed in dialogue and even in friction with the probabilistic constitution of the everyday.

PROBABILITY AND THE "TAMING" OF CHANCE

The deployment of chance as an instrument of realist representation participates in the long and complex history of thinking about chance, randomness, and order. As Jason Puskar explains, one "simply cannot define chance once and for all, for chance is nothing other than a moveable category demarcated and applied in different ways in different contexts" (5). Puskar's reminder that all definitions of chance "must be historical definitions" (5) helps draw attention to how these ideas underwent particularly significant changes during the nineteenth century.[7] As Ian Hacking has influentially argued, chance was "tamed" over the course of the nineteenth century. By "tamed," Hacking means that the recognition and management of chance were one and the same process: The idea of chance as pure randomness came into being through modes of probabilistic thinking that demonstrated how such randomness conformed to regularities in the aggregate, thus mitigating the most radical implications of the aleatory. While literary studies of chance have tended to focus on specific historical periods, this era of the taming of chance in the nineteenth century has only recently begun to receive the attention it deserves.[8] Several studies have examined the relationship between modern probability theory and the early novel through to the end of the eighteenth century, while another body of scholarship has explored how the novel engaged the more radical meaning of pure chance from the late nineteenth century onward.[9] Recent work by Maurice Lee (on thinking about chance in nineteenth-century America), Paul Fyfe (on accidents and the Victorian metropolis), and Michael Tondre (on counterfactual spaces of possibility within the Victorian novel)

---

7. My discussions of the history of probabilistic thinking draw on the work of Campe; Daston; Desrosières, *Politics*; Gigerenzer et al.; Hacking, *Emergence* and *Taming*; Hald; Poovey, *History* and *Making*; Porter, *Rise* and *Trust*; and Stigler.

8. Maurice Lee notes that "literary studies of chance and related concepts have appeared irregularly over the last several decades, making the growing subfield, if one can call it that, more of an archipelago of interests than a central area of inquiry" (10).

9. Works on eighteenth-century ideas of chance and probability include Thomas Witmore on accidents in the early modern period; Douglas Lane Patey on philosophical and literary probability in the Augustan period; Rüdiger Campe on the imbrication of literary and scientific discourse in early probability theory; Thomas Kavanagh on chance, the novel, and the culture of gambling in eighteenth-century France; and Jesse Molesworth on chance and the eighteenth-century novel. Studies of later ideas include Jason Puskar on the "production" of chance in late nineteenth- and early twentieth-century America; Leland Monk and Julia Jordan on chance and the modern British novel from the late nineteenth century; and Brian Richardson on causality and modern narrative. Ross Hamilton traces transformations of the idea of "accident" from Aristotle through to the twentieth century.

have made important contributions to our understanding of literary responses to chance during the nineteenth century. Although Tondre's study does not examine "diegetic depictions of 'chance'" (2), it demonstrates how the Victorian novel embraced the profound sense of possibility that accompanied the "intensifying interest in probabilities" (12) across a range of sciences in the second half of the nineteenth century. Focusing on the novel's cultivation of potentiality and possibility—particularly through "marginal, abased characters" (16) who challenge the developmental logic of *bildung*—Tondre makes a compelling case for how the importance of "multitudinousness" (17) and alternate possibilities to the mid-century novel reflected the infusion of statistical conceptions of indeterminateness into the Victorian mindset. Overall, recent scholarship has moved beyond the oversimplified dichotomy of determinism/indeterminism in understanding Victorian dispositions toward chance, but theories of realism have yet to incorporate these more sophisticated reckonings with chance. With its fundamental associations with randomness, disorder, and a-causality, chance remains problematic for realism.[10]

Much of the difficulty of thinking about chance in the context of the realist novel stems from the fact that, during the nineteenth century, chance was—as Tondre succinctly puts it—"an idea in transition" (9). The relationship between the conceptual fields denominated by the terms *probability* and *chance* underwent a profound transformation over the course of the nineteenth century, as the two terms began as being closely aligned and then shifted to being opposed to one another. At the end of the eighteenth century, probability and chance were broadly overlapping or synonymous terms that designated the limits of human knowledge in a world that was understood to be deterministic. *Chance* was the name applied to events whose causes were unknown yet were assumed to be constant in their operation; *probability* delineated a field that rationalized decision making under these conditions of uncertainty. The world was understood to operate according to uniform laws,

---

10. Chance and coincidence have long been read as reflections of a writer's belief in providence, or what Thomas Vargish calls the Victorian novel's "providential aesthetic." John Reed, for example, concludes that "Victorians frequently attributed accident, chance and coincidence—all involving unexpected events—to providence" (132). Although chance can certainly be read at times as a reflection of an author's belief in providence, this framework oversimplifies the complex and shifting understanding of causality, order, and contingency in the nineteenth century. As Fyfe suggests, only recently have scholars begun to move beyond the "dated but persistent simplification that only with twentieth-century modernism can writers register the cultural impact of what science has revealed" (21). As an example of such oversimplification, Fyfe offers Stephen Kern's claim that "in the nineteenth-century novel, chance or coincidence was invariably a sign of some transcendent controlling destiny if not divine plan," while in modernism chance becomes "evidence of life's fundamentally stochastic nature" (Kern, qtd. in Fyfe 21).

but human knowledge of those laws was imperfect—chance and probability were ways of talking about this imperfect knowledge. By the beginning of the twentieth century, the two terms had become oppositional. Chance started to be understood as a feature of the world itself, while probability mitigated the idea of pure randomness by revealing how order and regularity existed in the aggregate.[11] This transformation in ideas does not, of course, occur in clearly identifiable or even progressive steps. Yet the instability of these terms (and the relationship between them) during the nineteenth century highlights their importance for understanding how novelists grappled with questions of agency, causation, and order. As Fyfe has argued in the context of urban accidents, "The unstable definition of accident between 1830–1870 is precisely what helped Victorians to interrogate metropolitan upheaval from multiple viewpoints—philosophical, legal, actuarial, and theological—resulting in complex notions of probability that have yet to be adequately recognized" (16). Likewise, the unstable meanings of chance in the nineteenth century reflect emerging recognitions of contingency, variation, and difference.

The unstable and shifting meanings of chance during the nineteenth century can be distinguished from how chance and probability were conceived within the modern theory of probability that emerged in the late seventeenth century. Lorraine Daston has called this early theory the "classical interpretation" of probability, which continued to develop through the eighteenth century and culminated perhaps in the 1814 publication of Pierre-Simon Laplace's *Essai philosophique sur les probabilités* [*A Philosophical Essay on Probabilities*]. This classical interpretation of probability was codified by a flurry of thinking that utilized games of chance to model rationality and expectation under conditions of uncertainty. Although ideas of probability (and games of chance) have existed since antiquity, documents such as the 1654 correspondence between Blaise Pascal and Pierre Fermat (regarding the equitable distribution of stakes in an interrupted game of chance) initiated a new way of conceiving probability.[12] The older notions of likelihood and probability meant, following

---

11. Charles Sanders Peirce articulated a modern belief in absolute chance in his 1892 essay "The Doctrine of Necessity Examined," and by the late 1920s an understanding that the world was irreducibly probabilistic had by been introduced by quantum physics and formalized by theories such as Heisenberg's uncertainty principle.

12. The relationship between the ancient meaning of probability and its modern incarnation has been a matter of some debate. Drawing on the work and theory of Michel Foucault, Hacking influentially argued that the emergence of mathematical probability in the seventeenth century was part of an epistemic shift—it was the invention of a new concept of probability rather than a reworking of an old one in modified terms (*Emergence*). For Hacking, the mathematical theory of probability is premised on a set of assumptions about the world and our knowledge of it that cannot be reconciled with the ancient idea of the probable as we find it from Aristotle through to Aquinas. Hacking's claim has been challenged, particularly by lit-

from the Latin *probabilis*, *"worthy of approbation"* (Patey 3; original emphasis) or "opinion warranted by authority" (Daston 11). The new mathematical notion of probability was, in contrast, quantitative and grounded in the evidence of the world. Although games of chance provided the primary context for this new mode of logic and mathematics, it was not developed in isolation and then applied to real-world situations and problems. Rather, thinkers such as Christiaan Huygens, Jakob Bernoulli, and Abraham de Moivre (along with Pascal, Fermat, and others) used stochastic situations like games of chance to develop a "calculus" or "doctrine" of chances that formalized rationality under conditions of uncertainty. While each individual trial (or "hazard") in such games appears random, that randomness can be rationalized according to a quantitative logic that follows from the fundamental properties of the game itself (e.g., dice have six even sides, etc.). The assumptions about causality and rationality that underpinned this theory allowed probability theory to be deployed across diverse contexts, from Gottfried Wilhelm Leibniz's work on jurisprudence to John Graunt's efforts to calculate the population of London. In its diverse manifestations and applications, probability theory reflected a new mindset that was both open to uncertainty yet committed to reasonableness—a mindset capable of fueling the rise of a commercial society.

The underlying assumptions about causality and human rationality within the classical interpretation are essential to understanding the implications of nineteenth-century shifts in ideas about probability and chance. In regard to causality, all of these early probabilists were strict determinists. Probability was not a measure of inherent randomness or chance in the world, but rather a corrective to human ignorance in a universe governed by necessary causes. Uncertainty was viewed as an epistemological condition of human limitation, not a fundamental property of the world. From the hypothetical point of view of God—or Laplace's notorious "demon"—probabilities did not exist; an omniscient view of the entire state of the universe would enable one to extrapolate both past and future because causes were mechanical and constant. Although these thinkers turned to probability in the recognition that certain knowledge was not possible in all realms, these probabilities were nevertheless seen as thoroughly rational due to the theory's assumptions about how the human

---

erary critics like Douglas Lane Patey and Robert Newsom, who are both concerned with the question (as I am) of aesthetic probability in the period of mathematical probability. The examples I have already adduced of how the Aristotelian idea of probability gets carried forward but reworked demonstrate how, despite significant differences, there are continuities between the ancient and modern conceptions of probability that render Hacking's claims of an epistemic shift unconvincing. See Patey, pp. 166–73, for a succinct summary of and argument against the "Foucault-Hacking hypothesis." For further challenges to Hacking's theory, see also Newsom, pp. 34–47, and James Franklin, pp. 373–83.

mind worked. The classical theory of probability united what we now see as the two distinct sides of probability: the subjective (or epistemic) dimension that refers to our beliefs about the world and the objective (or aleatory) dimension related to observed frequencies in the world. Over the course of the nineteenth century, these two facets of probability came to be seen as distinct. Today, when we talk about probability, we are talking either about the state of our beliefs or about objective phenomena, but we understand that these are two different things. The classical interpretation of probability, however, united an account of how the world worked and our beliefs about it through the workings of empiricist philosophy and the psychology of associationism. The classical interpretation was predicated upon the ideal of the reasonable man—*l'homme éclairé*—whose degrees of belief were inherently calibrated to the observed frequencies of the world. As one authority puts it: "John Locke, David Hartley, and David Hume created and refined a theory of the association of ideas that made the mind a kind of counting machine that automatically tallied frequencies of past events and scaled degrees of belief in their recurrence accordingly" (Gigerenzer et al. 9). Although the "artificial associations forged by early education, habit, convention, and prejudice" had the capacity to obstruct the rational reckoning of chances and lead to competing beliefs, *l'homme éclairé* remained the underlying ideal—both a presupposition and a goal—that rendered the protocols of the classical interpretation coherent (Daston 197). Therefore, while the classical interpretation appears to move inconsistently (and even incoherently) between the aleatory and epistemological facets of probability, the distinction between the objective world and our beliefs about it did not pose a problem to early thinkers in this tradition. The logic of associationist psychology not only enabled the development of the calculus of chances but also facilitated the application of probability theory to a wide array of areas and phenomena because it enabled nature to be treated as if it behaved like a game of chance.

Over the course of the nineteenth century, the classical interpretation of probability and its underlying assumptions of determinism and rationality were displaced by the frequentist model of probability, which underpinned the emergence and increasing predominance of statistical thinking. Whereas the classical interpretation uses quantification and odds to approach individual events, the frequentist interpretation is interested in the averages—or frequencies—that emerge as the number of trials increases. In the classical interpretation, probability applies to one throw of the dice; in the frequentist interpretation, probability refers to the trends that emerge as the number of throws approaches infinity. The classical interpretation assumes that there are constant, determinate causes but turns to probabilities simply because those causes cannot be known; the frequentist interpretation abandons the assumption that the world behaves deterministically, so it turns to probabilities to makes sense of how randomness yields to some kind of order in the aggregate. For frequentism, therefore, probability emerges from and makes sense only in the context of this aggregate. The transition that resulted in the triumph of frequentism was "neither sudden nor clear," and fundamental continuities remain between the respective models of probability (Daston 371).[13] The displacement of the classical interpretation by frequentism was less of a radical break than a transition whereby the quantitative intensification of activities (and the accompanying accumulation of data) caused a qualitative shift in the conceptual foundations of probability theory. Nineteenth-century thinking about causality—in both its philosophical and literary manifestations—grapples with this emerging understanding of a world that is knowable despite being contingent, variable, and unpredictable.

Historians have identified the decade between 1820 and 1830 as particularly significant in this transition. Hacking cites the "avalanche of printed numbers" that appeared during the decade (*Taming* 2), while others explain that "by about 1830 *l'homme éclairé* had given way to *l'homme moyen*," Adolphe Quetelet's iconic notion of "the average man" (Gigerenzer et al. 37). The numerical data that fueled this transition in ideas about probability was predicated, as Mary Poovey (*History*) and Theodore Porter (*Trust*) have demonstrated, upon the instantiation of "facts" and numbers as the foundation of systematic knowledge. The widespread movement to apply probability theory to social phenomena led to discoveries that challenged the underlying assumptions of the classical interpretation. Laplace's 1814 work marked the apogee of the classical interpretation while also straining that model to its breaking point. Laplace elided the differences between the natural and social sciences and suggested that both realms were governed by analogous causal structures: Not just natural but social phenomena as well could be treated as if they behaved like a game of chance. Yet instead of validating Laplace's theories, the ensuing wave of social data revealed variability rather than the presence of constant causes and the operation of underlying laws—at least at the individual level. In the aggregate, however, seemingly random phenomena exhibited a different kind of regularity and order. The discovery of consistency in the number of

---

13. For example, John Graunt's 1662 mortality tables can be considered statistical, as they tabulate social phenomena in a way that helped make statistics integral to the construction of the idea of the state in the eighteenth century. Moreover, even though the "law of large numbers"—the logical pillar of frequentism—was given that name by Siméon Denis Poisson in 1835 ("*la loi des grands nombres*"), its mathematical proof dated back to the work of Jakob Bernoulli at the beginning of the eighteenth century.

dead letters in the Paris postal system from year to year—to cite one famous example—revealed the ways in which phenomena that appeared unaccountable and even irrational in the single instance could display regularity in the aggregate. Instead of simply marking the limits of human knowledge, then, chance began to be seen as a property of the world itself, acquiring a "purported ontological status" (Puskar 7). This capacity to countenance chance, however, went hand in hand with the discovery that chance "disappeared in large numbers" (Gigerenzer et al. 37). The frequentist interpretation of probability thus made space for chance through its capacity to counterbalance its destabilizing power.

Frequentism altered the fundamental parameters of probability theory as the classical interpretation's assumptions about causal determinism and the rationality of the mind gave way to a recognition of the inherent randomness of the world. Whereas the classical interpretation united the subjective and objective dimensions of probability, they emerged as separate interpretations of the concept within the frequentist paradigm: The fundamental orderliness of the world could no longer be intuitively grasped through experience, and probability became more firmly tied to the aggregation of numerical data. The subjective dimensions of the classical interpretation thus came to be seen as liabilities that threatened the rational foundations of probability theory. According to Alain Desrosières, "a provisional boundary was erected" in nineteenth-century theories of probability, a boundary that entailed "rejecting the 'state of mind' side of probability and confining itself to the 'state of the world' aspect" (*Politics* 55).[14] In the process, the gradual "erosion of determinism" turned attention away from underlying causes to the patterns and regularity that emerged in the aggregate (Hacking, *Taming* 1). Whereas the classical interpretation of probability emphasized the position of the decision-making individual, the frequentist theory turned to the abstracted position of society viewed as a whole. At a basic level, the move away from the classical interpretation entailed abandoning its presupposition of causal determinism. The embrace of the law of large numbers supported a belief that observed phenomena reflected causes at work while acknowledging that the nature of those causes might not be knowable The possibility of chance necessitates a rejection of the hypothetical position of Laplace's "demon." Thus, in order to bring the "social body" into existence, the logic of frequentism constituted society as an independent entity that operated according to statistical laws that were distinct from those which obtained at the level of the individual. In tracing the

---

14. A subjective interpretation of probability was not formally theorized until the 1920s, independently but concurrently by Frank Ramsey in England and Bruno de Finetti in Italy. See Gillies, pp. 50–87.

foundational philosophical problems of statistics back to fourteenth-century debates between realists and nominalists, Desrosières identifies an inherent tension in the "magical transmutation of statistical work," which enacts a "transfer from one level of reality to another" through a "transfer from one language to another (from unemployed persons to unemployment)" (*Politics* 70). Statistics produces knowledge by granting "the status of reality" to the level of the individual and the level of the social in a manner that allows the two scales to "exist in partly autonomous ways." By the latter half of the nineteenth century—as we will see in chapter 5—probability theory was forced to confront the status and meaning of the "laws" of society: Could statistics really be considered a true science if the laws that it identified only obtained in the aggregate, rather than in every instance? Thus, as chance transitioned across the century from signifying the limits of knowledge in a deterministic universe into a true randomness that could nevertheless be managed through abstraction from individual instances, it also came to embody the core tensions of variation, scale, and order that defined ideas of probability.

THE NOVEL, CONTINGENCY, AND SCALE

The realist novel's engagement with ideas of probability speaks to the gulf that emerges between thinking about particularities and collectives, the individual and society. Chance provided novelists a narrative mechanism for thinking through and mediating the relationship between these scales of reality. The analytical partitioning of reality into distinct levels enabled statistics to bring into being a "society" that could be measured, analyzed, and even managed while also acknowledging variation and unpredictability at the level of the individual. By the end of the nineteenth century, ideas of the "average statistical type and its temporal regularity" (Desrosiéres, *Politics* 96) were deployed within an emergent sociological discourse to describe a "collectivity distinct from its members" (97). Yet the notion that we can describe reality at two distinct levels that operate in potentially independent and even incommensurate ways presents obvious problems for a literary mode that aims to "tell us what our world is really like" (Shaw, *Narrating* 94). Scholarship on literary responses to the emergence of statistics has demonstrated how novelistic representation was shaped by the specter of the collective that was both composed but paradoxically independent of its individual constituents.[15] This

---

15. Audrey Jaffe has traced how the notion of the "average" made available by the stock market graph offered an abstraction against which the individual and their inner life could take shape in novelistic representation. Tina Young Choi turns to the body to understand how

work has taken us beyond conventional ways of talking about the novel's representation of the individual and society, in large part by drawing attention to how notions of the individual could not be easily reconciled with the ways in which society was composed and conceived. In his reading of George Eliot's engagement with probability theory, for instance, Jesse Rosenthal suggests that while *Middlemarch* (1871–72) reflects Eliot's "implicit reliance on the ability [of the bildungsroman] to represent society as compiled inductively from individual units," *Daniel Deronda* (1876) illustrates her increasing skepticism toward this logic as she comes to understand that self and society cannot be understood on commensurate terms—one can no longer simply count up from individuals to arrive at an understanding of the social (159). *Improbability, Chance, and the Nineteenth-Century Realist Novel* explores how the idea of probability becomes a paradoxical standard for narrative representation as it becomes associated with collectives or aggregates that cannot be represented through individual instances. It shows how improbability becomes a means of accommodating the exigencies of particularity, difference, and scale that become suspended within statistical regimes.

Identifying chance as *a name for the tension between individual variation and aggregate order* helps us to see that realism requires an approach attentive to the dialectical relationship between randomness and order that characterized probabilistic thinking during the nineteenth century. Incorporating chance into our understanding of realism offers new and more robust ways of understanding how causality works in realist novels and, more generally, in narrative. Causality is central to discussions of literary probability, yet critics have erred in too readily adopting Aristotle's belief that narratives must eliminate chance in order to represent causal relations. For Aristotle, probability ensures that the literary work can reveal the causal connections between actions and events, and thus provide a form of instruction about how the individual ought to comport themselves to the fundamental order of the world. Chance is thus seen as problematic for narrative because it is an event whose cause cannot be known. While the logic of this idea can be reconciled with the foundations of the classical interpretation of probability, it is incompatible with an emergent nineteenth-century recognition of how order emerges *through* chance. Criticism has been unable to adequately account for this idea

---

the anonymous masses shaped understanding of social belonging and social interaction. And Emily Steinlight has argued that nineteenth-century novels "at once presuppose and challenge the principle of population" (12) by conceiving of mass life in a manner that "exceed[s] the scope of society as such" (13).

of chance, as the paradigm of probabilism has defined realism through its opposition to chance.[16]

Approaching probability and chance historically requires us to see how causality begins to be conceived in *distributive* terms over the course of the nineteenth century. It is worth recalling that at the end of the eighteenth century chance generally denoted an event whose cause was unknown yet determinate; a century later, chance could be conceived as an event without cause—a "radical indeterminacy principle" (Puskar 7). This transition occurred as thinking about probability recognized and grappled with the problem of variation: Statistical thinking challenged ideas of determinism while revealing order at a higher level. Quetelet's *l'homme moyen* offers an instructive example. The "average man" became "the powerhouse of the statistical movement" (Hacking, *Taming* 105) by formalizing Quetelet's "unshakable faith that regular patterns invisible at the individual level would emerge at the societal level" (Daston 382). *L'homme moyen* extended the idea of the "mean" or average that had emerged through the "law of error" developed by Carl Friedrich Gauss at the beginning of the century. Gauss established how measurements (e.g., of astronomical phenomena) produce a distribution of data points that reveals a true value—the imprecision of our instruments and errors in our measurements produce variation, but individual errors conform to a pattern in the aggregate. Quetelet embraced the idea that this normal distribution—the "bell curve"—could be extended to social phenomena to reveal the laws of society. Working from the chest measurements of soldiers in a Scottish regiment, for instance, Quetelet found a similarity between the curve representing the law of error and the distribution of those chest measurements. Such discoveries resulted in the application of this idea of the distribution to a whole range of physical attributes and social phenomena: The averages could say nothing of specific individuals but described the prevailing characteristics of the population or nation. Such a theory relies upon the assumption that there are "lots of minute and varying causes" that determine phenomena and that "a multitude of interacting independent causes tends in

---

16. Speaking of the shared concerns of Darwinian thought and novelistic representation, for example, George Levine asserts that "realism is programmatically antagonistic to chance, but like Darwin must inevitably use it to resolve its narrative problems" (*Darwin* 19–20). Similarly, J. Jeffrey Franklin extends Thomas Kavanagh's work on chance and the eighteenth-century novel to claim that "any narrative form, but especially that of novelistic realism, *must* work against chance and coincidence to the extent that it stages the intersection of characters and events that appear casually related" (44; original emphasis). And in order to set up his study of modern narratives where chance is foregrounded, Brian Richardson argues that nineteenth-century realism "led to the suppression of providential theology and the marginalization of chance" (42).

a large number of cases to produce a Gaussian curve" (Hacking, *Taming* 112). As Hacking notes, Quetelet's extension of the law of error to social phenomena is "not very coherent" philosophically, but it illuminates how statistics both created and mitigated the threat to "a deterministic world view" that accompanies the recognition of chance (114). My point about causality here is that probability and chance are no longer being conceived in reference to individual events but require an aggregation that allows order to emerge—chance refers less to the causality of an individual event than to how causes produce variation across a distribution of events. Thus, J. Jeffrey Franklin is incorrect to extend eighteenth-century ideas of probability to an account of realism by suggesting that "the 'unreality' of chance and coincidence was *produced* in the process of inventing what came to be recognized as 'reality' within a worldview shared and propagated by the ethos of novelistic realism and the ethos of scientific rationality" (44; original emphasis). Nineteenth-century scientific discourse—and, as this book argues, novelistic representation—constituted reality not by eliminating chance but rather by incorporating it.

By demonstrating how chance is essential to how the realist novel constructs oblique, complex, and diffuse causal relations, this book offers narrative theory more robust ways to think and talk about how causality works in narrative, particularly in the realist novel. If realism is defined in part by its effort to create causal networks and relationships, chance is a problem only if we think about causality very narrowly as a direct, proximate link between two discreet events. For E. M. Forster, the narrative "The king died and then the queen died of grief" provides a minimal definition of a plot because it offers a sense of causality, but this way of thinking about causality conflates it with the most basic idea of plot (82). A novel's plot is one facet of its representation of the world, but only part of how we interpret and infer causal relationships within a narrative. As Shaw argues in his elaboration of historicist realism, plots are "not the key to realism, or its cornerstone": "Their primary function is not to embody or impose meaning, but to lend force to our imaginings" and "to move us through the world of a novel" (*Narrating* 129). A characteristic example of Hardy's use of chance helps us to see why realist novels necessitate more capacious ways of interpreting narrative causality. Tess's attempt to communicate her history to Angel Clare on the cusp of their marriage fails by chance in chapter 33 of *Tess of the D'Urbervilles* (1891), as her letter is accidentally "thrust beneath [. . .] the carpet as well as beneath the door," preventing Angel from receiving it (211). While this event certainly belongs to the sequence of happenings that culminate in Tess's murder of Alec and her subsequent execution, to say that it causes or determines that "fate" in some way is to work with an impoverished idea of narrative causality. Any meaningful discussion of causality in Hardy's novel needs to account for the ideological and material forces that the novel works so exhaustively to render: the forces that cause Tess to choose to conceal her past and then communicate it later by letter, that cause Angel to react in the way that he does when he eventually learns of her past, that cause Tess to return to Alec when Angel departs, and so on.

Or, to return to *The Mill on the Floss*: The flood is the immediate cause of Maggie's death, but no sound reading of Eliot's novel would claim that the impossibility of Maggie's self-realization is caused solely by the flood. Her death is preceded by a sequence of events in the plot which bring her to that point: her love of Tom and the mill, which cause her to return to St. Ogg's when the flood begins; Tom's rejection of her following her elopement with Stephen, which leads to their separation; the movement of the "swift, silent stream" that carries Maggie and Stephen past Luckreth; and so on (431). More important, these events—to borrow Shaw's phrase—"move us through the world" of the novel, where Eliot paints the forces that obliquely but resolutely shape Maggie's life: the domestic ideologies that constrain female identity, the spirit of capitalist advancement embodied by her uncle Dean and later Tom, the imbrication of nature in legal constructions that initiate her father's feud with Wakem, and even an attention to energy regimes that "recognizes and emphasizes the distinct temporality of a steam-generated economy as opposed to a water-generated one" (E. Miller 86). All of these are, in some way, causally responsible for Maggie's demise. If we are to understand how realist novels construct "'contingent' (that is, historical) and systematic relationships," then we need to analyze how they establish causal networks in which causes are both direct and diffuse (Shaw, *Narrating* 101).

The "incongruity" of *The Mill*'s flood foregrounds the problem of scale that besets thinking about causality and representation in the period, and it suggests that while metonymy remains the foundation of realism's capacity to construct systematic relations, metonymy cannot fully mediate two levels of reality that are conceived on autonomous terms. The sense of incongruity—or improbability—that accompanies the flood is tied to the fact that the flood's destruction of Maggie is imbued with significance, but that significance exceeds the operations of metonymy. Eliot's novel constructs strong metonymical relationships between Maggie, Dorlcote Mill, and the River Floss, as well as between the mill, the river, and the social and economic forces that define Maggie's milieu. However, the flood's embodiment of the impact of those forces on Maggie's life and identity moves toward the metaphorical or symbolic. But if this amounts to a "defect" as James claims, it is one that points to the limits of metonymy to grasp the relationship between levels of reality—the individual and the social—that are constituted and understood as autonomous. For nineteenth-century probability theory to describe reality in a manner that allowed chance to be acknowledged yet tamed, it needed to forgo the ability to know the causal relationship between individual events and the abstract forces that produce order in the aggregate.

This problem of mediating a view of the individual and the social aggregate is a central one for realist representation. Tina Young Choi, for instance, has demonstrated how in the 1840s there was a shift "from a statistical emphasis on whole numbers that correspond, one-to-one, to persons [. . .] and toward an emphasis on percentages and proportions" (21–22). This shift, Choi suggests, was at odds with a liberal ideology that elevated individual agency and choice, as risk moved from something that could be managed through rational decision making and instead came to be distributed across the social field. Choi reads the famously bifurcated form of Elizabeth Gaskell's *Mary Barton* (1848)—a novel that begins as a "Condition of England" novel and shifts to a novel focused on individual moral agency—as registering the "epistemological shift" required to comprehend events as at once inevitable (from the perspective of the long run) and as a matter of individual choice (29).[17] Gaskell's novels rely upon sympathy to bridge the gulf between the individual and the nameless masses and to configure the aggregate process of social transformation in terms of individual action. Yet the formal divisions of a novel like *Mary Barton* attest to a fundamental incommensurability of scale that in some instances quite literally pulls narrative perspective apart. Perhaps the most dramatic example of this incommensurability is *War and Peace* (1867), where Tolstoy, on one level, represents the lives of individuals like Prince Andrei Bolkonsky, Countess Natasha Rostov, and even Napoleon, and, on another level, offers his notorious philosophical discourses on the shape and movement of history. In its extended reflections on historical causality, such as the effect of Napoleon's cold on the Battle of Borodino, Tolstoy's novel demonstrates that it is "centrally concerned with the problem of uniting the disparate levels of human existence, a problem which it knows to be insoluble but feels compelled to solve" (Shaw, *Forms* 123).[18] Likewise, as the novelist perhaps most

---

17. Fyfe, pp. 100–131, also provides a reading of *Mary Barton* in the context of probability, insurance, and statistics.

18. Drawing on the philosophical work of Siegfried Kracauer, Shaw's *The Forms of Historical Fiction* defines the mediation of different levels of human experience as the "problem" with historical fiction, arguing that no representation can capture and unite all levels of human existence. He also offers a lucid critique of Lukács's theory of "typicality" which I discuss below.

immersed in the impact of contemporary scientific and social discourses on thinking about causality,[19] Eliot's novels (and their narrators) move between different perspectives on events and actions in order to contextualize them in relation to abstract social developments and processes. Although I have used Eliot's flood as a point of departure here, her novels play no further part in this study—the ending of *The Mill* is noteworthy precisely because it deviates from Eliot's characteristic techniques. Whereas the following chapters focus on novelists who embrace the improbable for strategic representational ends, Eliot is typically careful to contextualize events that might appear coincidental or improbable so as to situate them within broader patterns or causal networks.[20]

In the realm of literary criticism, Georg Lukács presented an early and philosophically ambitious effort to theorize realism's capacity to represent—and mediate—the levels of individual experience and "the totality of society" (*Realism* 100). While his discussions of realism remain important because of his emphasis on realism's historicizing potential, the totalizing ambitions of his theory of realism offer a useful point of comparison for my interest in how improbability encodes the limits of realist representation. Lukács's belief in realism's capacity to render social totality hinges upon his understanding of "typicality," which he explains in the following terms:

> The *typical* is not to be confused with the *average* (though there are cases where this holds true), nor with the *eccentric* (though the typical does as a rule go beyond the normal). A character is typical, in this technical sense, when his innermost being is determined by objective forces at work in society. Vautrin or Julien Sorel, superficially eccentric, are *typical* in their behaviour: the determining factors of a particular historical phrase are found in them in concentrated form. Yet, though typical, they are never crudely "illustrative." There is a dialectic in these characters linking the individual—

See *Forms*, pp. 19–50, for the critique of Lukács based upon Kracauer's work; see pp. 117–27 for his discussion of *War and Peace*. While Shaw engages this problem of representation on philosophical grounds, I am interested in how this problem first emerged in nineteenth-century thinking about probability and chance and thus in how novels themselves grappled with its implications.

19. Accordingly, Eliot's work has drawn the most attention from scholars thinking about chance and statistics in the Victorian novel. See J. Jeffrey Franklin, pp. 34–79; Monk, pp. 46–74; Rosenthal, pp. 153–90; and Tondre, pp. 126–64.

20. For example, in *The Mill on the Floss*, Aunt Pullet's discovery of Maggie's secret meetings with Philip in the Red Deeps in Book V is preceded by the narrator's discussion of probabilities, coincidences, and "fatality" (313). Book VI of *Daniel Deronda* (1876) opens with an epigraph from Aristotle's *Poetics*: "This, too, is probable, according to that saying of Agathon: 'It is a part of probability that many improbable things will happen'" (509).

and all accompanying accidentals—with the typical. (*Realism* 122; original emphasis)

Lukács's approach to realism—which takes Scott's historical fiction as its point of departure—emphasizes the mode's capacity to represent historical necessity: "The complex interaction of concrete historical circumstances in their process of transformation, in their interaction with the concrete human beings, who have grown up in these circumstances, have been very variously influenced by them, and who act in an individual way according to their passions" (*Historical* 58). Although the world itself only exists in its "individual particularity," the individual "may become typical in its literary presentation" (*Realism* 124). As opposed to the *average* (who embodies the characteristics of an entire population), or the *representative* (who stands in for a class or species within a society), the Lukácsian type can mediate the particularities of lived experience and the material but abstract forces that govern society. While it is the idealist (i.e., Hegelian) underpinnings of Lukács's thought that motivate his belief in literature's capacity to render the social totality of relations and causes, it also requires him to adopt a peculiar stance toward contingency and chance.²¹ As chapter 2 will argue in more detail, Lukács's scattered discussions of chance offer some of the most insightful reflections on contingency and causality in the realist novel, yet they always culminate in a claim that an "intricate network of causal connections" creates a "necessity which nullifies chance" (*Studies* 56). My approach to realism takes its cue from Lukács's belief in realism's capacity to grasp, through narrative form, the contours of historical existence, but it also shows how realism figures the "dialectics of freedom and necessity" not by nullifying chance but rather by foregrounding it to figure the oblique causal relation between individual experience and abstract social forces (*Historical* 147).

The following chapters demonstrate how the turn to chance or the improbable is not inevitably a failure of the realist imperative; these novelists rely on the improbable in recognition of the limits of probable representation to grasp

---

21. Lukács admits that "the ideal of totality in art can never, of course, be more than a guiding principle" (*Realism* 100) and claims elsewhere that "the structure of objective reality" constitutes a "wealth [that] we can never adequately grasp and reflect with our ever all too abstract, all too rigid, all too direct, all too unilateral thinking" (*Studies* 58). Nevertheless, the Hegelian underpinnings of his thinking lend a totalizing logic to his theorizations. As Terry Pinkard observes, "Hegel has nothing to say about probability theory and its role in inductive logic," even though—given his knowledge of Leibniz and his interest in the modern state—he "should have known about it" (24n7). I would suggest that probability theory, in its nineteenth-century manifestations, is defined by a skepticism and commitment to uncertainty that is anathema to Hegel's systematic philosophy.

the terms of a particularized, historical, and contingent reality. Uncoupling realism from the standard of probability opens space for a theory of realism that is attuned to the shifting meanings of probability and chance during the nineteenth century. It allows us to see how chance enables these novelists to figure the relationship between lived experience and "concrete historical circumstances in their process of transformation" because it disrupts the probabilistic image of the world as universal, ordinary, or given (Lukács, *Historical* 58). In *The Antinomies of Realism,* Fredric Jameson highlights the "increasing tension between universalism and particularity (or even singularity) in modern times," a tension that results in a "curious and dialectical process" of negation within the realist tradition (144). When a genre takes hold, it "eventually comes to be identified as the universal" and becomes a "target of critical isolation and eventual demolition" by subsequent works (144). "Any consequent realism," Jameson claims, "will therefore aim formally at dispensing with such stereotypes, at penetrating to the unique situations, cityscapes and individuals which make up the reality of a given moment of language, nationality and history" (144). Whereas the critical discourse of probabilism emphasizes realism's commitment to a shared vision of the world as it exists across geographic space and historical time, this book foregrounds the realist desire to "penetrat[e]" the unique milieus novels represent. In this way, chance functions as what Jason Puskar calls a "rhetorical strategy" within the realist novel (8). Chance is rhetorical not in the sense that it is being used to make a direct argument or claim—say, about providence or (in)determinism—but rhetorical in the sense that it creates specific types of engagement with the worlds novelists create.[22] While each of these writers turns to chance and improbability for their own particular aesthetic ends, the chapters collectively demonstrate how the realist novel participated in the effort to negotiate the tension between contingency and scale that characterized probabilistic thinking during the nineteenth century.

22. It is common to discuss narrative probability in terms of the expectations generated by genre—that is, our evaluation of what is probable within a given narrative is determined by the codes and conventions established by genre (see Rabinowitz). This approach has considerable value in helping us understand the interplay of textual dynamics and readerly experience, but it also relies upon the probabilist assumption that realist texts strive, in the first instance, to accord with the reader's sense of the real. Consider Monika Fludernik's definition of realism in terms of mimesis: "Realist texts are, in the standard definitions, mimetic texts: they re-present a fictional reality which iconically reflects our image of what is real. Yet our understanding of what is real derives precisely from well-worn clichés of what should happen, has been known to happen, conventionally does happen, reflecting an array of frames and scripts, conventionalized expectations, moral attitudes and commonsense notions of the agentially and psychologically verisimilar" (162).

METHODOLOGY AND SCALE

The tension between the individual and the social, between the particular and the representative, not only defines probabilistic thought from the nineteenth century onward, but also shapes current methodological developments within literary studies and the digital humanities. My methodology in this book is fairly traditional—each chapter is organized around close readings of a handful of novels—but each chapter shows how problems of representativeness, induction, and modeling are taken up *within* the nineteenth-century novel. The increasing prevalence and sophistication of computational methodologies has prompted critics to reconceive how we approach the relationship between our particular objects of study, the corpora to which they belong, and the cultures in which they were produced. In moving beyond oversimplified debates about "close" versus "distant" reading, scholars have demonstrated the value of computational approaches to literature—not just in working with large corpora but also at the scale of the individual text.[23] Andrew Piper frames his own contribution to this field by arguing that as scholars "we spend precious little time reflecting on the process of generalization itself, of how we move from the luminous detail to arguments about the larger social contexts in which those details are imbedded" (9). If computational methods seem to work at a level of abstraction that distances us from how individual texts make meaning, Piper reminds us that this emphasis on the individual text also "exiles us from an understanding of the representativeness of our own evidence" (7). In presenting his case for a recursive process of computational modeling, Piper acknowledges the philosophical complications of the model's capacity to "mediate between ourselves and our observations" (9), but he also (understandably) forgoes an engagement with the longer history of these ideas. The very idea of the "representative" was "unthinkable during most of the nineteenth century," and came into being as statisticians attempted to reconcile comprehensive views of society with individual case studies (Hacking, *Taming* 6).[24] It is not just that computational methodologies typically make use of forms of statistical analysis that have their basis in nineteenth-century developments in probability theory:

---

23. English and Underwood provide an overview of the shifts in methodology and scale. See Jockers, especially pp. 3–32, for a helpful overview of macroanalytic approaches; and Allison, especially pp. 1–35, for an explanation of the value of "reductive reading" for approaching individual works and authors. Babb traces the roots of digital humanities methodologies to nineteenth-century statistical thought.

24. See Kruskal and Mosteller.

The nineteenth-century novels that form the basis of many computational projects themselves frequently grapple with the problem of "representativeness." Each of the following chapters shows how the realist novel takes up the problem of representativeness—of moving between particularities, the groups to which they belong, and the contexts in which they are embedded. They thus not only trace the longer history of these ideas but also help us to refine our understanding of what our methodological approaches can accomplish as they attempt to model the landscape of nineteenth-century literature and culture.

This book is divided into two parts that trace the realist novel's engagement with ideas of probability from the decline of the classical interpretation of probability at the beginning of the century to the impact of abstraction and aggregation that define probability from mid-century onward. Part 1, "Realism and Difference," argues that Austen and Scott develop a realist mode that challenges the philosophical and psychological foundations of the classical interpretation of probability through a commitment to the cultivation of difference. Realism's historicist mindset is predicated upon a departure from the assumptions underlying Aristotelian and Enlightenment models of literary probability. If 1814 marked the apogee of the classical interpretation of probability through the publication of Laplace's *A Philosophical Essay on Probabilities*, it also marked a turning point in the history of the novel, with the publication of Scott's *Waverley*. The year was also the mid-point of Austen's career as a novelist (seeing the publication of *Mansfield Park*). The manner in which both address probability—as an aesthetic criterion related to representation and as a category of judgment—establishes the importance of the concept for how they conceived their novelistic practices. Whereas Scott invokes questions of probability frequently in his critical essays (particularly when discussing the gothic), Austen's novels dramatize the activity of probabilistic judgment and, through narratorial asides, reflect on questions of narrative probability. Both writers' engagements with ideas of probability challenge the model of rationality that is the foundation of the classical interpretation of probability; they turn to improbability as a means of addressing questions of difference—temporal variation and cultural otherness.

Chapter 1 demonstrates how Austen's novels consistently interrogate probability as a standard of judgment and representation. It argues that even though Austen's novels ultimately fulfill the expectations established by convention, her handling of characterization and closure reflect skepticism about the didactic capacity of the novel, as she repeatedly exposes and exploits the gap between probabilistic knowledge and the experience of the particular. The chapter begins with analysis of Richard Whately's 1821 review of Austen, which illustrates how the early critical discourse of realism reconfigures the idea of narrative probability through the quantitative logic of the classical interpretation of probability. The remainder of the chapter reads Austen's novels against Whately's review to highlight how Austen challenges both the rationalism and didacticism of this model.

Chapter 2 demonstrates how Scott's historical novels leverage the causal ambiguity of chance to create encounters with historical and cultural otherness. Scott harnesses the competing causal interpretations that chance elicits—the opposing ways characters "read" or interpret chance—to juxtapose culturally embedded modes of cognition. Drawing on Todorov's theory of the fantastic, the chapter analyzes chance events in *The Bride of Lammermoor* (1819), *Redgauntlet* (1824), and "The Two Drovers" (1827) to show how Scott mediates supernatural and rational causal frameworks to create encounters across historical and cultural divides. Scott's novels do not directly represent or map the movement of history but instead use chance to render historical forces that are more diffuse and cannot be directly represented.

Part 2 of the book, "Chance and Scale," explores how the Victorian novel confronts the questions of scale that emerge as probability becomes increasingly tied to processes of abstraction and aggregation. Although the Victorian novel is often characterized by its attention to a broad social landscape and its purported drive toward a position of omniscience, it must generate its picture of the social through a selection of individuals. As Jonathan Culler suggests, the omniscience that is often ascribed to nineteenth-century realist novels is perhaps better defined as an "accumulation" of people and perspectives (32). The chapters in this section address three genres of the realist novel—the novel of the city, the bildungsroman, and the provincial novel—to explore how chance becomes an instrument for figuring the relationship between the individual and social in each. Rather than working to generate the "illusion of repetitive everydayness" (McWeeny 17), these novelists use improbability to disrupt that illusion and to define the historical contours of the milieus they represent. In the same way that the absence of direct causation enables Scott to capture causal relationships that are more diffuse, chance provides these writers a mechanism to capture incongruities of scale that emerge as probability becomes a means of managing variation and randomness through aggregation.

Although Dickens and Trollope both turn to improbability as a way of confronting the figurational challenge of the social body, their differing uses of chance reflect competing concerns related to linking individual choice to aggregate social processes. Chapter 3 reclaims Dickens's use of coincidence as a narrative technology for representing the vertiginous experience of the modern metropolis. It provides a detailed reading of *Martin Chuzzlewit* (1843–44) that shows how Dickens uses coincidence to juxtapose the subjective experience of urban anonymity and autonomy with a broader view of social interconnection. By demonstrating how improbability facilitates the novel's effort to historicize and reform selfishness, the chapter reads Dickens's use of coincidence in *Chuzzlewit* as a hinge between what critics have seen as his recognition of modern contingency in his earliest works and the "networked" vision of society that had emerged by the 1850s.

Whereas Dickens leverages coincidence to assert a social interconnectedness whose scope cannot be directly experienced, Trollope's use of chance registers disconnection, marking the limits of the bildungsroman to link individual development to social progress. Chapter 4 analyzes the competing languages of probability in *Phineas Finn* (1869) to show how they represent a disjunction between causality and choice. The chapter argues that the novel's formal divisions are reflected in its competing language of odds (which are linked to an Enlightenment discourse of probability focused on decision making) and the language of statistics; ultimately, the formal divisions of Trollope's novel reflect the problem of translating risk and variation across the social body into individual choice and action.

Reading Hardy's realist aesthetic against the post-Darwinian probability theory of John Venn, the fifth and final chapter argues that the causal structures of Hardy's narratives reflect an emerging emphasis on the causal impact of environment and on how abstract, deterministic laws get enacted through contingent circumstances. The chapter offers a corrective to readings that oversimplify Hardy's use of chance through a reading of *The Return of the Native* (1878) that shows how the chance-filled plot foregrounds the social forces that attenuate characters' agency. While Hardy's novel attests to the absence of transhistorical structures of order, its form cultivates modes of cognition that can grasp the contours of existence within a nonteleological history.

As the chapters explore the important role of chance and improbability for these particular novelists, they collectively demonstrate how the internalization of the problem of probability was integral to the development of the realist mode. While the discourse of probabilism offers one way of approaching the nineteenth-century novel and the idea of realism, it cannot make sense of the fact that so many novels in the realist canon are preoccupied with chance and so resolutely defiant of the probable. Theorizing realism as improbable acknowledges the nineteenth-century novel's sophisticated awareness of the limits of narrative representation—the inherent gaps between cognitive models (linguistic as well as statistical) and the reality they aim to describe—but it also preserves its capacity to generate modes of apprehending the world in its irreducible, contingent historicity.

PART 1

∾

Realism and Difference

THE REALIST mode developed by Jane Austen and Sir Walter Scott in the early decades of the nineteenth century embodies a historicist mindset attuned to the specificity of periods, places, and cultures. Historicism, as Shaw explains, is fundamentally about the acknowledgment and comprehension of difference: "a sense of the systematic wholeness and otherness of different cultures in time, and a sense that despite difference, we can encounter them in a productive manner" (*Narrating* 130–31). Rather than subsuming particulars beneath transcendent structures or categories, realism cultivates a sense of plurality and contingency that is in tension with both the Enlightenment model of probability theory and the Aristotelian conception of probabilistic representation. Realism's commitment to difference reconfigures the relationship between notions of probability and the aims and techniques of fictional representation. For Aristotle, probability enabled tragedy to achieve its aims by ensuring it transcended the contingencies of history. By organizing the causal relationship between events in the plot, probability ensured that tragedy could trace the consequences of action, evoke pity and fear, and as a result provide a form of instruction about life. Catherine Gallagher has argued that this kind of internal probability was integral to the emergence and codification of the conceptual category of fictionality in the eighteenth century. According to Gallagher, the fictionality that defined the early novel required freedom from the pressures of historical accuracy and referentiality that had governed adjacent genres to that point. The probability of a fictive story enabled it to solicit belief while simultaneously allowing it to remain disburdened of claims of referentiality. As Gallagher explains: "The fictionality defining the novel inhered in the *creation* of instances, rather than their mere selection, to illustrate a class of persons. Because a general referent was indicated through a particular, but explicitly nonreferential, fictional individual, the novel could be judged generally true even though all of its particulars are merely imaginary" (342; original emphasis). As Gallagher notes, the Aristotelian foundations of this conception of fictionality are strong, and writers embraced probability to accomplish this peculiar coupling of the believable yet nonreferential.

If probability helped consolidate the idea of fiction's autonomy and truth in the eighteenth century, it did so by positing the fictional world's capacity to model meaningful causal relationships. This understanding of fictionality enables us to see how Aristotelian ideas of literary probability could be made intelligible within the parameters of the modern, mathematical theory of probability, despite their differing philosophical foundations. According to Douglas Lane Patey's account of probability and Augustan literary theory, literary form of the period adopted the underlying principles of rhetoric. These principles were modeled upon a doctrine of circumstances that used probable knowledge to counter the recognition of contingency and uncertainty. "Signs" were the fulcrum upon which the ancient meaning of probability ("backed by authority") turned into the modern, evidence-based (and ultimately quantitative) approach to probability. With the emergence of empiricist philosophy in the wake of the Renaissance, nature itself came to be seen as offering a testimony that could be read and interpreted based upon the evidence it presented to observation.[1] In Patey's account, the literary work—and narrative in particular—was regarded in the eighteenth century as "a hierarchic structure of probable signs, signs which at once constitute narrative structure and reveal meaning" (89). Reading the text became a proxy for reading the world at large, as the probable structure of the literary work became the vehicle of its didactic aims. According to Patey, both Henry Fielding and Samuel Richardson "attempt to lead their readers to infer to generalizations about the nature of [divine] design and, further, [. . .] to reshape their expectations [so] that they may act in such a manner as may with probability lead to happiness (earthly justification) and salvation" (214). This view of narrative as a hierarchy of probable signs shares with Aristotelian theory an emphasis on the internal probability of the work—the way it organizes and relates its parts. But it also draws on the assumption, central to the classical interpretation of probability, that there are underlying (deterministic) laws in the world and that probability affords the means of grasping those structures through the contingencies of lived experience. Just as the repeated events of the world wore grooves on the mind of *l'homme éclairé* to instruct probable belief, the literary text could operate as a model of the world and promote understanding of its fundamental order.

The following two chapters show how Jane Austen and Sir Walter Scott's engagements with probability are driven by skepticism about the ideal of rationality that underpinned the classical interpretation of probability and that persists in the critical discourse of probabilism. Writing as contemporaries, Austen and Scott set the course of the realist novel on two different trajectories at the start of the nineteenth century: Austen working on her "little bit (two Inches wide) of ivory [. . .] with so fine a Brush" (Austen, *Letters* 337) on the depiction of psychological and domestic interiority, and Scott developing the "Big Bow-wow strain" (Scott, *Journal* 155) of the historical novel that depicts expansive social landscapes and cultural transformation. Yet despite the significant differences in the scope and scale of their novelistic worlds, both writers invoke probability to think through the relationships between

---

1. See Hacking, *Emergence*, pp. 39–48.

belief, narrative structure, and fidelity to the external world. On the one hand, both writers at times seem to acknowledge probability as a commitment to a shared, empirically apprehended reality. Austen, for instance, sarcastically dismisses Mary Brunton's *Self-Control* (1810) in a letter to her sister Cassandra as "an excellently meant, elegantly-written Work, without anything of Nature or Probability in it" (*Letters* 244). Likewise, many of her "Corrections" to her niece Anna Austen Lefroy's manuscripts concern matters of probability: A character should not "walk out" immediately after having a broken arm set, and a town name should be changed since "Lyme is towards 40 miles distance from Dawlish & would not be talked of there" (280). Scott's 1830 introduction to *The Lady of the Lake* (1810) echoes Austen's talk of Lyme and Dawlish as he recalls the "uncommon pains" he took to "verify the accuracy of the local circumstances" of the poem: "I recollect, in particular, that to ascertain whether I was telling a probable tale I went into Perthshire, to see whether King James could actually have ridden from the banks of Loch Vennachar to Stirling Castle within the time supposed in the poem" (*Poetical* 155). On the other hand, both demonstrate an acute awareness that probability is not an innate standard of rationality but instead a variable threshold of belief prone to irrational distortions. Probability is Austen's point of engagement with the gothic romance in *Northanger Abbey* (1817), as Catherine's deductions about General Tilney and the happenings within the Abbey are repeatedly couched in the language of probability. However, when Henry Tilney implores her to "'consult [her] own understanding, [her] own sense of the probable'" in the novel's climactic scene, it is clear that that is what she has been doing all along—Henry appeals to an innate rational core that the novel shows to be illusory. The gothic also offers Scott an opportunity to probe the foundations of belief, as his criticism and fiction display a fascination with fiction's capacity to activate superstitious or irrational beliefs. For example, although Clara Reeve "condemns" Horace Walpole for the "extravagance" of *The Castle of Otranto* (1764), Scott does not see the need to restrict "the realm of shadows by the opinions entertained of it in the world of realities" (I. Williams 96–97). Whereas for Reeve "there is a verge of probability, which even the most violent figment must not transgress," Scott wonders: "Where [. . .] is the line to be drawn? Or what are the limits to be placed to the reader's credulity, when those of common sense and ordinary nature are once exceeded?" (97). Probability is central to both Austen's and Scott's novels not as an intuitive, stable, or absolute standard but as a space for negotiating the relationships between belief, textual representation, and world.

As an aesthetic standard, the ideal of probability is opposed to difference through its appeal to the universal. For Aristotle, this appeal is explicit: Probability ensures that tragedy can create a particular type of experience for the audience precisely through its capacity to partake of the universal. For later theorists of narrative and critics of realism, probability entails an implicit appeal to and correspondence with the reader's sense of how the world works. By internalizing and interrogating the idea of probability within their novels, Austen and Scott demonstrate that their realism is instead committed to difference. For Austen's fine brush, difference resides primarily in the particularity of individuals and experience, while for Scott it is about difference at the level of culture and history. Their engagements with probability occur at the level of content, as their novels dramatize scenes of probabilistic judgment and interpretation, and also at the level of form, as they reflect upon or draw attention to the mechanics of their representational techniques. Both novelists demonstrate an awareness of and openness to variation that defined the changing landscape of thinking about probability and chance during the nineteenth century. While the paradigm of probabilism privileges the correspondences between belief, representation, and world, improbability allows us both to acknowledge incongruities between them and to analyze how these writers negotiate those gaps. To create meaningful encounters with difference realism had to move beyond the limits of the probable.

CHAPTER 1

Probability, Particularity, and the Uncertain Futures of Austen's Very Minor Characters

> The anxiety, which in this state of their attachment must be the portion of Henry and Catherine, and of all who loved either, as to its final event, can hardly extend, I fear, to the bosom of my readers, who will see in the tell-tale compression of the pages before them, that we are all hastening together to perfect felicity. The means by which their early marriage was effected can be the only doubt: what probable circumstance could work upon a temper like the General's?
>
> —*Northanger Abbey*, chapter 31

PROBABILITY ILLUMINATES key aesthetic and philosophical questions that animate Jane Austen's novels. In concluding her first completed novel by invoking a "probable circumstance" to resolve the plot, Austen draws attention to the tension between her narrative's internal coherence and its fidelity to the external world (233). Within the novel's diegesis, Catherine and Henry remain in a state of uncertainty about the eventuality of their union, yet readers—armed with the knowledge of generic convention and the "telltale compression of the pages" in their hands—intuit the inevitability of that union. Austen's production of a "probable circumstance" to reconcile this disjunction constitutes a double move toward the idea of the probable. On the one hand, it acknowledges probability as an aesthetic standard by preserving the internal coherence of her narrative and refusing the turn to the accidental or improbable to bring about closure. The identification of the "circumstance which chiefly availed" in this instance—Eleanor Tilney's marriage to a "man of fortune and consequence" (233)—maintains the consistency of the General's character[1] and ensures that the plot, to cite Ian Watt's criteria for "formal

---

1. Henry Fielding defines the criterion of "conservation of character" in his discussion of probability in Book 8 of *Tom Jones* (1749): "Actions [. . .] should be likely for the very actors and characters themselves to have performed: for what may be only wonderful and surprizing in one man, may become improbable, or indeed impossible, when related of another" (328).

realism," uses "past experience as the cause of present action" (22). On the other hand, by posing the question in this way, Austen highlights that the "circumstance" is no less contrived for being plausible within the parameters of the storyworld she has constructed. Austen, in other words, does not just produce the probable circumstance within the diegesis; she calls attention to its production in a way that reminds readers that the pages before them are a "fictional 'creation'" rather than a "'re-creation'" of the world (Dannenberg 25). Austen's move here indicates that maintaining the internal consistency of the narrative amounts to a constructed artificiality, problematizing the relationship between narrative representation and the external reality it claims to apprehend. The "only doubt" is resolved, but it is replaced with a deeper skepticism about the adequacy of narrative form to the richness and particularity of the world.

This chapter argues that Austen's realism is defined by a commitment to particularity and difference that departs from the philosophical foundations of the classical interpretation of probability. Her engagements with probability show how nineteenth-century realism defined itself in dialogue with the core epistemological questions that shaped contemporary thinking about probability. The classical interpretation of probability was predicated on the ideal of *l'homme éclairé*, and it can be summed up by Pierre-Simon Laplace's dictum that the theory of probability is "at bottom only common sense reduced to a calculus; it makes us appreciate with exactitude that which exact minds feel by a sort of instinct" (Laplace 196). Although Douglas Lane Patey locates Austen as the "last and greatest novelist" (218) in the eighteenth-century didactic tradition grounded in this theory, more recent scholars have aligned Austen with a Romanticism attuned to the contingency and uncertainty of the present and future. Emily Rohrbach, in particular, has shown how Austen develops a poetics that breaks with Enlightenment theories of historiography (and probability) that assumed stable patterns of cause and effect. According to Rohrbach, Austen (alongside Keats and Byron) promotes a sense of "uncertain futurity" (14) by acknowledging the "impossibility of anticipating the future based upon patterns of the past—or the future based on patterns of the present" (26). While Rohrbach turns to *Persuasion* (1818) and its precise historical setting in the post-Waterloo moment to establish the "historical and historicizing import of her novels" (107), this chapter locates in Austen's interrogation of probability a commitment to contingency, uncertainty, and unpredictability that runs through her entire oeuvre. Her novels trouble the relationship between literary structure and the world, challenging the assumptions about rationality and the reliability of probabilistic knowledge. The tension between the probable and the particular drives the unfolding of her narratives, and while she recognizes the implicit authority of the probable, her realism draws attention to its limitations in its effort to cultivate an appreciation of contingency and difference. Although Austen's novels do not make explicit use of chance in the way that the subsequent chapters will explore, the way she leverages the particular against probabilistic knowledge displays the same openness to variation that defined the changing landscape of ideas about probability and chance in the early decades of the nineteenth century.

The ending of *Northanger Abbey* identifies two facets of narrative where the dynamic interplay of the probable and the particular is especially significant: characterization and closure. Austen's novels repeatedly confront—and dramatize—the two interconnected problems of induction: on the one hand, making inferences about how a character will act based upon typological categories and, on the other, extrapolating didactic principles from the resolution of the novel's plot. In drawing attention to readerly expectations, the ending of *Northanger Abbey* foregrounds the fundamental role narrative conventions play in this dynamic movement between the particular and the general (or typical). From the playful burlesques of her juvenilia such as "The Mystery" (a short drama written at the precocious age of twelve) through to her 1816 "Plan of a Novel," Austen was firmly aware of the degree to which the experience of narrative is governed by convention. Even though her novels generally fulfill the expectations engendered by the conventions of genre, her interrogation of the conventional underpinnings of probabilistic expectation reflects her frustration with the constraints such conventions impose. While Stuart Tave reads Austen's invocation of a "probable circumstance" at the end of *Northanger Abbey* as evidence that "Austen's own art is not yet good enough to produce all it seems to promise" (37), her repeated encounters with the same problem through the rest of her novels demonstrate that she never manages to resolve the paradoxical imperatives of probabilistic representation. After all, the final chapter of her final novel, *Persuasion,* begins by essentially repeating the same gesture that concludes *Northanger Abbey*: "Who can be in doubt of what followed?" (232). Austen's self-reflective preoccupation with probability shows her wavering uneasily between embracing probability as a form of fidelity to the world and exposing probability as little more than the hardened accretions of convention.

In foregrounding the limits of probabilistic expectation and representation, Austen's novels show how the realist mode developed through the recognition of the limits of narrative representation. If, as Catherine Gallagher has argued, probability was essential to the emergence of the category of fictionality because it enabled texts to be "judged generally true" (342) despite being nonreferential, Austen's interrogation of probability confirms that by the early nineteenth century, fictional texts could concern themselves with something other than soliciting belief in the general truth of their representations. By reading Austen's engagement with probability against an Aristotelian framework, this chapter adds to a growing body of scholarship that, like Rohrbach's, finds Austen's realism to be defined by a commitment to uncertainty, unpredictability, and possibility. In an important account of Austen's relationship to probability, for instance, William Galperin identifies a resistance to the probabilistic that constitutes a break with the tradition of the female novel that Austen inherited from Frances Burney. Galperin links the probabilistic to the "'naturalizing'" (48) discourse of the picturesque and argues that the "oppositionality" (61) of Austen's work—a form of "counterhegemony" (85)—resides in its cultivation of possibility against the normative force of the probable. Matthew Wickman has also suggested that Austen challenges the probabilistic; in a brief but rich account of *Love and Freindship*, Wickman argues that Austen's early novella "deconstruct[s] the difference between the romantic and the probable" (77) and thus "divulges the artificiality of the kinds of narrative conventions that structure both romantic *and probable* relations to the world" (75; original emphasis).[2] More recently, Christopher Miller has identified the importance of surprise to Austen's aesthetic, arguing that it constitutes a "locus of pleasure, both in lived experience and in narrative mediation" (142) and that surprise challenges the probable through a mixture of "knowing and unknowing" (165). This chapter extends this work by attending more carefully to how Austen represents the contours of probabilistic expectation within her novels. It adds to these political, literary historical, and affective readings of Austen's resistance to the probable an understanding of its philosophical and epistemological foundations, situating Austen's attention to the "heterogeneity of the real" (Galperin 8) within the longer history of probabilistic thought.

To establish Austen's break with the philosophical underpinnings of the classical interpretation of probability, I read her novels against Archbishop Richard Whately's 1821 review of her works. The first section of this chapter analyzes Whately's praise of Austen in light of "the precepts of Aristotle" in order to establish the status of probability within critical discourse in the early

---

2. See also Loveridge, who provides an extended reading of *Northanger Abbey* that sees "Nature" and "Probability" as the opposing terms structuring the novel. He argues that Austen "play[s] with the idea of probability in order first to provoke and then destroy the reader's expectations of probable conclusions" (25). However, while he reads the novel against the backdrop of eighteenth-century theories of literary probability, he does not consider how these aesthetic matters relate to the broader history of probabilistic thought that concerns me here.

decades of the nineteenth century (96). Whately's critical account is important for three reasons: it demonstrates that discussions of narrative probability become inflected by the logic of quantification that increasingly characterizes philosophical theories of probability in this period; it dramatizes the tension in the early discourse of realism between a commitment to concrete particularity and the revelation of general truths; and it exemplifies the values and assumptions that accompany the discourse of probabilism as it both carries forward and redefines the Aristotelian emphasis on probability. While the first section of this chapter identifies what it meant for Austen's novels to be praised for their probability by her contemporaries, the remainder of the chapter reads those novels' engagement with probability against this critical framework to demonstrate an alternative set of aesthetic commitments. The second section of the chapter shows how Austen's novels interrogate this theory of knowledge and interpretation through dramatized scenes of probabilistic judgment. Austen's representations of probabilistic judgment reflect the eroding foundations of the classical interpretation of probability. Whereas the logic of associationist psychology "had initially joined the two sides of probability, frequencies and degrees of certainty," emphasis had shifted by the end of the eighteenth century "from accurate tallies to distortions and illusions" (Gigerenzer et al. 35). In both her characterization and her plotting, Austen mobilizes the tension inherent in the process of induction—the movement between particular instances and general knowledge. Rather than educating probabilistic judgment, her novels expose its fallibilities. The chapter concludes by extending this argument to the question of closure and the endings of Austen's novels. The final section analyzes Austen's introduction, at the end of her novels, of what I call "very minor" characters that destabilize the sense of finality and closure. These characters—Margaret Dashwood, the third sister in *Sense and Sensibility* (1811); Fanny Price's younger sister, Susan, in *Mansfield Park* (1814); and Anna Weston, the daughter born to Mrs. Weston at the end of *Emma* (1815)—are barely noticeable (or are nonexistent) throughout much of the novel but are foregrounded in the closing pages as a strategy for turning attention to the future and its uncertainty. Although Austen's plots tend to fulfill and validate conventional expectations, these characters inscribe uncertainty into the ends of their respective novels. They attenuate their didactic force by serving as doubles (or iterations) of the heroines who foreground the limits of extrapolating knowledge of the future from the unfolding of the past. The interrogation of probabilistic knowledge and judgment within Austen's works thus informs both the structures of her plots and the modes of interpretation they solicit from readers.

I. NARRATIVE, PROBABILITY, AND "REAL LIFE": ARISTOTELIAN THEORY IN 1821

Richard Whately's 1821 review of Austen in *The Quarterly Review* demonstrates how the Aristotelian discourse of probability gets reinterpreted within the mathematical, quantitative framework of modern probability theory. The review takes its cue from Sir Walter Scott's 1815 review of *Emma,* and it is perhaps the most important early assessment of Austen after Scott's. According to Claudia Johnson, Whately's review began the long tradition of praising Austen on account of "what she does *not* do," namely, address political issues directly or develop an overtly didactic agenda like many of her fellow female novelists in the period (xx; original emphasis). But it is significant also for the way it highlights the complexity—even incoherence—of theorizing literary probability, especially at the time of its publication. Whately's philosophical background and his approach to literature as a logician establish the intersections of literary and philosophical thinking on probability. His 1826 *Elements of Logic* was influential in reviving the study of logic in England, and subsequent figures in the history of probabilistic thought—John Stuart Mill, George Boole, and Augustus De Morgan among them—acknowledged its influence. It was as a result of disagreements with Whately's *Logic* that William Whewell was prompted to develop his influential approach to inductive reasoning, and Charles Sanders Peirce was first introduced to the study of logic through Whately.[3] If Whately's *Logic* can be seen as a foundational text in the history of probabilistic thought, his review of Austen displays the logic that grounds the critical discourse of probabilism that still shapes certain discussions of realism. In this review, Whately approaches narrative—as he does the subjects of rhetoric and logic—as a committed Aristotelian, and the extended discussion of literary form that opens the essay reads as a standard recapitulation of the account of plot and probability in Aristotle's *Poetics*. However, his discussion of narrative probability in terms of the *"overbalance of chances"* being for or against a particular event reflects a quantitative logic that collapses the distinction between the internal coherence of a narrative and its fidelity to the external world (*"Northanger"* 90; original emphasis). In doing so, it identifies probability as the means by which narrative representation can grasp general principles of experience and therefore provide didactic instruction.

Whately repeats Scott's identification of Austen's fiction as a "new kind of novel" that presents "a correct and striking representation of that which

---

3. On Whately's influence on nineteenth-century logic and probabilistic thought, see Fisch; McKerrow; and Snyder, pp. 34–42.

is daily taking place around [us]" (Scott, "Review" 418), but he also extends it by arguing that the novels' probability lends them an *"instructive"* quality that "guides the judgment, and supplies a kind of artificial experience" (*"Northanger"* 87–88; original emphasis). This view follows from Aristotle's belief in the philosophical value of poetry: By presenting incidents as they happen according to probability and necessity, narrative and "dramatic poetry" can "furnis[h] general rules of practical wisdom," whereas history "details what has actually happened, of which many parts may chance to be exceptions to the general rules of probability" (38). Austen's novels, according to Whately, are to be praised on two counts in particular. The first is their avoidance of "those sundry little violations of probability which are to be met with in most novels" and "lower their value, as models of real life" (88). Unlike Fielding and Radcliffe, Austen does not resort to improbable events and the "machinery of accidents" in the orchestration of plot, and as a result she generates "a clear and *abstracted* view of the general rules" that govern human affairs (93; original emphasis). Their second virtue is the absence of overt didacticism. According to Whately, Austen is "evidently a Christian writer" (95) but is not "obtrusive" with her religion or purpose, unlike Maria Edgeworth, who is "too avowedly didactic" and "press[es] every circumstance of her story [. . .] into the service of a principle to be inculcated" (93). The "moral lessons" in Austen's works "spring incidentally from the circumstances of the story." They present an "unpretending kind of instruction which is furnished by real life; and certainly," Whately claims, "no other author has ever conformed more closely to real life, as well in the incidents, as in the characters and descriptions" (95–96). There is "little or nothing that is not probable" in Austen's works, and for this reason no other author has illustrated Aristotle's precepts so successfully.

Although Whately appears to faithfully articulate the principles of Aristotelian theory in his exegesis of Austen's works, his discussion of probability reveals important tensions that accompany the attempt to apply Aristotelian principles to an emerging realist mode. In particular, Whately's account of fictional probability threatens to collapse the foundational distinction between poetry and history. Whately begins by upholding this distinction to preserve the philosophical value of literature and its capacity to provide knowledge of "general rules," yet he describes Austen's fiction in terms that also align it with history. Austen's narratives are "a kind of fictitious biography" that present us "with the general, instead of the particular,—the probable, instead of the true" (93), but Whately then also lauds their conformity to "real life" and their ability to provide the "instruction which is furnished by real life" (95). "The perfect appearance of reality" achieved by Austen's works comes from the "vivid distinctness of description," "the minute fidelity of detail," and the "probability of incident" (96). Whereas for Aristotle the value of poetry and tragedy resides in the fact that they are not "real life," Whately yokes the novel's instructive quality to its fidelity to reality. This slippage hinges on his quantitative characterization of probability and improbability. When comparing Austen to Fielding, for instance, Whately decries the improbability of the plot of *Tom Jones*: "Circumstances are such as it is incalculably improbable [they] should ever exist: several events, taken singly, are much against the chances of probability; but the combination of the whole in a connected series, is next to impossible" (91). For Whately, the improbable can be distinguished from the unnatural according to whether "the *overbalance of chances* is against it" (90; original emphasis). "What happens according to probability" comes to refer not only to the causal relationship between events and the internal coherence of plot (as it does for Aristotle), but also to the narrative's fidelity to "real life" through a (proto)frequentist logic.

Although Whately's discussion of probability in terms of the "overbalance of chances" might appear synonymous with Aristotle's notion of "what happens for the most part," his rearticulation of probability in quantitative terms enacts a categorical shift. The category of the "probable" that plays such a central role in *The Poetics* is not quantitative—it is not something that is calculated or counted. The modalities of the necessary, probable, and chance that appear in Aristotle's discussion of plot are derived from his broader philosophical system, where they account for the relationship between causality and knowledge. Although they appear as three distinct categories, they are in fact better understood as two. As Dorothea Frede explains: "What happens for the most part is [. . .] not a kind or class of events that differs fundamentally from the events that happen of necessity; it is rather of the same type. For both together are opposed to what happens *by chance*" (201; original emphasis). Aristotle first introduces the category of the probable as "what happens for the most part" (*hōs epi to polu*) before replacing it with the term *eikos*, the "probable" (or "likely") (206). His dictum that plots be constructed according to probability and necessity—and exclude chance—follows from his argument for the philosophical value of poetry and tragedy. Chance and accidental events are, in the strict sense, beyond scientific knowledge within Aristotle's philosophical system. They must therefore be excluded from the poetic work if it is to attain its proper ends and be "not an imitation of persons, but of actions and of life" in order to illustrate how people "achieve well-being or its opposite" (Aristotle 11). In Frede's words: "It is the possibility of depicting events undisturbed by accidents that establishes the superiority of tragedy over history and makes it an important philosophical enterprise, because it can depict the universal, i.e. what is not distorted by the incalculable vicissitudes of everyday life" (205). Although necessity would be preferable to the merely probable, necessary relations typically obtain only in nature, whereas human affairs and actions are restricted to probable relations. The probability that governs plot allows it to transcend the particularity of history and to provide knowledge about life in the world by reaching toward the universal. Whately's quantitative concept of probability thus implies a different model of knowledge: The probable is no longer categorically distinct from the "incalculable vicissitudes of everyday life" but now derived *through* the quantification and calculation of "real life."[4]

In carrying forward and reframing Aristotle's discussion of plot and probability, Whately's review reveals the extent to which the modern mathematical notion of probability had shifted the conceptual foundations of probability by the beginning of the nineteenth century. As a founding document of the mathematical approach to probability, the 1662 Port Royal *Logique* presented one of the first attempts to "actually quantify the ancient dictum 'most of the time'" (Daston 39). The "climate of near quantiphrenia" that ensued saw the application of the mathematical theory of probability to an ever-increasing range of phenomena, as things like belief and testimony were reimagined through the dominant metaphors and models of gambling (47–48). Yet some phenomena lend themselves to quantification more easily than others, and verisimilitude—the appearance of truth or illusion of reality—was one familiar sense of probability that was not "proto-quantitative" in the seventeenth century, remaining untouched as mathematical ideas of probability spread (48). Written at the apogee of the classical interpretation of probability, Whately's review offers proof that verisimilitude could be understood in quantitative terms through a peculiar application of quantitative logic to the events of fictional plots. Whately's attempt to calculate the probability of the events that constitute the plot of *Tom Jones* is logically incoherent—the odds of fictional events (and most real-world ones, for that matter) cannot be calculated as if

---

4. Frede notes that Aristotle's "what happens for the most part" potentially admits a quantitative interpretation, although she explains that this interpretation is not viable within the system presented by *The Poetics*: "In order to get a better grasp on the tragedian's specific kind of 'likeliness' we have to delve more deeply into the peculiarities of the elements of drama to which Aristotle refers [. . . since] the poet's striving for universality is of a quite special kind. Firstly, the events and circumstances that form the plot are far from the usual human experience. Secondly, the persons involved, the agents, are not the average types of human beings. It is, rather, the poet's task to present the unusual as necessary or at least as likely. This, to put the cards down finally, must be the peculiarity in tragedy that explains the terminological shift to '*eikos*.' A scientific 'statistical' conception of what 'happens for the most part' would certainly not do to capture the poet's striving for the 'unusual likeliness'" (209).

they conformed to the logic of a game of chance.⁵ Noting this incoherence is not, of course, the point. The fact that Whately is able to imagine narrative probability in these terms reflects the theory of mind that subtends the classical interpretation of probability. "Normal psychology" in the period, Daston reminds us, "was both inherently probabilistic and empirical" in its operations: "The more constant and frequent the observed correlation, the stronger the mental association, which in turn intensified probability and belief. Hence, the objective probabilities of experience and the subjective probabilities of belief were, in a well-ordered mind, mirror images of one another" (197). This is good sense—and the representation of "real life"—reduced to a calculus. In this context, we can see that when Whately speaks of the "overbalance of chances" being against a particular event, then, he is not making an appeal to an imaginative set of trials whereby circumstances are iteratively repeated. Rather, he is making an implicit appeal to experience itself: The plot of *Tom Jones* is improbable not according to a rational reckoning of the odds but rather according to the well-ordered empirical mind, which assesses the verisimilitude of the plot against the associations formed by experience.

II. PARTICULARITY AND PROBABILISTIC JUDGMENT: BETWEEN ONE AND "SUCH A ONE"

Whately finds in Austen's novels a fidelity to "real life" that enables them—through their probabilistic operations—to become instructive about life in the world. Yet his quantitative logic exposes the emerging gap between the subjective and objective meanings of probability. Rather than finding the "'unusual likeliness'" (Frede 209) of Aristotelian tragedy—whereby actors and events are unusual particularities capable of embodying the universal—Whately identifies something more akin to an aggregate likelihood that reflects the frequentist logic which displaced the classical interpretation of probability over the

---

5. Rüdiger Campe argues that the modern mathematical understanding of probability remains consistent with the Aristotelian understanding of probability in the idea that probability refers to a representation that transcends the contingency of what has happened to portray general laws that can be observed in their effects but never known with scientific certainty. However, it departs from Aristotle by construing the contingency of the world according to the logic of the game. According to Campe, the "aestheticization of probability is only possible [. . .] because the interpretation of the game of chance as probability enabled the play of contingency to turn into the theory of probability" (251). The collapsing distinction between *probabilis* ("the search for confirmation and evidence") and *verisimilis* ("the reference to truth and its manifestations") follows from the ability of "appearance" to mediate these categories of manifestation and representation.

early decades of the nineteenth century. The remainder of this chapter argues that it is Austen's commitment to particularity that prompts her to interrogate the relationship between literary form and the ideal of rationality that underpins the classical interpretation of probability. While Austen certainly "conducts her novels in the Augustan vocabulary of probable inference, of sagacity in reading signs and circumstance" (Patey 218), she is concerned more with troubling the empirical foundations of probabilistic expectation than with rectifying expectation for didactic aims. Her exploration of the foundations of probabilistic judgment in dramatized scenes of interpretation exposes the limits of induction, as her narratives are driven by characters whose particularity confounds probabilistic expectation. This approach to characterization, in turn, underwrites her efforts to attenuate the didactic force of her narratives by revealing the ways in which probability imposes an artificial order on "real life." The "probable circumstance" that is conjured to bring *Northanger Abbey* to a satisfactory conclusion preserves the consistency of General Tilney's character and the internal coherence of the diegesis, but it exposes the "compression" that narrative performs on the heterogeneity of the world.

Austen's point of attack is the model of mind that enables Whately to assess literary structure according to normative rationality. Her exploration of how probabilistic judgment is prone to the distortions of desire reflects the emerging gap between distinct interpretations of probability conceived either as a matter of belief or as a matter of quantitative frequency. Although it was not until the 1830s that this distinction between subjective and objective probability began to appear explicitly in the theory of probability, Austen's dramatizations of probabilistic reckoning reflect the shifting conceptual foundations of probability. In his *Treatise of Human Nature* (1738–40), David Hume acknowledged the role of habit, education, and prejudice in the formation of probable judgments, suggesting famously that "custom be the foundation of all our judgments" (147). Nevertheless, Hume maintained that the associations formed by experience were capable of correcting such distortions to the understanding, at least in "wise men" (150).[6] In other words, although the same psychological mechanisms governed both philosophical and unphilosophical probabilities, "the wise man knew to correct for the vagaries of the imagination, the immediacy of impressions, or the 'general rules' of prejudice, all of which deceptively heightened the vivacity of a given idea" (Daston 202). In the second half of the eighteenth century, however, this tension became more pronounced, and early nineteenth-century probabilists abandoned the assumption that the rational reckonings of the unprejudiced mind mirrored

---

6. On Hume's view of probability and custom, see Morris; and Daston, pp. 191–210.

the frequencies of a world governed by deterministic laws. The theory of the "normal mind" in associationist psychology changed, and emphasis shifted away from the idea that the mind operated as a "kind of counting machine that automatically tallied frequencies of past events and scaled degrees of belief" to focus instead on the "illusion[s] and distortions that prejudice and passion introduce into this mental reckoning of probabilities" (Gigerenzer et al. 9–10).

Scenes that explicitly invoke probability show how Austen challenges the theory of probable signs that sustained a narrative tradition focused on the rectification of expectation. In staging scenes where characters—and, by extension, readers—must adjudicate between competing forms of evidence and the distortions of that evidence by desire, Austen foregrounds the process of probabilistic inference but also exploits its unstable foundations. Take, for instance, the following scene from chapter 26 of *Emma,* in which Emma and Mrs. Weston debate the latter's conjecture about a possible match between Mr. Knightley and Jane Fairfax following the mysterious arrival of the pianoforte. Having observed Knightley's behavior toward Jane and her relations during the Coles' party, Mrs. Weston confesses that "'The more I think of it, the more probable it appears.'" Emma in her stunned disbelief asserts that "'Mr. Knightley must not marry!'":

> "My dear Emma, I have told you what led me to think of it. I do not want the match—I do not want to injure dear little Henry—but the idea has been given me by circumstances; and if Mr. Knightley really wished to marry, you would not have him refrain on Henry's account, a boy of six years old, who knows nothing of the matter?"
>
> "Yes, I would. I could not bear to have Henry supplanted.—Mr. Knightley marry!—No, I have never had such an idea, and I cannot adopt it now. And Jane Fairfax, too, of all women!"
>
> "Nay, she has always been a first favourite with him, as you very well know."
>
> "But the imprudence of such a match!"
>
> "I am not speaking of its prudence; merely its probability."
>
> "I see no probability in it, unless you have any better foundation than what you mention. His good-nature, his humanity, as I tell you, would be quite enough to account for the horses. He has a great regard for the Bateses, you know, independent of Jane Fairfax—and is always glad to shew them attention. My dear Mrs. Weston, do not take to match-making. You do it very ill." (209)

It is a striking passage for a number of reasons; in particular, the vigor of Emma's objections to the idea of Knightley and Jane marrying stands out—it is perhaps the first flicker of recognition of her desire for Knightley. There is also an intriguing echo of Henry Tilney's rebuke of Catherine in his mother's room: "'Dear Miss Morland, [. . .] what have you been judging from?'" (*Northanger* 186). The passage stages a confrontation between two forms of evidence: While Mrs Weston's conjectures are based on what we might call circumstantial evidence (her immediate observations of Knightley's behavior), Emma relies on her long-standing knowledge of Knightley and his character. Emma's objections are initially grounded in the consequences that would attend the union—its supposed implications for little Henry—but she eventually considers the merit of Mrs. Weston's evidence on its own terms, concluding that causes other than romantic desire (i.e., Knightley's "good-nature," his humanity") account sufficiently for his behavior.

This is one of many scenes within *Emma* where evidence is weighed in this manner—a few pages prior finds Emma and Frank Churchill discussing the "'great probability'" of Emma's conjectures about Jane and Dixon—but its explicit juxtaposition of probability and prudence is especially significant (203). This scene does not just invoke the language of probabilistic judgment; it also confounds the procedures of interpretation that govern the process of inferring from probable signs. As Patey shows, probability was the governing norm within Augustan literary theory because it was the means by which a work became a viable model of reality that could educate probable judgment and cultivate prudence. Narrative in this view fulfills its didactic aims by "placing characters and readers in a world in which the conditions of knowledge are such as to render all knowing, all learning, a process of inference from signs," "teach[ing] certain capacities of judgment by dramatizing those capacities in action" (Patey 179). Yet rather than reinforcing the operations of inference from probable signs, the scene shows how Austen, as William Galperin puts it, consistently allows "readers to draw improbable inferences from probable signs" (95). The object of scrutiny in the debate between Emma and Mrs. Weston is, of course, not the procedures of inference themselves but rather Knightley's actions and intentions. Yet the terms of the debate suggest that probability and prudence might be at odds: For Knightley—the paragon of rationality and sound judgment—the prudent course of action and the probable course of action ought to be one and the same. The available evidence and signs admit different interpretations that cast the foundations of Knightley's character into doubt, as his past behavior potentially becomes an unreliable indicator of his future action. Just as the evidence that Harriet later adduces to support her belief that Knightley loves her must appear probable in order for Emma to experience the pang of jealousy that prompts her to recognize her own desire, the passage at hand cultivates uncertainty precisely because Mrs. Weston's conjectures appear probable.

The scene is constructed to generate uncertainty within the larger dynamics of the novel—it confounds probabilistic judgment rather than educating it. It is possible to read the passage as revealing the illusions, distortions, and prejudices that play an important role in all of Austen's novels. The novel as a whole is governed by a controlling irony—orchestrated by Austen's pioneering use of the free indirect mode[7]—that situates the reader in complex relation to any judgment or inference that is made, particularly by Emma (the novel's primary focalizer). Between Mrs. Weston's pronouncement that she has "'made a match between Mr. Knightley and Jane Fairfax'" and the incongruity of Emma's response ("'I could not bear to have Henry supplanted'"), it is possible to read this as one of the first moments where the reader is being led to infer Emma's desire for Knightley and thus the inevitability of their eventual union. Yet the dynamics of this moment are categorically different from other similar moments in the novel where Austen creates critical distance between readers and characters, such as when Emma misinterprets Mr. Elton's charade as evidence of his desire for Harriet in chapter 9. This earlier scene presents a clear discrepancy between evidence and interpretation ("Humph—Harriet's ready wit!") that creates incongruity and thus critical distance from Emma (70). The later debate between Emma and Mrs. Weston, in contrast, produces competing signs without clearly providing a hierarchy of interpretative significance. The novel's manipulation of evidence frustrates the effort to categorically distinguish illusions or distortions from sound judgments. Even if we see that Emma's judgment here is distorted by her (unacknowledged) desire for Knightley, the question of Knightley's potential interest in Jane remains unresolved. Similarly, although there are signs that potentially point to some kind of relationship between Frank and Jane, to infer their secret engagement prior to its revelation late in the novel requires the reader to indulge in the conjectural work of an "imaginist" like Emma—to engage, in other words, in the same imaginative play that is the object of ironic demystification throughout the novel (314).[8] Rather than working to stabilize clear distinctions between rational inferences and ungrounded conjectures, the dynamics of the

---

7. See Ferguson for an influential account of the free indirect mode in *Emma*.

8. Kay Young attends to the "neuroaesthetics" of *Emma* in a reading that links the role of imagination to the prediction of the future: "As an imaginist, Emma imagines and makes predictions about the future: she engages in 'speculation,' 'foresight,' and 'anticipation'—all acts

novel produce a proliferation of possibilities that all have—to borrow Frank Churchill's phrase—"'an air of great probability'" (324).

As they foreground modes of attention and acts of observation, then, Austen's novels question the rational foundations of inference and induction. We begin to move away from a view of a fundamentally stable world that can be rationally (if imperfectly) apprehended by the well-ordered mind, and toward a dawning appreciation of the world's potential variability and capacity to surprise. While the Enlightenment model of probable judgment relies upon a foundation of past experience as the basis for interpretation, Austen withholds these foundations, particularly in the presentation and assessment of characters at pivotal moments in her plots. A key scene from chapter 18 of *Sense and Sensibility* provides an exemplary instance of this strategy; here, Elinor and Marianne notice Edward Ferrars wearing a ring "with a plait of hair in the centre," and the reader is drawn into the various conjectures about what this might mean for Elinor:

> "I never saw you wear a ring before, Edward," [Marianne] cried. "Is that Fanny's hair? I remember her promising to give you some. But I should have thought her hair had been darker."
>
> Marianne spoke inconsiderately what she really felt—but when she saw how much she had pained Edward, her own vexation at her want of thought could not be surpassed by his. He coloured very deeply, and giving a momentary glance at Elinor, replied, "Yes; it is my sister's hair. The setting always casts a different shade on it you know."
>
> Elinor had met his eye, and looked conscious likewise. That the hair was her own, she instantaneously felt as well satisfied as Marianne; the only difference in their conclusions was, that what Marianne considered as a free gift from her sister, Elinor was conscious must have been procured by some theft or contrivance unknown to herself. She was not in a humour, however, to regard it as an affront, and [. . .] resolved henceforth to catch every opportunity of eyeing the hair and of satisfying herself, beyond all doubt, that it was exactly the shade of her own. (96)

As Elinor and the reader will learn shortly, the plait of hair belongs to Lucy Steele. This passage exemplifies why Austen has drawn so much attention from critics interested in the cognitive, intersubjective dimensions of narra-

---

of seeing not what is before her but what might be in the future—these are her ideas as dreams and plots." See Young, pp. 29–50.

tive, as the reader must untangle the assumptions and motivations of three characters operating on different planes of knowledge.[9] In the context of probabilistic judgment, it is Elinor's "instantaneous" feeling that the hair is her own that is significant. There are three possible explanations: the plait belongs to either Fanny, Elinor, or another woman. The first possibility is easily dismissed since—as Marianne clumsily proclaims—Fanny's hair is darker, and Edward would have little reason to be self-conscious or embarrassed if it were his sister's. The other two possibilities are each plausible, yet both are problematic insofar as they contradict Elinor's understanding of Edward's character as it has been established by prior experience. Marianne's conjecture—or, rather, the conjecture attributed to Marianne by Elinor—that the hair is Elinor's is justified since she does not know that Elinor has not offered Edward a ribbon of her hair. From Elinor's perspective, however, either Edward is attached to another woman, which no evidence supplied by his past behavior would support, or he has surreptitiously acquired Elinor's hair by "theft or contrivance," an act that would also challenge her established understanding of his character. His embarrassment could be read as evidence of either. The point is that neither Elinor nor the reader possesses the requisite foundations upon which a reliable inference might be made. In this absence, it is desire that structures a belief that is "instantaneously felt" by Elinor and presumably accepted by the reader. As with the scene from *Emma*, the intuitive judgment is not rational but rather driven by desire, yet the manner in which the reader is drawn into the drama of interpretation destabilizes the grounds upon which they might distinguish between the two.

This recognition of the subjective foundations of probabilistic judgment not only foregrounds the way in which desire distorts judgment, but also privileges the particularity of characters, circumstances, and experience over the general knowledge that might be arrived at through the process of induction. Nothing that Elinor has experienced or knows about Edward prepares her for the possibilities opened by the ring. As Harry E. Shaw argues in his case for "reading through the grain" of Austen's narratives: "For Austen, nothing is ever essentially the same as anything else. She is always making distinctions; we can think of her linguistic practice as constituting a 'difference machine'" (*Narrating* 159). The power of difference is particularly important to Austen's modes of characterization, which challenge stable typologies of character. *Pride and Prejudice* (1813) thematizes this issue in a conversation about "intricate" characters between Elizabeth, Bingley, and Darcy in chapter 9. When Bingley confesses

---

9. See, for example, Zunshine.

that he considers himself "quite fixed" at Netherfield, Elizabeth's coy reply initiates the following exchange:

> "This is exactly what I should have supposed of you," said Elizabeth.
> "You begin to comprehend me, do you?" he cried, turning towards her.
> "Oh! Yes—I understand you perfectly."
> "I wish I might take this for a compliment; but to be so easily seen through I am afraid is pitiful."
> "That is as it happens. It does not necessarily follow that a deep, intricate character is more or less estimable than such a one as yours." [. . .]
> "I did not know before," continued Bingley immediately, "that you were a studier of character. It must be an amusing study."
> "Yes; but intricate characters are the *most* amusing. They have at least that advantage."
> "The country," said Darcy, "can in general supply but few subjects for such a study. In a country neighbourhood you move in a very confined and unvarying society."
> "But people themselves alter so much, that there is something new to be observed in them for ever." (42–43; original emphasis)

Irony suffuses the early part of the exchange, as Elizabeth playfully hints at what she "understands" about Bingley (i.e., his desire for her sister Jane); the latter part of the conversation, however, anticipates the larger thematic concerns of the novel. It is not just that Elizabeth and Darcy are misled by prejudice in their initial assessments of each other. The novel as a whole highlights Austen's investment in "deep, intricate" characters who defy expectations and who support the idea that there is always "something new to be observed in them for ever." Elizabeth is stunned, for instance, when she learns that Charlotte Lucas is going to marry Mr Collins: "The possibility of Mr. Collins's fancying himself in love with her friend had once occurred to Elizabeth within the last day or two; but that Charlotte should encourage him, seemed almost as far from possibility as that she should encourage him herself" (122). The "depth" and intricacy that accompanies such moments relates not only to characterization but also to the novel's themes, as Charlotte's choice complicates the assessment of marriage by serving as a backdrop to Elizabeth and Darcy's eventual union. Although Austen restricts herself to the depiction of social worlds that are "very confined" and look to be "unvarying" in their appearance, her narratives work to cultivate an appreciation of their unplumbed depths, richness, and unpredictability.

It is Darcy himself who proves to be the most intricate character in *Pride and Prejudice*. Elizabeth's inferences regarding him—especially as the novel moves toward its resolution—reveal how Austen uses such intricacy to challenge probabilistic judgments. As Elizabeth works through the fallout of Lydia's elopement with Wickham and learns of Darcy's role in bringing about their marriage, she finally becomes fully alive to her desire for him. In the process, she convinces herself—through a sequence of conjectures and probabilistic inferences—that her desire for him "could not in rational expectation survive such a blow as this," and that "there seemed a gulf impossible between them" (295). When she learns of Darcy's presence at her sister's wedding, "conjectures as to the meaning of it [. . .] hurried into her brain; but she was satisfied with none. Those that best pleased her [. . .] seemed most improbable" (302). Indeed, although "her heart did whisper that he had done it for her," it is a desire soon "checked by other considerations" that lead to the conviction that Darcy "must" not be able to connect himself with her family (308). This is an exemplary moment of probabilistic judgment in Austen in its subtle positioning of the reader in relation to Elizabeth. It is also significant for the way that Elizabeth consciously removes her desire from the process of probable judgment. Given "such a one" as Darcy, it is improbable that he would want to attach himself to Elizabeth given the circumstances of her sister's elopement. The pleasure of the novel, however, follows from the difficulty of reducing Darcy to a stable and fully knowable character type—he is, after all, Fitzwilliam Darcy, not "such a one" as Darcy. If an ironic distance opens between the reader's judgment and Elizabeth's at this moment, it arises from our capacity to intuit Austen's larger narrative design, not from an inherent fault in Elizabeth's probabilistic inferences. Austen, in other words, seems to be playing two orders of probabilistic expectation off of one another to create this richly satisfying moment: This differential knowledge heightens our pleasure in the seemingly improbable outcome that awaits Elizabeth in her uncertainty about Darcy's intentions. Rather than reinforcing each other through a shared appeal to rational order, literary structure and the procedures of interpretation are placed in ironic tension.

This tension returns us to the ending of *Northanger Abbey* and the problem posed by the character of General Tilney. If we see Austen as supporting a normative, Enlightenment model of probabilistic judgment, then the novel's burlesque of the gothic mode might be read as an endorsement of the empiricist mode of observation and judgment championed by Henry Tilney. Stuart Tave, for instance, sums up the matter neatly in the assessment that "the order of probability at Northanger Abbey has been imported by Catherine from romance" (53). Yet Austen's treatment of probabilistic inference places Henry's admonitory corrective—"'Consult your own understanding, your own sense of the probable, your own observation of what is passing around you'"—in a more complicated light. The mechanisms of probabilistic judgment that are eventually brought to bear on the General's character during Catherine's visit to the Abbey are explored at the beginning of volume II, when Henry interrogates Catherine's assessment of other people's motives. When Catherine first meets Henry's brother Frederick, she fails to comprehend his gallantry toward Isabella, misinterpreting his flirtation as mere politeness. After hearing Frederick express a disinclination toward dancing and Isabella assert that she will not dance, Catherine sees the two dancing and cannot interpret it as anything other than a capitulation to social form. Yet Henry's diagnosis of Catherine's faulty inferences also points up the limitations of his own methods: "'With you,'" he tells Catherine, "'it is not, How is such a one likely to be influenced? What is the inducement most likely to act upon such a person's feelings, age, situation, and probable habits of life considered?—but, how should *I* be influenced, what would be *my* inducement in acting so and so?'" (126; original emphasis). Catherine poignantly "'do[es] not understand'" what Henry means here because she lacks the experience of the world necessary to make such inductive inferences; she can only assess other people's actions based upon her own experience. Put differently, when she interprets the events at the Abbey, she is indeed consulting "her own sense of the probable"—her experience, which includes what she has encountered in novels, does not validate the inherently rational foundations of the mind embodied by *l'homme éclairé*. While Henry's methods of imaginative conjecture yield accurate interpretation in this particular scene, their limits are revealed when he confronts Catherine about her inferences about "such a one" as his father. By "judging from" the gothic romance, Catherine misjudges the General, but Henry's exhortation to "'remember the country and age in which we live [. . .] that we are English, that we are Christians'" also fails—as many critics have noted—to grasp the particularity of the General (186).[10] It is not simply that Catherine's gothic imaginings tap into the underlying violence of the patriarchal order. Rather, the General's particular character fails to be adequately accounted for by the typological or characterological categories that both Catherine and Henry bring to bear on it. The difference between Catherine's and Henry's

---

10. Diane Hoeveler, for example, argues that "the net effect of mingling the gothic with the domestic and sentimental romance produces a strange hybrid—the awareness that the domestic is gothic or that we cannot think any more about the domestic without at the same time recognizing its gothic underpinnings, its propensities for violence, abuse, and exploitation of women" (129). Or, as Galperin succinctly puts it: "Catherine is fundamentally correct in treating the general with apprehension" (86).

judgments is a difference in degree, not kind. The "real" General emerges through the interstices of Catherine's inferences and the telling silences of Henry, Eleanor, and even the narrator.

III. UNCERTAIN FUTURES: ANNA, SUSAN, MARGARET

The manner in which Austen leverages the particular against probabilistic knowledge reflects a commitment to difference and heterogeneity, a commitment that has aesthetic and philosophical implications. On a basic level, the pleasure of working through the unfolding of one of Austen's novels is tied up with the processes of discrimination they force us to perform. Her plots gain their energy from the distinctions they make between "such a one" as the General and General Tilney himself, and from the tension they exploit between how "such a one" as Darcy ought to behave toward the Bennets and his improbable love for Elizabeth. The fineness of Austen's brush participates in an epistemological shift whereby the more attention that was paid to particulars, the more variation and irregularity were discovered. Her investment in differences and distinctions embodies a general skepticism about the process of induction—of deriving general knowledge from observed particulars. This is a problem that has implications for the representation of character as well as for the organization of plot.[11] As I have argued, Austen's plots mobilize the potential for the future to look different from the past in the process of their unfolding; they also draw attention to how convention dictates action within the "tell-tale compression" of a novel's pages. Although her novels offer strong forms of closure in spite of these challenges to the probable, there is nevertheless a complexity with which she orchestrates her endings that anticipates later critical discussions of "open" and "closed" narrative forms. In *Aspects of the Novel* (1927), for instance, E. M. Forster promotes an elevation of character over plot that is characteristic of modernist sensibilities: "In losing the battle that the plot fights with the characters, it often takes a cowardly revenge. Nearly all novels are feeble at the end. This is because the plot requires to

---

11. It is not coincidental that Austen's works have been central for developing broader theories of how narrative works, and in particular the relationship between concepts such as "character" and "plot." Both Alex Woloch and James Phelan provide extended readings of *Pride and Prejudice* in works that aim to elaborate the functions of major and minor characters (Woloch) and the mimetic, thematic, and synthetic aspects of characters (Phelan). Both are interested in the tension between the treatment of characters as singular individuals and as embodiments of attributes or thematic qualities. See Woloch, pp. 43–124, and Phelan, *Reading*, pp. 43–60.

be wound up. [. . .] [The novelist] has to round things off, and usually the characters go dead while he is at work" (91). The invocation of the "probable circumstance" needed to bring *Northanger Abbey* to a satisfactory end indicates Austen's self-consciousness about such "cowardly revenge": It allows the plot to be "wound up" in a probable manner, but in the process the General "go[es] dead" by becoming flat. To conclude this chapter, I show how Austen introduces "very minor" character at the end of her novels to pry open their "closed" forms. These young women prompt us to question the reliability of the past for predicting the future and thus represent a subtle but profound aesthetic challenge to probabilistic representation that shows how an openness to an uncertain future runs through all of Austen's works.

One of the most important things at stake in this analysis of probability in this historical context is the question of fiction's didactic function. As Whately and Aristotle contend, a narrative's didactic force—its ability to provide an "unpretending kind of instruction"—depends upon the degree to which it meets the demands of probability. To argue, as I have done here, that Austen interrogates the aesthetic implications of probability entails a claim about the didacticism—or lack thereof—of her works. The question of Austen's didactic intentions has been explored most fully by those critics interested in Austen's place within her contemporary political matrix, as well as by those critics concerned with her relationship to the didactic tradition of the novel that she inherits.[12] I would contend that Austen's primary concerns are aesthetic and that she remains skeptical about the didactic function of fiction. This is not to say that these investments are not in themselves ideological or do not have ideological implications; rather, it is simply to assert that her realism is shaped by aesthetic rather than didactic concerns. Reading Austen alongside her contemporaries, Mary Waldron has made a similar point, arguing that Austen aims "to produce a critique of fictional figures who control the action of the story because the narrative assumes them to be endowed with special *vertù*" (114). For Waldron, the very range of ideological positions attributed to Austen by her critics testifies to the moral ambiguity of her works, an ambiguity that Waldron sees as their innovative and defining feature. All of Austen's major characters—George Knightley and Fanny Price included—"are morally inconsistent, threading their way through conflicting courses for which there proves to be no systematic guide" (14). Waldron's claim that even the most vir-

---

12. Feminist criticism has been a particularly generative field in this regard; see Butler and Johnson. Jan Fergus emphasizes Austen's didactic intentions and sees her continuing the tradition she inherits; however, she also suggests that while Austen "accepts the eighteenth-century doctrine that literature should educate the emotions and judgment, she rejects most of the literary conventions associated with the doctrine, and particularly the exemplary character" (5).

tuous of Austen's characters act inconsistently resonates with my attention to her skepticism about the foundations of probable judgment: Austen abandons the assumption that the "wise man" can overcome the distortions of prejudice and desire to act in a consistently rational manner.

Closure is one area where a text's didactic intentions might be clearly expressed, as a plot's confirmation of an abstract moral principle (e.g., "Virtue Rewarded") announces the narrative as a form of instruction about "real life." Austen's resistance to strong closure in favor of contingency is most evident in *Persuasion,* a novel that presents two significant structural deviations from her earlier works. First, the temporal shift in the novel's setting alters the dynamics of interpretation and judgment that galvanize the narrative. Rather than bringing general experience and knowledge of the world to bear on the character of a new individual, Anne assesses Wentworth's ambiguous behavior in the present against the backdrop of her prior knowledge of him. Although we know from the outset that Anne "thought very differently from what she had been made to think at nineteen" (29), she also tempers her expectations and compels herself to "be feeling less" (56) in Wentworth's presence with the recollection that the world is changeable: "Eight years, almost eight years had passed, since all had been given up. [. . .] What might not eight years do? Events of every description, changes, alienations, removals,—all, all must be comprised in it; and the oblivion of the past." The culmination of the novel is not simply the recognition of mutual desire but the rediscovery by both Anne and Wentworth of the constancy of their own feelings and the other's love. They are "more tender, more tried, more fixed in a knowledge of each other's character, truth and attachment; more equal to act, more justified in acting" (225). This is not constancy amid change, but constancy *through* change. Second, as Emily Rohrbach so deftly shows, the novel's precise historical setting—opening in "the summer of 1814" (10) with Napoleon presumably in exile on Elba—contextualizes and tempers their interpersonal certainty with a broader uncertainty that arises from this specified historical context.[13] "The dread of future war" that "dim[s]" the sunshine of the novel's ending adds a rich complexity to the novel's affective force, one consistent with its attention to contingency (236). *Northanger Abbey* challenges its own didacticism directly through

---

13. Rohrbach's reading of the novel highlights how the importance of "anticipated retrospection" in the novel reflects an openness to contingency and uncertainty characteristic of the future anterior: "Austen and any post-1815 reader would know that, although the British military engagement in the 1815 warfare with Napoleon was relatively brief and the navy not involved, the characters' perception of their moment *will have been* a false sense of peace" (106; original emphasis). For a theoretical account that locates the future anterior as the defining structure of narrative temporality, see Mark Currie's excellent book *The Unexpected: Narrative Temporality and the Philosophy of Surprise.*

sustained irony, concluding with the narrator wryly "leav[ing] it to be settled by whomsoever it may concern, whether the tendency of this work be altogether to recommend parental tyranny, or reward filial disobedience" (235). *Persuasion,* however, aims for similar ends through a redistribution of certainty and uncertainty. The eroding foundations of probabilistic judgment, in other words, reflect a genuine sense of social and historical transformation.[14]

The endings of *Northanger Abbey* and *Persuasion* thus take quite different approaches to mitigating the didactic force that accompanies narrative closure. The novels in between tackle the problem in a formally innovative way through the introduction of "very minor" characters who serve as doubles—or iterations—of their novels' respective heroines. If "closed" forms promote didacticism, they do so by asking us to see particular plots as the expression of general principles, so that the novel attains the "instructive" quality privileged by Whately. As I have argued, this inductive process is at odds with Austen's effort to attend to and maintain differences, to foreground the distinction between "such a one" as the General and the General himself. The introduction of these very minor characters reinforces Austen's investment in particularity. They inscribe uncertainty into the novel's conclusion—and pry open its closed form—by prompting the reader to speculate on the contours of their unmapped futures and to see that the heroine's fate cannot be taken as a reliable predictor of the future.

Emma provides the most robust example of this structure through the figure of little Anna Weston, whom Mrs. Weston (formerly Miss Taylor) delivers safely into the world at the beginning of chapter 53 (the novel's antepenultimate chapter). The news of Anna's birth provokes an important debate between Emma and Knightley about Emma's own development, as Emma suggests that Anna will provide Mrs. Weston with the opportunity to put her educative "powers in exercise again":

"[Mrs. Weston] has had the advantage, you know, of practicing on me," [Emma] continued—"like La Batonne d'Almane on La Comtesse d'Ostalis, in Madame de Genlis' *Adelaide* and *Theodore,* and we shall now see her own little Adelaide educated on a more perfect plan."

---

14. The processes of "persuasion" in the novel depend on probabilistic expectation and judgment, and the contingency of these processes is central to the novel's primary concerns Anne's initial decision to break off her engagement to Wentworth is based in part on the "anxiety attending his profession, [and] their probable fears, delays and disappointments" that would attend their engagement (29). In addition to Rohrbach, John Wiltshire has also offered an account of contingency in the novel; see Wiltshire, pp. 147–68.

> "That is," replied Mr. Knightley, "she will indulge her [daughter] even more than she did you, and believe that she does not indulge her at all. It will be the only difference."
>
> "Poor child!" cried Emma; "at that rate, what will become of her?"
>
> "Nothing very bad.—The fate of thousands. She will be disagreeable in infancy, and correct herself as she grows older. I am losing all my bitterness against spoilt children, my dearest Emma. I, who am owing all my happiness to *you*, would not it be horrible ingratitude in me to be severe on them?"
>
> Emma laughed, and replied: "But I had the assistance of all your endeavours to counteract the indulgence of other people. I doubt whether my own sense would have corrected me without it."
>
> "Do you?—I have no doubt. Nature gave you understanding;—Miss Taylor gave you principles. You must have done well. My interference was quite as likely to do harm as good." (431–32; original emphasis).

The newborn Anna is not the real concern here, or at least the concern only insofar as her future provides the occasion for reflection upon Emma's own development. The scene poses a basic question: To what extent can we infer the arc of Anna's future development based upon the development we have seen Emma undergo? Rather than offering a clear answer to this question, however, the debate about the causality of Emma's development actually foregrounds the lack of clear causal structures and thus frustrates the effort to use Emma's development as a framework for understanding Anna's. The inability to inductively extrapolate a general model of development from Emma's that could be used to reliably project Anna's future recursively foregrounds the particularity and contingency of Emma's own development. While Emma's reference to Anna as a "poor child" mitigates any sense of real danger by tapping into the novel's most sustained joke ("Poor Miss Taylor!" are the first words of dialogue in the novel, spoken of course by Mr. Woodhouse), the subsequent question—"what will become of her?"—echoes Knightley's reflections on Emma's fate in chapter 5: "'There is an anxiety, a curiosity in what one feels for Emma. I wonder what will become of her!'" (39). By chapter 53, the reader knows of course "what [has] become" of Emma, but the iteration of this developmental process prompts the reader to speculate on the contours of Anna's future.

Yet rather than offering a clear indication of the causality of Emma's development—which could then be applied to the mapping of the infant Anna's future—the debate between Emma and Knightley highlights the complexity and contingency of Emma's maturation, confounding the effort to extrapolate general principles from it. Ultimately, we cannot predict the arc of Anna's development because we cannot identify the causes that have determined what Emma has become. The crux of the debate is the nature of Knightley's influence on Emma's development: Has Emma "correct[ed] herself" or was the external corrective of Knightley necessary for Emma to become the woman she has developed into by the novel's end? Is "understanding" a natural faculty, or a capacity supplied by education? These are the core questions of the novel, but rather than supplying clear answers, the texture of the debate here shows that they are unanswerable. There are clearly compelling psychological reasons that might explain Knightley's repudiation of any purported influence over Emma. More to the point, though, his suggestion that Anna's will be "the fate of thousands" highlights the tensions between the particular and the general, returning us to the question of whether Emma is herself exceptional or simply another one of those thousands. If Emma has been corrected by Knightley, then has her exceptionality—the "sauciness" (94) and imagination that set her apart from her milieu—been extinguished by her subjection to Knightley's moral (and masculine) vision? Or, if Emma's developmental arc reflects that of spoiled children everywhere, then has there been anything exceptional about her all along? Again, we can view Knightley's abnegation cynically, but the very dynamics of the debate appear to support his claims, as the scene dramatizes the unique dialogic reciprocity of Emma and Knightley's relationship. Amid *Emma*'s cacophony of monologic voices (Miss Bates, Mr. Woodhouse, Mrs. Elton, Isabella, etc.), Emma and Knightley seem to be the only pair capable of genuine dialogue. This dynamic is on full display in this scene, confirming that while Knightley might be seen as exerting some disciplinary force over Emma, she remains defined by her resistance to Knightley's authority. The introduction of Anna and the speculation about her future development direct attention to the causality of Emma's development. Yet rather than clarifying those causal structures—or distilling general principles—the scene performs several turns of the screw that heighten the causal ambiguity of that development. This scene, in other words, articulates the central didactic question of the novel and then explores it in a manner which shows that it cannot be answered. The act of "off-line" simulation of imagining the forking paths of Anna's future heightens the sense of Emma's particularity, confounding the effort to extrapolate general principles from her development.[15]

---

15. *Emma* provides a striking example of such "off-line" simulation at the beginning of chapter 31, when Emma tries to reflect upon and determine whether or not she is in love with Frank Churchill by imagining the potential ways their relationship might progress. Although she "form[s] a thousand amusing schemes for the progress and close of their attachment [. . .]

Both *Mansfield Park* and *Sense and Sensibility* attenuate narrative closure in a similar manner by turning attention to the younger sisters of the heroines. Although Lady Bertram cannot "willingly" part with Fanny, who has settled at Thornton Lacey with Edward, she can "part with her, because Susan remained to supply her place" and become the "stationary niece" (438). Several sentences are devoted to describing Susan's "fearless disposition and happier nerves" and how they contribute to her becoming "useful to all" at Mansfield Park. The narrator concludes by noting how Susan's "usefulness"—coupled with the general thriving of all the characters involved—lead to Sir Thomas's self-satisfied celebration of "what he had done for them all" and the "advantages of early hardship and discipline" (439). While the patriarch of the family derives a clear lesson from the preceding events, Susan's introduction prompts us to contemplate the role of Fanny's character in the production of that conclusion, and more specifically whether her influence is the product of her circumstantial upbringing or of her inherent qualities. As with Anna Weston in *Emma*, then, the introduction of Susan Price enables Austen to recapitulate the central thematic and causal questions of the novel; instead of eliminating ambiguity, this strategy cultivates it by questioning the degree to which the future might be reliably projected from the past.

The same strategy can be seen in the reintroduction of Margaret Dashwood at the end of *Sense and Sensibility*. After ironically announcing the "extraordinary fate" of Marianne Dashwood, a fate that entails discovering "the falsehood of her own opinions" and submitting to a second attachment in her marriage to Colonel Brandon, the narrator of *Sense and Sensibility* describes the ensuing domestic felicity of the novel's primary characters (379). Although Marianne has managed to escape the dangers that accompany unrestrained sensibility—dangers that the fates of the two Elizas in the novel remind us are very real—Austen nevertheless highlights the contingency of Marianne's fortune by gesturing toward the uncertain future of her younger sister Margaret. Margaret may be the most superfluous character within Austen's rigorous characterological systems—she is absent for most of the novel, and the only necessity she serves is that her existence justifies Elinor and Marianne's decision to leave their mother and travel to London under the guardianship of Mrs. Jennings. Yet the narrative returns to Margaret in the penultimate paragraph of the novel, with the narrator's comment that "fortunately for Sir John and Mrs. Jennings, when Marianne was taken from them, Margaret had reached an age highly suitable for dancing, and not very ineligible for

the conclusion of every imaginary declaration on his side was that she *refused him*" (245; original emphasis).

being supposed to have a lover" (381). The predominant tone here is certainly humorous, yet the moment nevertheless reminds us of the contingency of Marianne's extraordinary-in-being-ordinary fate: The ostensibly benevolent raillery of Sir John Middleton and Mrs. Jennings presents a real threat to the vulnerable young girls. Just as Anna Weston's entrance onto the scene highlights the inscrutable causality of Emma's development and forces us to imagine other outcomes under slightly different circumstances, the introduction of Margaret—who notably does not have the benefit of Elinor's presence—into the environment that Marianne has just escaped reminds us that Marianne's fate might have unfolded differently, and that it cannot be a reliable predictor of Margaret's future. While the uncertain futures of these very minor characters perhaps do little to temper the happy endings of their respective novels, they do mitigate their didactic force. In doing so, they represent a sophisticated attempt to navigate the complex matrix of issues that attend the notion of probability at this moment in literary and intellectual history. As readers speculate upon the probable fates of these young women, we do so without being able to determine whether our conjectures are those of a "mathematician" or an "imaginist" (*Emma* 313–14).

CHAPTER 2

Reading Chance, Encountering Otherness in Scott

> Sir Walter Scott, an orthodox cosmolater, is always half and half on these subjects. The appearances [of spirits] are so stated as to be readily solved on the simplest principles of pathology[,] while the precise coincidence of the event so marvellously exceeds the ordinary run of chances, as to preserve the full effect of superstition for the reader and yet the credit of unbelief for the writer.
> —SAMUEL TAYLOR COLERIDGE, MARGINAL NOTE IN *WAVERLEY*

COLERIDGE'S NOTE on Fergus Mac-Ivor and the apparition of the Bodach Glas in chapter 59 of his copy of *Waverley* specifies how Scott's equivocal handling of the supernatural brings together questions of probability, belief, and genre. Although the novel seems to approach spirits and ghosts from a position of rationalist "unbelief," Scott nevertheless turns to improbability— here in the form of a "precise coincidence" that "exceeds the ordinary run of chances"—to produce the "full effect of superstition for the reader." Fergus's belief in the haunting specter of the Bodach Glas can be "solved" and dismissed simply as "pathology": it is the result of his irrational superstition. Yet the circumstances surrounding the spirit's appearance exceed a rationalist framework to the point where this purportedly "marvellou[s]" occurrence becomes credible. Like Richard Whately's review of Austen, Coleridge's invocation of the language of probability demonstrates how notions of aesthetic probability were articulated in quantitative terms in the early decades of the nineteenth century. It also shows how realism is conceived in relation to a normative model of the everyday—an "ordinary run of chances"—that novels themselves deliberately challenge. Scott's historical fiction presupposes a rationalist framework that acknowledges that spirits and supernatural events are not real but then presents circumstances that are so highly coincidental that they evoke the "pathology" of superstition. The novel itself internalizes this tension between a putatively realist framework of unbelief and irratio-

· 69 ·

nal superstition in the figure of Edward Waverley. When Fergus first informs Edward that he has seen the Bodach Glas and explains the belief among his clan that the spirit "'crosse[s] the path of the Vich Ian Vohr [. . .] before [his] approaching death,'" Edward asks his friend how he could "'tell such nonsense with a grave face'" (294). However, when Waverley reflects upon Fergus's uncertain fate the next day following the skirmish at Clifton, "the superstition of the Bodach Glas recur[s] to Edward's recollection," and he finds himself with "internal surprise" contemplating the possibility that Fergus's superstition might be valid (297). It is not just Scott, then, who is "half and half" on these matters: Edward here dramatizes the process that Ian Duncan has identified as characteristic of the Waverley Novels as a whole, a process whereby the reader too becomes "doubled and divided between mental states of enlightened freedom and a primitive, irrational bondage" (*Shadow* 280).[1]

This chapter demonstrates how Scott uses improbability to balance the realist "credit of unbelief" with the "full effect of superstition," arguing that this evocation of superstition through "precise coincidences" is a key tool his historical novels use to stage encounters with historical and cultural otherness. It thus shows that Scott's realism is defined not by its rejection of the irrational or supernatural, but rather by the way it uses improbability to strategically leverage the effects of superstition. By dissolving rather than reinforcing the boundary between "enlightened freedom" and "irrational bondage," Scott's realist method both acknowledges the parameters of a rationalist worldview and moves beyond it to expose the irrational superstition that remains latent within it. Devin Griffiths has recently argued for Scott's importance to the development of a "comparative historicism" (89) that replaced Enlightenment theories of history as "progressive, providential, and stadial" (84) with an "uncertain network of analogies—a history of difference and differentiation as well as resonance—that exposed modernity as a tense and uneven composite" (88). Scott's strategic deployment of chance becomes a mechanism for orchestrating this method of comparative historicism. It thus shows how the novel form emerges in dialogue with the epistemological problems that accompanied shifting models of probability at the start of the nineteenth century. As Mary Poovey has suggested in her reading of Samuel Johnson's *Journey to the Western Islands of Scotland* (1775), the assumptions of universality and typicality that accompanied Enlightenment approaches to history came

---

1. Ina Ferris has demonstrated more than any other critic the profound implications of this "generic doubleness" for the legitimization of the novel form through Scott's historical romances; the Waverley Novels, Ferris argues, "offer a generic doubleness that allows male subjectivity to enter into a female genre without losing its masculine purchase on truth and fact" (88).

to be challenged at the end of the eighteenth century as cultural otherness was encountered in increasingly particularized and countable forms.[2] Scott negotiates probability through chance and coincidental events that court competing interpretations, grappling with challenges to the rational model of mind that had grounded the classical interpretation of probability and Enlightenment philosophy more broadly. Whereas Austen explores the subjective underpinnings of probabilistic expectation, Scott engages these foundations through the problem of cultural and historical differentiation. Because his fiction foregrounds "the forces that bind together individuals into historically distinctive societies," Scott is particularly attuned to the ways in which values, beliefs, and epistemologies are embedded within contingent cultural formations (Shaw, *Forms* 128). As Scott uses chance to differentiate and thus historicize dispositions toward the supernatural, he creates resonances that challenge the supposed "enlightened freedom" secured by modernity.

Scott is clearly aware of the degree to which narrative probability is tied intimately to genre, but he challenges both the stability and the authority of realism's ostensible commitment to a fully rational worldview. Scott's artistic identity was forged through his relationship to the gothic, beginning in the 1790s with his translations of German dramatic works and his imitations of supernatural ballads in collaboration with Matthew "Monk" Lewis. As critics such as Fiona Robertson and Michael Gamer have shown, Scott positions himself in intricate ways vis-à-vis the gothic, drawing on its imaginative, affective, and commercial power while also establishing literary and cultural authority by treating it with requisite critical distance. According to Gamer, Scott's early career "involves a full-scale appropriation and recasting of popular gothic materials into a respectably historical, national, masculine, and poetic mould" (156). As Scott's 1811 introduction to Horace Walpole's *The Castle Otranto* (1764) demonstrates, the project of "recasting" the gothic is built upon the recognition of both continuity and difference between the past and present. While Walpole's purpose was to present "domestic life and manners, during the feudal times" as it was "chequered and agitated by the action of supernatural machinery, such as the superstition of the period received as a matter of devout credulity," this superstition also lingers into the present in spite of rational skepticism toward the supernatural (91). Walpole's novel appeals "to that secret and reserved feeling of love for the marvellous and supernatural, which occupies a hidden corner in almost every one's bosom" but which can be evoked only through technical artistry (91). For Scott, Walpole's success resides in his ability to produce in "a well-cultivated mind" the

---

2. See Poovey, *History*, pp. 249–65.

"surprise and fear" evoked by the supernatural (91): Superstition becomes "contagious" (92), and the reader's feelings become "for a moment identified with those of a ruder age" (93).

Scott repeatedly revisits these ideas in his reviews and criticism, where probability defines the unstable boundary between the rational and the superstitious. In his entry on Ann Radcliffe in *Lives of the Novelists* (1821–24), which I discuss at greater length below, Scott acknowledges that he writes in "an age of universal incredulity" (I. Williams 116) and confirms the distinction between narratives that abide by "natural principles" and those that indulge in the supernatural or the gothic. Likewise, in his review of Mary Shelley's *Frankenstein* (1818), Scott asserts that a distinction is "sufficiently obvious and decided" between works that "bound the events they narrate by the actual laws of nature" and those that surpass these bounds and are "managed by marvellous and supernatural machinery" (260). Despite this distinction, however, Scott asserts that a narrative can still be probable if it contains the unnatural, as in some genres the reader accepts the marvelous on the grounds established by the author: "The *probable* is far from being laid out of sight even amid the wildest freaks of imagination; on the contrary, we grant the extraordinary postulates which the author demands as the foundation of his narrative, only on condition of his deducing the consequences with logical precision" (262; original emphasis). This discussion frames probability primarily as a matter of internal coherence related to genre: Whether a work commits to the "laws of nature" or uses "supernatural machinery," the aesthetic concern is simply whether events unfold logically within those parameters. Yet in practice Scott exploits the ambiguity and instability of such parameters. For example, in his essay "On the Supernatural in Fictitious Composition," Scott explores the various ends toward which the supernatural might be put, and by delineating a series of gradations between the ostensibly "realist" and the indulgently "marvellous," he reframes the distinction between the two as a difference in degree rather than as a categorical difference in kind. As Coleridge suggests, his fiction is consistently "half and half on these subjects." Edward's "internal surprise" as he entertains the possible validity of Fergus's superstitious belief in the Bodach Glas reflects Scott's broader understanding that our sense of the probable is composed of knowledge of natural laws that never fully surmounts irrational structures of belief.

Scott consistently exploits casual ambiguity to foreground the unstable distinction between the "actual laws of nature" and the marvelous. An earlier scene in *Waverley* also involving Edward and Fergus demonstrates the structures of belief implicated in the Bodach Glas, revealing how Scott's treatment of causality is central to the comparative historicism that grounds his realist method. During his first excursion into the Highlands, Edward suffers a sprained ankle during a stag hunt with Fergus and his clan. A shout in Gaelic alerting the hunters to stampeding deer is "lost" on Edward, and he is saved from more serious injury only by the timely interposition of Fergus (123). Edward's subsequent convalescence is an important cog in the larger causal gears of the novel—it contributes to the delays and complications that force him to resign his commission in the king's army, leading him to align himself with the Jacobites. However, Scott also leverages the occasion to juxtapose superstitious and rational causal interpretations. The "old smoke-dried Highlander" who is summoned to treat Edward's injury begins by performing the ceremonial deasil, muttering Gaelic incantations as he prepares an embrocation (124). Edward cannot discern whether these words are "prayers or spells," dismissing it all simply as "gibberish." The treatment works, however, and Edward's pain subsides. Yet *how* it works elicits different interpretations: Whereas Edward "imputed [success] to the virtue of the herbs, or the effect of the chafing," the Highlanders in attendance "ascribed [it] to the spells with which the operation had been accompanied." This juxtaposition does more than mark Edward's cultural distance from the superstitious Highlanders, as it adds to the rich characterization of Fergus and his precarious cultural position. To Edward's surprise, Fergus concurs with the "superstitious ideas of his countrymen" despite his "knowledge and education," because "like most men who do not think deeply or accurately on such subjects, he had in his mind a reserve of superstition which balanced the freedom of his expressions and practice on other occasions" (125). Thus, the ambiguous causal link between the application of the embrocation and the cessation of Edward's pain allows Scott to mark the cultural distance between Edward's rationalism and the Highlanders' superstition. But it also enables the novel to collapse that distance through Fergus. If Fergus's "reserve of superstition" signals his incomplete acclimatization to modernity, the "internal surprise" Waverley later experiences as he contemplates the Bodach Glas might be read as a cognitive trace of the acts of cultural and historical negotiation the novel performs as a whole.

This chapter analyzes the ways in which Scott utilizes the inherent causal ambiguity of chance and coincidence to develop a mode of comparative historicism that both locates sites of cultural difference and also evokes resonances that reveal modernity to be (in Griffiths's terms) "an uneven composite." Chance events and "precise coincidences"—between, for instance, prophecies or legends like the Bodach Glas and the events narrated—can be interpreted through both rational and supernatural causal schema,[3] and thus they embody the doubleness that is more broadly characteristic of the generic hybridity of Scott's historical romances. As the scene of Edward's treatment illustrates, a causal interpretation through a rational or supernatural causal schema situates a character within a particular cultural formation. Although Scott's realist mode generally remains committed to plotting events according to naturalistic causation, he relies upon causal ambiguity to elicit and incorporate other modes of interpretation (and the cultural formations of which they are artefacts) within that realist mode. The different dispositions toward freedom and fatalism conjured by Scott's improbable realist aesthetic not only challenge the rationality that underpinned the classical interpretation of probability but also anticipate the conflicting attitudes chance would elicit as it was "tamed"—both recognized and mitigated—over the course of the nineteenth century. Scott's evocation of seemingly surmounted modes of belief and dispositions toward causality is more than a matter of historical curiosity—an effort to dramatize for readers what those in the past used to believe. Edward's "internal surprise" at his superstitious inclinations and Fergus's "reserve of superstition" reveal the incomplete ascendancy of rationality, and they suggest the complexity of the dynamics of readerly experience created by the generic doubleness of Scott's fictions. Each of the three sections of this chapter focuses on a particular text—"The Two Drovers," *Redgauntlet,* and *The Bride of Lammermoor,* respectively—to establish how "reading chance" becomes a central structure within Scott's works as they construct encounters with cultural and historical otherness. The first section shows how Scott creates encounters with cultural otherness by using chance to sustain causal ambiguity in line with Tzvetan Todorov's theorization of "the fantastic." The second section engages with Georg Lukács's discussions of chance and realism to develop an approach to realist causality that recognizes the capacity of chance to facilitate the representation of abstract social forces. The third and final section of the chapter returns to the problem of the supernatural to argue that Scott's gothic mode challenges readerly credulity by provoking the reader's "reserve of superstition." Scott's realism is distinctive not simply because it attempts to accommodate causal structures seemingly at odds with realism's commitment to naturalistic causation. Scott's use of causal ambiguity and his

---

3. A causal schema is a "conception of the manner in which two or more causal factors interact to produce a specific type of effect" (Ritzema and Young 36); they are our cognitive scaffolding for making sense of causal relations in the world and our means of attributing causes to observed effects. Scott exploits the ways in which moments of chance and coincidence can be explained in terms of naturalistic or rational causation ("event[s] caused by the environment [a] person [is] in or by psychological factors within the person") but also in terms of superstitious or supernatural causation ("event[s] caused by some force beyond those in the environment and within the person") (38).

courtship of supernatural causal interpretations might be seen as constitutive of his realism insofar as they become the narrative mechanisms through which cultural and historical otherness can be experienced.

I. CASUAL AMBIGUITY AND THE FANTASTIC IN "THE TWO DROVERS"

To argue that Scott's plots perform important cognitive work is to counter a long critical tradition of dismissing Scott's craftsmanship out of hand. E. M. Forster's praise of Scott's capacity to "tell a story" (33) in *Aspects of the Novel* is accompanied by censure: "He cannot construct" (32). "Unlike the weaver of plots," a storyteller like Scott "profits by ragged ends" according to Forster (34). Harry E. Shaw, one of Scott's most perceptive readers, claims that he is "frivolous about narrative" and constructed his plots "haphazardly" ("Problem" 182).[4] And speaking of Scott's efforts to write himself out of debt in the last decade of his life, Stuart Kelly claims that "you can almost hear the effort of dragging the quill across the page, churning out sub-clauses and eking out the details" (286). Such views only gain added force in cognitive approaches to realism, which are inclined to evaluate highly coincidental events in light of concepts like Marie-Laure Ryan's notion of the "cheap plot trick." Scott himself at times reveals his self-consciousness about his works' potential flaws in his elaborate editorial apparatuses. The "Introductory Epistle" to *The Fortunes of Nigel* (1822), for instance, stages a conversation between the figure of Captain Clutterbuck and the "Eidolon" (or specter) of "The Author of Waverley" in which the two discuss the manuscript the reader is about to begin. After the Author concedes that he has no desire to "[row] against the stream of popular opinion," he promises that—in contrast to *The Monastery* (1820)—he has abandoned "the mystic, and the magical, and the whole systems of signs, wonders, and omens" and has not relied upon "dreams, or presages, or obscure allusions to future events" (6). The two then discuss probable plotting, with the Author dismissing the practicality of a plot that flows like a river, "gliding on, never pausing, never precipitating [. . . ,] widening and deepening in interest as it flows on; and at length arriving at the final catastrophe." Clutterbuck sums up the Author's views with a (misquoted) epigram from the Duke of Buckingham's *The Rehearsal* (1671): "'What the devil does the plot signify,

---

4. Shaw's comments are not leveled as criticism of Scott's practices but rather aim to defend him from critics who emphasize his lack of seriousness as a novelist by linking his "frivolousness" about narrative to his insights about the limits of narrative and historical understanding. See Shaw, "Problem."

except to bring in fine things?'" (7). Even "The Two Drovers"—the tale that interests me here—seems to preempt consideration of its formal complexity. In *Chronicles of the Canongate* (1827), it is introduced by a vignette in which the *Chronicle*'s narrator, Chrystal Croftangry, admits to producing the tale in haste when he learns that "'the little Gillie-whitefoot was come from the printing office [. . .] to torment me for *copy,* for so they call a supply of manuscript for the press'" (123; original emphasis).

Yet the "copy" that follows does more than fulfill Croftangry's purpose of "throw[ing] some light on the manners of Scotland as they were, and to contrast them, occasionally, with such as now are fashionable in the same country" (51). The story's sophisticated use of chance mobilizes competing probabilistic interpretations to generate a rich and complex engagement with cultural otherness. The story relates a conflict between the eponymous drovers, the Highlander Robin Oig and his English friend Harry Wakefield. "Touched in point of honour" after Harry assaults him in an alehouse, Robin takes revenge and kills Harry, and he is subsequently executed after an English court deems the act premeditated murder (124). The tale opens by painting a complex portrait of Robin, who is—like Croftangry—a "borderer," caught between generations and geographies because his profession places him in an uncertain cultural position that straddles the boundaries of the Highlands and modernity (50). Robin's defining characteristic is "pride of birth." Yet while his genealogy and reputation make him something of a celebrity in his Highland community, his travels to England "had given him tact enough to know that [such] pretensions" would be "both obnoxious and ridiculous if preferred elsewhere" (126). Robin's conflicted identity is on display when his aunt Janet insists on performing the ancient ritual of the deasil to bless his impending journey with Harry south into England. Robin is "rather impatient of her presence," but "half embarrassed, half laughing," he yields to her insistence to "soothe her humour" (127). In the middle of the ritual, Janet stops in horror and exclaims to Robin that "'there is blood on your hand, and it is English blood.'" Robin dismisses Janet's "Taishataragh (second sight)" with a "'Prutt, trutt'" and maintains his rational skepticism as Janet pleads with him to abort his journey. Robin refuses, but, "determined to close [the scene] at any sacrifice," he agrees to surrender his dirk to Hugh Morrison, another drover who will be following behind (128). From a narratological perspective, this transaction is highly structured, though it is also highly contingent, a point reinforced by Hugh's later reference to the dirk as "'wanchancy'" (139)—dangerous, but also unlucky or uncanny.[5]

---

5. *OED, s.v.* "wanchancy, *adj.*"

Chance and coincidence are essential to how the story stages a conflict between traditional and modern self-understanding, as Scott utilizes a highly contingent sequence of events to precipitate the conflict between Robin and Harry. As the two friends travel south, they are pressed by circumstances to secure separate fields in which to rest their flocks:

> Unhappily *it chanced* that both of them, unknown to each other, thought of bargaining for the [same] ground [. . .]. The English drover applied to the bailiff of the property, who was known to him. *It chanced* that the Cumbrian Squire, who had entertained some suspicions of his manager's honesty [. . .] desired that any inquiries [. . .] should be referred to himself. As, however, Mr Ireby had gone the day before upon a journey of some miles' distance to the northwest, the bailiff chose to consider the check upon his full powers as for the time removed [. . .]. Meanwhile, ignorant of what his comrade was doing, Robin Oig, on his side, *chanced* to be overtaken by a well-looked smart little man upon a pony [. . . and] asked him whether he could let him know if there was any grass-land to be let in that neighbourhood [. . .]. He could not have put the question to more willing ears. The gentleman of the buckskins was the proprietor with whose bailiff Harry Wakefield had dealt. (131; added emphasis)

The use of the verb *chanced* three times in this short sequence draws attention to the contingency (and constructedness, of course) of the circumstances. When the mistake comes to light, Harry reluctantly acknowledges the primacy of Robin's claim, but his pride is deeply wounded. Later in the evening, his anger is inflamed at the alehouse "by the bailiff [. . .] as well as by the innkeeper, and two or three chance guests," who heighten his "resentment against his quondam associate" (133). Robin refuses Harry's invitation to spar, proposing instead "'to go before your shudge, though I neither know his law nor his language'" (136). Harry proceeds to strike the smaller Scotsman several times before his "placability" prompts him to try to make peace with his defeated friend (137).

While Harry is mollified and eager to be "'better friends than ever,'" Robin believes that his reputation has been indelibly marred by this encounter in which the rules of fair play have not been followed (137). He flees from the alehouse with an ambiguous gesture: "He shook his hand at Wakefield, pointing with his fore-finger upwards, in a manner which might imply either a threat or a caution" (138). The exact meaning of Robin's gesture and thoughts remain obscure to the bystanders and the reader alike; soon after, though, the narrative enters his experiential field:

But there remained one party from whose mind that recollection [of the scuffle] could not have been wiped away by possession of every head of cattle between Esk and Eden.

This was Robin Oig McCombich.—"That I should have had no weapon," he said, "and for the first time in my life!—Blighted be the tongue that bids the Highlander part with the dirk—the dirk—ha! the English blood!—My muhme's word—when did her word fall to the ground?"

The recollection of the fatal prophecy confirmed the deadly intention which instantly sprang up in his mind. (138)

The recollection of the prophecy gives Robin's "impetuous spirit [. . .] a fixed purpose and motive of action" (139). He walks a dozen miles round trip to retrieve his dirk from Hugh and returns to the alehouse, where he slays Harry. The time that it takes Robin to retrieve his weapon is ultimately what condemns him in the eyes of the English law to which he is subsequently subjected. The story concludes with an extended description of the trial, in which the English judge acknowledges that Robin's "'rooted national prejudices [. . .] made him consider himself as stained with indelible dishonour'" (144). Yet Robin cannot be exonerated: The "'pinch of the case lies in the interval of two hours interposed betwixt the reception of the injury and the fatal retaliation'" (144–45). Immediate retaliation may have been justified, but according to the judge the elapsed time is "'an interval sufficient for [Robin] to have recollected himself.'" His attack on Harry is deemed "'predetermined revenge,'" and Robin is sentenced to death (145).

The plot of "The Two Drovers" is at once highly contingent and overtly constructed—it strategically deploys chance to construct causal ambiguity. If the plot is a vehicle "to bring in fine things"—in this case, a fight, a murder, and an execution—the manner in which the story calls attention to the mechanics of its unfolding is equally significant. The contingency creates an asymmetry between the "unhappy" chance events that initiate the plot and their ultimate consequence, one that facilitates the story's exploration of the incongruity between Robin's identity and the English legal code that determines his fate. Just as the bystanders at the alehouse are horrified by Robin's retaliatory assault, "the provocation being, in their opinion, so utterly inadequate to the excess of vengeance," the discordance between the initiating events ("unhappily it chanced") and their consequences is essential to how the story works.

More importantly, the ambiguous causal relationship between Janet's prophecy and the subsequent conflict between Robin and Harry enables Scott to dramatize how Robin's agency and identity are circumscribed by his traditional Highland culture. The "precise coincidence" between omen and event raises a basic but troubling interpretive question: What, ultimately, causes Robin to kill Harry? The causal ambiguity of the story creates the structure of interpretive hesitation that Tzvetan Todorov identifies as the condition of possibility for "the fantastic." According to Todorov, the fantastic denotes a duration of hesitation—by readers and characters alike—between competing causal interpretations of seemingly supernatural occurrences: 'There is an uncanny phenomenon which we can explain in two fashions, by types of natural causes and supernatural causes. The possibility of a hesitation between the two creates the fantastic effect" (26). Whereas "total faith" in the supernatural produces *the marvelous* and "total incredulity" leads us to *the uncanny* (or the supernatural explained), a hesitation between the two constitutes the fantastic—"it is hesitation which sustains its life" (31). The duration of this hesitation can be managed in a variety of ways (and for a variety of ends), and it may or may not entail the hesitation of a character.[6] The "first condition of the fantastic," however, is the hesitation of the reader between competing causal explanations for the events represented. Todorov is concerned not with the particular beliefs or actual reading experiences of embodied readers but rather with "the role of the reader implicit in the text," what narrative theorists working in the rhetorical tradition of Wayne Booth would call the *implied reader*. The hesitation, in other words, is the product of the particular manner in which the events are presented and thus "implies an integration of the reader into the world of the characters." As with Austen's dramatized scenes of inference and probabilistic judgment, the reader's complex and uncertain positioning vis-à-vis the character is crucial.

Todorov's structural account of the fantastic illuminates how Robin's recollection of the prophecy creates a moment of hesitation where the causal relationship between the prophecy and the fight in the alehouse becomes ambiguous. As Robin laments the absence of his dirk after being beaten, he suddenly recalls Janet's prophecy: "'Blighted be the tongue that bids the Highlander part with the dirk—the dirk—ha! the English blood!'" Robin's attitude toward the prophecy alters dramatically, and the narrative states explicitly that this change is the cause of subsequent events, as "the recollection of the fatal prophecy confirmed the deadly intention which instantly sprang up in his mind." The interval between "the dirk" and "the English blood" (demarcated textually by the repetition of "the dirk") constitutes a moment of hesitation

---

6. According to Todorov, this hesitation can be experienced by characters as well, but it is not a necessary condition of the fantastic. It is also possible for an individual character to reflect the role of the reader and their hesitation, in which case that hesitation might become a thematic element of the narrative.

where the relationship between Janet's prophecy and Robin's situation becomes an object of scrutiny. Although Robin is initially skeptical of Janet's "second sight," the "precise coincidence" between her prophecy and his situation produces a moment of hesitation, which dissolves as he comes to see his impending retaliation as predetermined ("ha!"). If Robin's hesitation resolves into an acceptance of what Todorov calls a *pandeterminism* that negates chance (45), the reader's hesitation is dispelled by the naturalistic causes that the narrative subtly brings to attention. Robin's "deadly intention" exists prior to his recollection of the prophecy, but it is the recollection that "confirm[s]" this intention—his recollection of the prophecy is thus the proximate cause of his retaliatory assault. Although the story never explicitly debunks a supernatural explanation, it guides the reader to an interpretive position different from Robin's. The reader is aligned with Robin as the Highlander recalls the prophecy and is thus prompted to consider its significance, but then the reader sees how Robin's subsequent decisions and actions are the causal factors in determining his fate. If Robin initially regards the prophecy with skepticism, then the same judgment remains available to him when he remembers it later. He could, in other words, interpret the relationship between the prophecy and the scuffle as a mere coincidence and nothing more. But the coincidence activates something akin to Fergus's "reserve of superstition" and, in effect, causes Janet's prophecy to become self-fulfilling. The prophecy is not "fatal" in itself, but it becomes so through Robin's sudden belief in it; his agency is attenuated not by a predetermined fatalism but by his inability to contemplate the possibility of chance. Robin's assignation of supernatural causation—that he is fated to murder Harry—becomes the foundation (as a psychological factor) of a naturalistic causal explanation for the reader.

"The Two Drovers" demonstrates how Scott leverages the causal ambiguity produced by chance and coincidence to explore the conflict between rationality and superstition and to structure a complex engagement with Robin's cultural otherness. Just as Todorov notes that "accident or coincidence" can "erode the case for the supernatural" since "in the supernatural world, instead of chance there prevails what we might call 'pandeterminism'" (45), Scott identifies coincidence—between dreams and reality, for instance—as a particularly potent source of superstition in past ages. In his *Letters on Demonology and Witchcraft* (1830), Scott diagnoses "concatenation[s]" like those seen in "The Two Drovers" and *Waverley* as the source of "general belief" in the supernatural, acknowledging its psychological power while accounting for it on rational grounds (7). Scott explains, invoking the same quantitative, probabilistic language used by Whately and Coleridge: "Yet perhaps, considering the many thousands of dreams, which must, night after night, pass through the imagination of individuals, the number of coincidences between the vision and the real event, are fewer and less remarkable than a fair calculation of chances would warrant us to expect." Beginning with the presumption of the reader's "incredulity," Scott works to unsettle this disbelief in order to create a complex engagement with Robin Oig. Even as the reader is distanced from Robin in the recognition that it is his response to the prophecy that leads him to kill Harry (and not a predetermined fate that the prophecy announces), the momentary act of identification with Robin foregrounds the cultural limitations of the rationality that grounds the juridical condemnation of Robin's act. As Shaw has argued in an extended reading of the story, "'The Two Drovers' demonstrates that we can often see far beyond our own cultural grid, but that our vision may in the end have little effect on our actions" (*Narrating* 212). This tension is displayed most vividly in the concluding trial scene, where the judge, despite his sympathy, cannot think beyond a notion of justice that profoundly fails to account for Robin's being and actions. Like the *Letters on Demonology*, "The Two Drovers" resists "a crude opposition between superstitious past and rational modernity," as it harnesses the inherent causal ambiguity of chance to facilitate this ideological negotiation (Maxwell-Stuart 7).

II. CHANCE AND THE "DIALECTICS OF FREEDOM AND NECESSITY" IN *REDGAUNTLET*

The competing interpretations that chance elicits in "The Two Drovers" create structures of difference and resonance across cultures, allowing Robin's otherness to be cognized but not subsumed within the rationalist framework of modernity. The highly contingent events that structure the plot evoke opposing dispositions toward causality that nevertheless reveal a common substrate. If Robin's rational skepticism is overpowered by his "reserve of superstition," the reader's presumed incredulity is challenged by the hesitation that allows for a momentary identification with Robin. While the Enlightenment understanding of probability presupposed the fundamental rationality of the mind, Scott's fiction taps into the "reserve of superstition" that subsists beneath probabilistic judgment. In doing so, his method contradicts the claim that realist causality operates by rigorously excluding chance and coincidence, showing instead how these mechanisms can be used to represent diffuse causal structures.

Redgauntlet offers a more systematic example of this method and amplifies its representational stakes. The "'accident—lucky or unlucky'" that brings Darsie Latimer into contact with his uncle Hugh Redgauntlet structures the novel's plot, and in doing so it also becomes the means by which the novel represents, through a series of mediations, the historical processes that lead to the disappearance of Jacobitism that the novel conjures through its fictional, failed rebellion (301). *Redgauntlet* does not explicitly court the possibility of supernatural causation (or reflect the structure of the fantastic); however, chance structures Scott's effort to represent the disappearance of Jacobitism by eliciting competing causal schemata that are metonymically linked to the cultural positions that constitute the horizon of the novel's political and historical landscape. Georg Lukács's analysis of chance and realist representation will help illuminate the sophisticated relationship between plot, individual agency, and historical process in Scott's third and final Jacobite novel. Despite the limitations of his rigid Hegelian framework, Lukács reveals the power of chance to grasp abstract causal structures and thus how it helps figure the "dialectics of freedom and necessity" that constitutes realism's strongest claim on historical existence (Lukács, *Historical* 147). In Scott's novel, a single chance event becomes a vehicle for representing the movement of history.

Conflicts between different modes of seeing the world are at the heart of Scott's novelistic method, and *Redgauntlet* has been regarded as Scott's most thoroughgoing reflection on his narrative practice because of its formal self-consciousness. Critics have characterized the dialectical interaction of opposing narrative modes in the Waverley Novels in different ways: James Kerr sees "fiction" and "history" as competing forms of understanding that Scott uses to grasp and shape the past, while Ian Duncan argues that the relationship between "romance" and "history" in the Waverley Novels is "complicated and delusive" since "neither carries total authority, [and] their dialectical complicity is insisted upon" (*Romance* 59–60). For many, *Redgauntlet* is Scott's greatest work because it is at once the most fictional and the most historical of his novels: It stages a counterfactual third Jacobite rebellion two decades after the 1745 Uprising, but it does so with the aim of helping readers grasp the historical processes that have undermined the material and social foundations of Jacobitism. The novel's formal heterogeneity—consisting of epistolary correspondence, third-person narration, and interpolated tales—foregrounds the conflicting perspectives of different narrative modes, particularly in the epistolary exchanges between Darsie and his friend Alan Fairford that open the novel. Alan calls attention to the power of Darsie's imagination and implores him to "view things as they are, and not as they may be magnified through thy teeming fancy" (13), reminding readers that we are receiving competing accounts of the same events from differing perspectives. Scott is not only reminding us that our experience of reality is mediated by interpretive frameworks; he is exploring the incongruities that emerge between competing modes of seeing and understanding.

The ideological displacement of Darsie, the rightful heir of the Redgauntlets, from his uncle Hugh is the primary mechanism *Redgauntlet* uses to represent the obsolescence of Jacobitism. Their distinct and opposing conceptions of identity embody what James Chandler calls "cultural-historical typologies of character and agency" (96). On the one hand, Hugh—a "decayed gentleman"—remains devoted to the restoration of the Stuarts despite the failure of the 1745 Uprising and the consequent necessity that he remain in hiding (26). His political allegiances structure his understanding of heredity and social identity. He believes that the blood in his and Darsie's veins—and the "fatal sign" of the horseshoe on their brows—links their fates to the Stuarts (192). His fatalism is revealed when he commands Darsie to "'abandon [himself] to that train of events by which [they] are both swept along, and which it is impossible that either of [them] can resist'" (168). Darsie, on the other hand, rejects this determinism and feels himself instead to be a "solitary individual" who is "in the world as a stranger in the crowded coffee-house, where he enters, calls for what refreshments he wants, pays his bill, and is forgotten" (4). Darsie's reference to the *locus classicus* of the modern public sphere—the coffeehouse—is apt, since his modern bourgeois sense of self arises from his initial ignorance of his genealogy and his legal training in Edinburgh. His ideological displacement from Hugh embodies the same cultural tensions at play in "The Two Drovers," and it reflects the process that Andrew Lincoln has called the "disembedding" of identity "from the social, material, and cultural grounds that governed individuals in earlier ages" (9).

Darsie's ideological displacement from Hugh is predicated upon geographical displacement, so their encounter on the Solway Firth that brings them into contact is a compositional necessity on the most basic level. However, Lukács's distinction between "narration" and "description" illuminates how Scott integrates the event into the wider dramatic action of the novel and its depiction of historical processes. In "Narrate or Describe?" (1936), Lukács ponders what "is meant by 'chance' in fiction," and compares the horse races in Émile Zola's *Nana* (1880) and Leo Tolstoy's *Anna Karenina* (1875–77) to explicate the difference between narration and description (*Writer* 112). The difference between the two novelists is how they integrate the horse race into their novel's representation of reality. Zola's horse race displays his "virtuosity" in detailed description, but the scene remains "mere filler" since the "events are loosely related to the plot and could easily be eliminated" (110). The race is not random, of course: It is linked to the main plot insofar as the heroine and the victorious horse have the same name. But this "tenuous chance association" is merely symbolic (i.e., the horse's victory is symbolic of the heroine's social triumphs). In contrast, the race in *Anna Karenina* is "no mere tableau but rather a series of intensely dramatic scenes which provide a turning point in the plot" (111). It is representative of narration (as opposed to description) because it enables readers to experience events and to grasp "the general social significance emerging in the unfolding of the characters' lives" (116). The relationship between the race and the characters' lives is "itself a chance event," but it becomes "an occasion for the explosion of a conflict," as Vronsky's defeat is not merely symbolic but the culmination of a series of dramatic developments (112). Tolstoy, according to Lukács, "go[es] beyond crass accident and elevate[s] chance to the inevitable."

Two elements of Lukács's analysis here are important for analyzing how chance contributes to the "dialectics of freedom and necessity" in historicist realism. First, the categorical distinction between narration and description highlights (as in Todorov) the manner in which narratives "integrate" readers into the world of characters and makes them experiential participants in the dramas represented. Narration and description for Lukács are not "'pure' phenomenon" but rather "philosophies of composition" that govern particular novelists' methods of representation and emerge from their distinct positions within history (*Writer* 116). Scott, unsurprisingly, emerges in "Narrate or Describe?" as a writer whose methods exhibit realism's full potential. Lukács, for instance, examines how the opening scene of *Old Mortality* (1816) "exposes the contradictions" within each of the parties the novel represents. Second, the coupling of narration with metonymy and description with metaphor articulates the conceptual structures that Tolstoy uses to mediate the particular and the general. In Zola's more metaphorical or symbolic method, the fortuitous or accidental event is asked to "provide direct expression of important social relationships" but cannot bear the weight of such abstract and complex structures of relation (much like Eliot's flood, as we saw in the introduction). The implications of this distinction become clearer in Lukács's analysis of Honoré de Balzac's *Lost Illusions* (1837–43) in *Studies in European Realism* (1950). Here, Lukács analyzes the ways that Balzac grasps how the individual both determines and is determined by social processes, emphasizing that the relationship between the particular and the general is represented obliquely: "The aggregate of social determinates is expressed in an uneven, intricate, confused, and contradictory pattern, in a labyrinth of personal passions and chance happenings" (53). Each individual event in the plot is "in itself accidental," but collectively, events work to reveal the "underlying necessity" (57). The chance event thus comes to appear "inevitable" not because it confirms an abstract fatalism but rather because it makes accessible social forces and historical processes that cannot be represented directly through narration.[7] As the epigraph to chapter 22 of *The Fortunes of Nigel* (unattributed and thus likely penned by Scott himself) puts it: "Chance will not do the work—Chance sends the breeze" (240). Lukács's assumptions about social reality and the capacity of narrative to represent that reality are of particular importance for understanding the role of chance and metonymy in realist representation: "The many-sided influence of multifariously determined factors [in Balzac's novel] is in perfect conformity with the structure of objective reality whose wealth we can never adequately grasp and reflect with our ever all too abstract, all too rigid, all too direct, all too unilateral thinking" (58). Chance—precisely because it confounds straightforward causal attribution—enables more complex webs or structures of causation to become visible.

Lukács's theoretical framework can help us to see how Scott uses the "accident" that brings Hugh and Darsie together—coupled with the ensuing legal dispute regarding possession of Darsie's body—to represent the complex social processes that have led to the disappearance of Jacobitism. The chance encounter initiates chains of metonymic relation, beginning with the diverging causal schemata that Darsie and Hugh bring to bear on their interpretation of that event's significance. These interpretations are themselves linked to their diverging ideological positions. Whereas Darsie deems the encounter an "accident" and believes that it has no bearing on his agency, Hugh interprets it as evidence of destiny dictating the actions they must both perform (301). Lilias later tells Darsie that his eventual capture was "'doomed to be,'" but the specific circumstances of his appearance fuel Hugh's fatalism: "'Just before you came to the country, my uncle's desire to find you out, became, if possible, more eager than ever [. . .]. At this very time, your first visit to Brokenburn took place'" (310). The encounter and subsequent kidnapping thus create a striking juxtaposition of Hugh's determinism and Darsie's sense of freedom, a tension that Darsie himself articulates following his capture: "'I, as well as you, am actuated by impulses, the result either of my own free will, or the consequences of the part which is assigned to me by my destiny [. . .]—You perhaps feel yourself destined to act as my jailor. I feel myself, on the contrary, destined to attempt and effect my escape'" (194).

---

7. Ina Ferris makes a similar point in her analysis of the way "Scott's open and inconclusive starting points" imply a "profound distrust of the whole idea of the moment" (220). Ferris argues that moments for Scott "have neither a constitutive nor inherently revelatory power. They exist as traces, as highly complex traces of the working of diverse and unobservable forces that it is the business of the historical novelist to attempt to uncover" (221). See Ferris, pp. 199–222.

The conflict moves metonymically outward to another level of generality by producing a legal conflict which discloses the processes that have undermined the foundations of Jacobite ideology and makes visible the material forces that guarantee the failure of the unfolding rebellion. The question of who has legal right to Darsie's body exposes the gulf between Hugh's ideological position and his material social context. When Darsie learns the full extent of the planned rebellion, he is amazed that the participants are "'subjecting their necks again to the feudal yoke, which was effectively broken by the Act in 1748, abolishing vassalage and hereditary jurisdictions'" (309). Darsie's reference to the Heritable Jurisdictions Act that was passed in the wake of the 1745 Uprising is significant, for the Act dissolved the social influence of the clans and helped secure the legal structures that underwrite Darsie's self-understanding.[8] That Hugh views it as "'the act of an usurping government'" lays bare the inherent contradictions in his self-understanding and position: He must appeal to the very legal structures he is attempting to abolish in order to secure Darsie's participation in the rebellion. Although Hugh eventually compels Justice Foxley to recognize his legal guardianship over Darsie, Darsie himself views this as a mere "legal pretext" that violates his natural right of self-possession (198). Hugh can compel Darsie's physical participation but not his ideological assent. The rebellion is doomed by the very fact that Hugh must use a "legal pretext" to secure the rightful heir of the Redgauntlets to the Jacobite cause. The incongruity between Hugh's seeming power in local matters and the ultimate futility of his endeavors is on display when he himself is nearly arrested by the Justice. When he learns that there are warrants against him, he is surprised that the state should trouble itself with "'the unfortunate relics of a ruined cause'" (182). Although he can fling "the warrant into the fire" and intimidate the attorney who presents it, he cannot destroy the social structures that guarantee the authority of the warrant. The rebellion ends with General Campbell deciding to "'make no arrests'" and "'no further inquiries of any kind'" because such measures are unnecessary: The force of law need not be invoked to quash Jacobitism because the social and cultural structures that underpinned it have disappeared (373).

Thus, the chance encounter between Darsie and Hugh can be seen as the narrative mechanism that facilitates Scott's effort to represent the obsoles-

---

8. See Whetstone for an account of the effects of the reform of the Scottish sheriffdoms on Scottish legal practice. She suggests that "there was no real reason to suppose that the system [of heritable jurisdictions] was related to Jacobitism, but with attention finally turned to Scottish affairs such obvious anachronisms became a clear target of reform" (63). In other words, the legal and social reforms that followed the 1745 Uprising worked in both explicit and more diffuse ways to dissolve the foundations of Jacobitism.

cence of Jacobitism. The metonymic structures linked to this moment trace the contours of the "dialectics of freedom and necessity" in the novel, and in doing so enable us to read Lukács's insights back against his underlying assumptions, preserving the fundamentally ambiguous causal role of chance. In his statement about the "structure of objective reality" having a "wealth we can never adequately grasp and reflect," Lukács appears to accept the ultimate limitations of narrative representation. Yet in his assertion that chance gets elevated to the "inevitable," Lukács maintains a claim for narrative's capacity to grasp and represent the underlying structures of objective reality. In his discussion of Balzac, Lukács argues that the "necessity which nullifies chance consists of an intricate network of causal connections," and that this "aggregate necessity of an entire trend of developments constitutes a *poetic* necessity" (*Studies* 56; translator's emphasis). Accordingly, chance is "sublate[d]" by this poetic necessity (*Balzac* 55; translation mine).[9] This claim suggests that Lukács does not abandon the Aristotelian model of poetic probability so much as revise it: Whereas chance and necessity were opposing categories for Aristotle, Lukács argues that the complexity of modern social reality requires that chance be integrated into narrative representation. This follows quite logically from the Hegelian underpinnings of his dialectical model, and it reflects his commitment to the concept of "totality" and realism's capacity to comprehend the "totality of the social process" (55). Philosophical and political commitments aside, however, Lukács's insistence that chance is "sublated" negates the inherent causal ambiguity it generates, which is its most important feature in Scott's representational method.

Acknowledging this equivocation—preserving the instability and ambiguity introduced by chance—is essential for grasping the specific vision of historical process presented by *Redgauntlet*. The novel does not, like "The Two Drovers," leverage the causal ambiguity of chance to potentially challenge the reader's presumed "incredulity" by courting the possibility of a superstitious interpretation of events. From the outset, Hugh's pronouncements of fatalism are presented with ironic distance, and the novel does not structure a moment of hesitation for the reader. Nevertheless, the novel's depiction of the move toward modernity is not one of unequivocal difference and progress but one of resonance and return. The nature of Darsie's freedom remains circum-

---

9. Alfred Kazin translates this as "sublimat[ed]," but the original German is *Aufhebung*. The entire sentence in the original reads: "*Balzacs Form der dichterischen Aufhebung des Zufalls ist also noch 'altmodisch' und unterscheidet sich grundsätzlich von der Art neuerer Schriftsteller*" [Balzac's mode of the poetic sublation of chance is thus still "old-fashioned" and differs in principle from the method of recent writers] (*Balzac* 55; translation mine). Lukács's notion that necessity asserts itself through contingency is drawn from Hegel; see Hegel, pp. 541–71.

scribed by the forces of history and intimates a connection with his uncle's determinism. Darsie's encounter with Hugh has profound implications for his identity. He goes from being "a wandering, unowned youth, in whom none appeared to take an interest [. . .] to the heir of a noble house, possessed of such influence and such property, that it seemed as if the progress or arrest of important political events was likely to depend upon his resolution" (312). This newfound sense of influence and importance initially provides "more than a few thrills of gratified vanity," yet Darsie eventually finds that his "resolution" has little bearing on the circumstances in which he finds himself embroiled. Rather than place himself "in direct opposition to so violent a character as his uncle," Darsie chooses inaction as he comes to realize "that the conspiracy would dissolve of itself" without his intervention (346). Thus, while Redgauntlet's fatalism might appear to be a form of "irrational bondage," his belief that both Darsie and he are swept up in a train of events that they cannot control is more or less validated. The novel, like "The Two Drovers," rejects supernatural causation subtly rather than explicitly, allowing for a blending within Scott's realist mode that ratifies the present and its modes of cognition while establishing their contiguity with the past.

III. A FORMAL "COMPOUND BETWIXT ANCIENT FAITH AND MODERN INCREDULITY"

Scott's use of chance anchors the comparative historicism of his realist method by staging confrontations that produce contact between historically distinct ways of being. While these events draw attention to the plot's constructedness, they are important for the effects they facilitate. The causal ambiguity of chance elicits culturally defined modes of cognition that challenge the presumed rational "incredulity" of the reader and activate a "reserve of superstation" that attests to the incomplete ascendancy of modernity. Scott's complex handling of the supernatural suggests that while a detached and "fair calculation of chances" may enable us to dismiss extraordinary coincidences as just that, such concatenations reveal lingering forms of "irrational bondage" that negate the ideal of *l'homme éclairé*. *The Bride of Lammermoor* offers a sophisticated variant on the narrative structures and techniques that Scott harnesses to create encounters with otherness because it does not fully maintain the "credit of unbelief" in the supernatural. While it might seem perverse to consider *The Bride of Lammermoor* as a realist novel alongside works like *Waverley*—or even Austen's novels—we must recall that realism is, like modernity for Scott, a "tense and uneven composite" (Griffiths 88). If Scott deploys chance and coincidence in works like "The Two Drovers," *Redgauntlet,* and *Waverley* to evoke past modes of cognition in ways that demarcate structures of contiguity and difference, *The Bride* amplifies the destabilizing power of the past through a gothic mode that resists the forms of closure and distance cultivated by Scott's Jacobite novels.

Scott relies on chance in *The Bride* to structure a critical juncture in its plot: the "'singular event'" where Edgar Ravenswood goes to enact his revenge upon William Ashton, but instead saves Ashton and his daughter Lucy when he finds them threatened by a bull (45). More important to the novel, however, are second-order coincidental juxtapositions like those Scott discusses in *Letters on Demonology and Witchcraft* and deploys in "The Two Drovers." Just as "The Two Drovers" leverages the ambiguous causal relationship between Janet's prophecy and the conflict between Robin and Harry, *The Bride* situates narrative events alongside prophecies and omens that purportedly predict their occurrence. These include the legend of the Mermaiden's Well, Old Alice's prophecies, and—most importantly—Edgar's death in the quicksand of Kelpie's Flow, which fulfills the prophecy of Thomas the Rhymer. Events in the narrative can be accounted for by both naturalistic and supernatural causation, although (in contrast to "The Two Drovers") the novel sustains causal indeterminacy by resisting interpretive resolution. The novel does voice skepticism at times toward the supernatural and seems committed toward maintaining Coleridge's "credit of unbelief for the writer," but the precision of coincidence between event and prophecy goes further than any other of Scott's major works in provoking the reader's reserve of superstition.

If interpretation of *The Bride* hinges upon the novel's ultimate attitude toward the supernatural and its effects, then the novel's technical handling of chance and coincidence structures its "strange dualism" and formal ambivalence (G. Levine, "Exorcising" 380). Like many of the Waverley Novels, *The Bride* explores historical differentiation through competing modes of viewing and interpreting, but it is unique in the extent to which it both courts and dismisses superstitious interpretations. On the one hand, Caleb Balderstone and the blind sybil Alice stand as representatives of what James Kerr calls a "moribund feudal order" and are consequently the primary believers in supernatural necessity (91). On the other hand, the narrator Peter Pattieson writes from the standpoint of rational enlightenment and consistently treats the supernatural with skepticism. As George Levine has suggested, Scott seems in the novel to be "meticulous about maintaining an enlightened stance toward the mysterious" ("Exorcising" 382). This meticulousness is evident in the sustained attention to the circumstantial and psychological foundations of superstition. The introduction of Lucy Ashton, for instance, echoes the description of Edward

Waverley and the effects of his "desultory habit of reading" (*Waverley* 14). Greater emphasis, however, is placed on her predilection for the supernatural:

> Left to the impulse of her own taste and feelings, Lucy Ashton was peculiarly accessible to those of a romantic cast. Her secret delight was in the old legendary tales of ardent devotion and unalterable affection, chequered as they so often are with strange adventures and supernatural horrors. This was her favoured fairy realm, and here she erected her aerial palaces. But it was only in secret that she laboured at this delusive, but delightful architecture [. . .]. In her exterior relations to things of this world, Lucy willingly received the ruling impulse from those around her. (*Bride* 25)

Lucy's self-consciousness in this regard is also displayed by the narrator Pattieson. Although he resists dismissing Edgar's vision of the recently deceased Alice in chapter 25 as "delusive," he frames the event by reminding the reader of the need to present beliefs of past times with fidelity: "We are bound to tell the tale as we have received it; and, considering the distance of time, and propensity of those through whose mouths it has passed to the marvellous, this would not be a Scottish story, unless it manifested a tinge of Scottish superstition" (187). More explicitly than Chrystal Croftangry's frame narrative in *Chronicles of the Canongate*—or even Pattieson's introductory narrative in the first chapter of *The Bride*—this commentary frames and circumscribes belief in the supernatural as something securely in the past, or at least something fueled by a willful disconnection from the "ruling impulse" of reality.

Yet this kind of commentary is infrequent in the novel, and while Caleb and Pattieson represent the poles of credulity and skepticism, the main characters find themselves somewhere in the middle of that spectrum. Edgar Ravenswood and William Ashton are particularly interesting characters because their unstable interpretive frameworks are linked to the political turmoil that constitutes the immediate context of their personal conflict. Like Edward Waverley with the Bodach Glas, Ravenswood and Ashton find themselves struggling to suppress superstition when confronted with coincidences that challenge their skepticism by evoking the various legends and prophecies that surround their conflict. For instance, when Ashton looks to secure his ascendancy over Ravenswood at the outset of the novel by portraying Edgar's actions at his father's funeral as treasonous, he is coincidentally reminded of the legend of revenge that accompanies the Ravenswood family:

> While he was in the act of composition, labouring to find words which might indicate Edgar Ravenswood to be the cause of the uproar, without directly

urging the charge, Sir William, in a pause of his task, chanced, in looking upward, to see the crest of the family for whose heir he was whetting the arrows and disposing the toils of the law, carved upon one of the corbeilles from which the vaulted roof of the apartment sprung. It was a black bull's head, with the legend, "I bide my time"; and the occasion upon which it was adopted mingled itself singularly and impressively with the subject of his present reflections. (24)

At this point, the narrator briefly recounts the legend of Malisius de Ravenswood before returning to Ashton and speculating that "perhaps" Ashton himself recalls the legend at this moment, since he decides to reflect further upon his actions before proceeding. The presence of Malisius reasserts itself again in chapter 18. When Edgar arrives at the castle, young Henry Ashton is terrified by the resemblance between Edgar and the portrait of his ancestor, and he wonders if Edgar "'is come to say, with a hollow voice, *I bide my time,*—and is to kill you on the hearth as Malise did the other man'" (147; original emphasis). The elder Ashton is displeased to have "these disagreeable coincidences" between the past and his own situation forced upon him. Similarly, even though Edgar generally maintains an "antisuperstitious stance" (G. Levine, "Exorcising" 382), he becomes susceptible to superstition at particular moments, such as in his vision of Old Alice. Approaching the Mermaiden's Fountain, he recalls the "fatal influence which superstitious belief attached to the former spot," and subsequently struggles to control his response upon seeing Alice and learning of her recent death. Although "he banished, as much as he could, the superstitious feelings which the late incident naturally inspired," he is nevertheless shown to be 'considerably affected by a concurrence of circumstances so extraordinary" (190).

While these scenes foreground the residual force of the gothic, *The Bride* (like *Redgauntlet*) does historicize such views. The cause of Ravenswood's demise, most critics of the novel remind us, lies not in supernatural necessity but in the sociohistorical forces that Scott depicts in his characteristic realist mode. Just as *Redgauntlet* discloses the social processes that have undermined Jacobite ideology, *The Bride* foregrounds the changing economic and political conditions that have dissolved the foundations of Ravenswood's social identity. Nowhere is this work more evident than in Caleb's trip to Wolfshope in chapter 12, where he attempts to secure food for Edgar and Ashton after they are stranded at Wolfscrag as a result of a storm. Because the economic and ideological authority that once granted the Ravenswoods feu-rights has been displaced, Caleb is forced to steal hens from a villager in a pitiable attempt to sustain the dignity of the Raveswoods. "Emancipated from the chains of feudal dependence," the inhabitants of the village have begun in recent years "to grumble, to resist, and at length positively refuse compliance with the exactions of Caleb" (101), eventually presenting him not with offerings of eggs and butter but with the "awful form of Davie Dingwall, a sly, dry, hard-fisted, shrewd country attorney" (102). Thus, just as Redgauntlet's "fate" is materially grounded in his necessary appeal to the very legal authority he wants to overthrow, Edgar's fate seems inscribed in Caleb's need to steal that which was once the Ravenswoods' by right. These contradictions present naturalistic causes for Edgar's demise, even though, as David Brown argues, "for Edgar, a product of the feudal system, and for the other feudal characters [. . .] the economic causes of their downfall remain obscure" (149).

Although the novel seems committed to "demystifying Gothic consciousness" (Kerr 87–88), its form nevertheless resists securing that mode of experience in the past. An irreducible tension remains between naturalistic and supernatural causal accounts of its events. Superstition is historicized as a product of a "moribund feudal order" (Kerr 91), but the novel's events—and in particular Edgar's demise in the quicksand of Kelpie's Flow—cannot be accounted for causally by structures of metonymy. Interpretations of the novel's ending register the way in which Edgar's death eludes the network of causal structures that the Waverley Novels typically provide. Fiona Robertson, for example, argues that Edgar's death "*metaphorically* suggests his shifting and ambiguous social status" (216; emphasis added), while Bruce Biederwell argues that "*it seems fitting* that Ravenswood's own death is emptied of dramatic moment" (200; emphasis added). Thus, even though Edgar's inability to secure a social footing is consistent with the tumultuous social context the novel depicts, the "precise coincidence" of his death with the prophecy of Thomas the Rhymer elicits—without dismissing—a superstitious or supernatural explanation, one that is elsewhere subjected to demystification.[10] This singular power of the moment to overpower the attenuating circumstantial context and provide an "'instant and vivid flash of conviction'" is articulated by Peter Pattieson in his discussion with the painter Dick Tinto in the novel's opening chapter (13). The painting Tinto shows to Pattieson not only stands as its own form of prophecy (proleptically presenting a moment to which readers then know the action of the narrative will inevitably lead), but it also—as

---

10. A comparison with the ending of *Redgauntlet* is instructive. The return of Prince Edward to France and the departure of Hugh Redgauntlet represent the disappearance of Jacobitism metonymically (not metaphorically). These departures *are* the dissolution of Jacobitism and can be causally accounted for by the kinds of metonymic structures discussed above. The same cannot be said of Edgar's death.

Shaw argues—"implies a radical suppression of narrative in favour of immediate, atemporal perception" (*Forms* 217).

Many critics have noted and tried to account for the novel's ultimate ambivalence, and the aesthetic dimension of probability demonstrates the cognitive effects of its formal dualism.[11] We could return to Todorov's theory of the fantastic here: The novel's causal indeterminacy means that neither "total faith" nor "total incredulity" is possible, suggesting that the novel fosters the sustained hesitation that defines the fantastic (31). Sigmund Freud's essay "The Uncanny," however, is a more pertinent point of reference, for even though the narratological structures Freud elaborates are similar to (and even less sophisticated than) Todorov's, Freud's psychological framework allows us to contextualize Scott's efforts to tap into the reader's "reserve of superstition" within the broader history of probabilistic thought. Discussing the technical aesthetic elements of the Uncanny, Freud explains that 'in literature there are many opportunities to achieve uncanny effects that are absent in real life' because the space of fiction licenses the writer to choose "whether to present a world that conforms with the reader's familiar reality or one that in some way deviates from it" (156). The author can "prevent us from guessing the presuppositions that underlie his chosen world, or he may cunningly withhold such crucial enlightenment right to the end" (157). It is precisely by keeping open the question of whether the fictional world obeys the causal rules of "common reality" that the writer can evoke, even if momentarily, "primitive beliefs" that have been "surmounted" (155–56). Although Freud, Todorov, and the critical discourse of probabilism presuppose a clear difference between a "common" or "familiar" reality and what Scott calls "marvellous and supernatural machinery" (I. Williams 260), Scott's realism challenges the stability of the rationality that underwrites this distinction.

Scott himself, in fact, anticipates the cognitive elements of the theorization of the fantastic and the Uncanny. In his commentary on Ann Radcliffe's novels, Scott expresses his distaste for what Todorov refers to as the "supernatural explained," that is, the tendency in modern romances for all circumstances "however mysterious, and apparently superhuman, [to] be accounted for on natural principles, at the winding up of the story" (I. Williams 115). Scott inter-

---

11. Kerr concludes that "the novel ends without achieving historical balance" (98). Duncan locates the source of this imbalance in the particular historical period *The Bride* represents: Whereas Scott's novels typically depict "the middle road" of compromise, the action of the novel is set between the Glorious Revolution and the 1707 Act of Union, meaning that "the utopian settlement" that generally occurs "cannot take place in private life because it has not arrived in public life" (*Romance* 136). Shaw reads the novel biographically in the context of Scott's failed relationship with Williamina Belsches, concluding that "*The Bride* transmits feelings of radical ambivalence which Scott is usually careful to rationalize" (*Forms* 216).

rogates the impulse that writers like Radcliffe feel, having courted the possibility of supernatural causation for hundreds of pages, to fabricate naturalistic causes in the final pages to account for phenomena. As an alternative, he proposes that authors might be bold enough to claim "the knot as worthy of being severed by supernatural aid," offering justification for this "more simple mode" of "boldly avowing the use of supernatural machinery" (116). Since "ghosts and witches, and the whole tenets of superstition" were once the matter of "universal belief," then "it would seem," Scott suggests, "no great stretch upon the reader's credulity to require him, while reading of what his ancestors did, to credit for the time what those ancestors devoutly believed in." Despite readers' incredulity, in other words, simply asking them to indulge in supernatural causality might be more aesthetically satisfying than unravelling the complex "skein of adventures" through naturalistic explanation (115).

Scott, however, ventures one step further: The causal knot need not be severed by either the disavowal or the embrace of supernatural machinery. Some authors—and he could very well be alluding to his own practices in *The Bride of Lammermoor* (which he had not yet publicly acknowledged authorship of)—have endeavored to produce a "compound betwixt ancient faith and modern incredulity" (116). Rather than boldly accept supernatural machinery or fabricate naturalistic explanations, these authors "have exhibited phantoms, and narrated prophesies strangely accomplished, without giving a defined or absolute opinion, whether these are to be referred to supernatural agency, or whether the apparitions were produced (no uncommon case) by an overheated imagination, and the presages apparently verified by a casual, though singular, coincidence of circumstance." Scott admits that this method is "an evasion of the difficulty, not a solution," but nevertheless deems it "the most artful mode of terminating such a tale of wonder." This method does not simply appeal to readers both credulous and incredulous. As Scott suggests in his review of Charles Maturin's *Fatal Revenge* (1807), supernatural causation "appeals to the beliefs of all ages but our own; and still produces when well managed, some effect even upon those who are most disposed to contemn its influence" (I. Williams 210). This technique, then, does not simply ask the incredulous reader to indulge in "surmounted" beliefs. Instead, it assumes the possibility that they—like Fergus Mac-Ivor, Robin Oig, William Ashton, and even Edward Waverley—might possess a "reserve of superstition" that could be activated in the right circumstances.

Ultimately, then, the formal dualism of *The Bride* establishes a different disposition toward the past—and a different attitude toward modernity—than Scott's other works, a difference with significant implications for understanding realism and its capacity to represent historical modes of being in the world. Elsewhere, Scott uses chance and coincidence to elicit the possibility of supernatural causation, but then works to contextualize and historicize such explanations. This dynamic performs a double duty: It affirms the presumed incredulity of the reader while simultaneously contributing to Scott's characteristic attempt to incorporate historical and cultural otherness into a vision of modernity. In *The Bride*, however, the past and its modes of vision have not been surmounted and subsumed by rational incredulity but rather remain capable of return. The possibility of momentary belief in the supernatural is not an act of make-believe—that is, simply giving "credit for a time" to beliefs held by past generations but that have since been surmounted. Rather, it entails recognition that such structures of belief remain the active, if suppressed, foundations of the present. If Ravenswood's plight suggests the necessity of transcending the past, then the novel's refusal to dismiss superstition suggests the impossibility of complete transcendence.[12] By not adhering strictly to naturalistic causation and leaving open the possibility of supernatural causation, *The Bride* appears to depart not only from Scott's typical realist mode but also from the fundamental principles of realism more generally. Yet this deviation might in another sense be regarded as the apotheosis of Scott's realist project because it embraces the possibility that ostensibly "surmounted" beliefs may be felt and experienced. If Scott's works typically navigate probability by using chance and coincidence to coordinate opposing schemata within a realist mode, *The Bride* reveals how realism's capacity to facilitate the encounter with otherness is made possible by the improbable.

---

12. In contrast, James Kerr argues that Ravenswood must "somehow achieve a position of transcendence which places him outside of history" (91), while George Levine suggests that the novel "implies the necessity of transcending the past" ("Exorcising" 392).

PART 2

∽

Chance and Scale

THE MANNER in which Austen and Scott resist the demands of probable representation provides some basic principles for theorizing nineteenth-century realism in relation to notions of probability. On the most basic level, they illustrate the limitations of conceptualizing realism in terms of fiction's ability to "recreate" extratextual reality or to encourage readerly "immersion" by occluding its ontological status as fiction. As the previous chapters have demonstrated, it is precisely by drawing attention to the artificiality of their narratives that Austen and Scott cultivate modes of attention and cognition adequate to historical particularity. Austen's explicit reflections on probability and Scott's construction of highly contingent events provide examples of how questions of probability become internalized and thematized within the realist novel, complicating how we think about realism in relation to ideas of readerly belief. The turn to the improbable reflects the shifting philosophical foundations of probability in the early nineteenth century and points to the pressures these changes placed on the relationship between narrative representation and the world. As the probabilistic idioms invoked by Richard Whately, Samuel Taylor Coleridge, and even Scott himself demonstrate, the ascendancy of quantitative notions of probability meant that, by the outset of the nineteenth century, both the world and narrative representation could be construed in terms of an aggregate regularity—an "ordinary run" or "fair calculation" of chances. The evaluation of narrative in relation to this normative model reflects a set of assumptions about the nature of fictional representation and what it can achieve, assumptions that have their origin in Aristotelian theory and strong ties to Enlightenment philosophies of mind. This paradigm presupposes the inherent orderliness of the world and the rational mind's intuitive capacity to grasp that order, and it privileges—in turn—narrative's ability to provide some kind of instruction by aligning the well-ordered mind with the orderliness of the world. While it is easy to extend this framework to accommodate a basic concept of literary realism, doing so yields an understanding of realism that turns us away from how nineteenth-century novelists—or at least an important strain of them—orient themselves toward this matrix of ideas. The dynamics of Austen's and Scott's novels are geared toward strategically disrupting the illusion of the ordinary in their recognition that the probable's implicit appeal to the universal is at odds with their efforts to create engagements with embedded, historical experience.

The second half of this book extends this line of thinking by exploring how Victorian novelists turn to chance to address the representational challenges that attend a world whose scale cannot be reconciled with individual experience. If Austen and Scott test the limits of the probable, these later novelists construct plots that defy probability more overtly: *Martin Chuzzlewit* repeatedly stages coincidental encounters between characters on the streets of London; *Phineas Finn* presents its protagonist's rise as a gambler's improbable run of luck; and *The Return of the Native* exploits chance to the point that characters feel they are being "crushed by things beyond [their] control" (346). When narrative theorists frame questions of narrative probability in terms of "extratextual patterns of cause and effect" (Phelan, "Authors" 22) or "the statistical probability of external events" (Ryan 60), they demonstrate the persistence of the normative ideal that narrative events ought to conform to an "ordinary run of chances." These contemporary iterations of probabilism retain its Aristotelian foundations but are motivated more by an interest in aesthetic questions of authorial craft or readerly experience than by Aristotle's investment in narrative's philosophical value. Yet to predicate a narrative's ability to fulfill its representational ambitions on a more fundamental capacity to conform to extratextual patterns and frequencies disregards probability's historical dimension: Realist representation is shaped by the recognition of the incongruous relationship between particularity and the scale at which "the ordinary" emerges. Probability theory, from the nineteenth century onward, is defined by the recognition that aggregate regularity is incommensurable with the individual, both in the sense that it cannot be apprehended through the individual's immediate experience and in the sense that an individual cannot embody the aggregate. As probability theory comes to be associated with the frequentist identification of aggregate regularities, chance comes to signify a perspectival tension between two positions: an acknowledgment of contingency, variability, and even indeterminism that can be counterbalanced by the discovery of higher-order regularity. If probability theory underpinned statistical practices that helped "contribut[e] to the definition of society as an object of scientific study" (Gigerenzer et al. 39), then the aggregative frequencies that constitute and define society can be seen as consistent with the realist novel's "sociological imagination" (McWeeny 3). Yet the nineteenth-century realist novel only ever has one eye toward the sociological. These novelists' deployments of chance not only reflect a recognition of the incongruous perspectives of the sociological and experiential but also anchor narrative strategies that aim to accommodate these asymmetrical scales within novelistic representation.

As the following chapters establish the central role chance plays in the Victorian novel's efforts to render a social world undergoing rapid transformation, they also trace the novel's diminishing capacity to situate the individual's experience within the scale of the social. Chapter 2 showed how Scott leverages chance to reconcile perspectives across cultural and historical divides; his realist method operates on the premise that codified cultural formations can be coherently conceived in their distinctiveness but can also be brought into relation through underlying resonances. For these later writers, the divide they must bridge exists within a given historical moment. Dickens's handling of coincidence formalizes the contradictory perspectives that define the modern metropolis: Individuals experience the space of the city as one of anonymity and therefore autonomy, but that experience is in fact the product of the market economy's dense webs of interdependence and connection. While the surprise generated by improbable encounters registers that incongruity, it forces recognition of a scale of the social that cannot otherwise be apprehended. Whereas Dickens's realism acknowledges but overcomes the gulf that emerges between the individual and the collective, Trollope's bildungsroman introduces and confronts the question of temporality: The social body confronts the individual not only as an abstraction but also as something that is itself changing. If chance registers the incongruous scales of individual development and social progress in Trollope's novel, it also signals the limits of the bildungsroman's integrative function as these scales become irreconcilable within narrative form. Hardy's representational practice encodes the implications of temporal change in a more radical manner, as his realism marks the evacuation of any stable position from which the collective might be apprehended, or what John Plotz has characterized as the loss of a "portable" concept of culture. Yet in emphasizing an almost paradoxical recognition of the contingency and intransigence of social circumstances, Hardy's use of chance cultivates the modes of historical awareness that this book locates at the core of the nineteenth-century realist project. If Hardy's techniques point to an emerging modernist commitment to perspectivalism, they also demonstrate the importance of chance for tracing the dissolution of a shared sense of the everyday.

CHAPTER 3

Dickensian Coincidence, Cognitive Mapping, and the Victorian Metropolis

"Why, Mark!" [Mr Chuzzlewit] said, as soon as he observed it, "what's the matter!"

"The wonderfullest ewent, sir!" returned Mark, pumping at his voice in a most laborious manner, and hardly able to articulate with all his efforts. "A coincidence as never was equalled! I'm blessed if here ain't two old neighbours of ourn, sir!"

"What neighbours!" cried old Martin, looking out of the window. "Where!" [...]

"Here, sir!" replied Mr Tapley. "Here in the city of London! Here upon these very stones!"

—*Martin Chuzzlewit*, Chapter 54

THE CHANCE ENCOUNTER in the final chapter of *Martin Chuzzlewit* between Mark Tapley and his former neighbors in America epitomizes the type of coincidence that Dickens's critics have regarded with cynicism, if not disdain. Having left this nameless woman and her husband on the other side of the Atlantic in chapter 33, Dickens brings them back in this implausible encounter on the streets of London so that they can be incorporated into the novel's celebratory finale. George Gissing claimed that the "abuse of coincidence" was the "sin, most gross, most palpable which Dickens everywhere commits" (57) and remarked specifically of *Chuzzlewit* that it "aims at a series of 'effects,' every one void of human interest, or, at best, an outrage to probability" (50–51). Early in the twentieth century, Sinclair Lewis, in a review of John Dos Passos's *Manhattan Transfer* (1925), lauded the superiority of Dos Passos's narrative form over Dickens's "rigged" method of plotting, in which "by dismal coincidence, Mr. Jones had to be produced in the stage-coach at the same time with Mr. Smith, so that something very nasty and entertaining might happen" (70). The improbability of Mark's encounter with his former neighbors is tied to its distortion of narrative space, but its effects are predicated upon the material conditions of the urban environment in which it occurs. While the experience of the city is characterized by the collision with countless others who populate its streets, the fact that Mark meets "old neighbours" rather than strangers makes the encounter "wonderfu[l]." The sense of narrative improbability, then, is conditioned by a quantitative shift in the scale of the social. The moment defies the logic of causality in the sense that it appears to come from nowhere, but it also violates a quantitative logic that is determined by the population of London: Among the more than one million anonymous strangers Mark could meet, he happens to encounter this couple. Yet like Austen's reflections on probability at the end of *Northanger Abbey,* Dickens here draws attention to the moment he has constructed, as Mark and the elder Martin Chuzzlewit discuss this "coincidence as never was equalled" at considerable length. By foregrounding its improbability, Dickens also draws attention to the material conditions—the "very stones" of London's streets—that define the parameters of the probable.

If the reappearance of this couple defies the supposed unknowability of the urban mass, their continued anonymity within the narrative—the fact that they are never given names—affirms the tensions that Gage McWeeny has argued define "the newly crowded social sphere of the nineteenth century" (22). Departing from the critical tradition that has identified sympathy as central to the modes of identification and relationality nurtured by the realist novel, McWeeny shows how literature of the Victorian period dealt with the experience of anonymity that accompanied the "broad shift from a culture characterized by the predominance of kinship relations to the more contractual obligations associated with market subjectivity" (11). In identifying how literature gave form to gradations of affiliation and attachment that accompany this society composed of strangers, McWeeny also defines the almost paradoxical status of the stranger within the novel form. Although the stranger is "the bearer of a representativeness or generality that would seem to beg figuration within a literary genre, the realist novel, that is dedicated to depicting ordinary life as ordinary," the very ordinariness of the stranger is "threatened by the specifying effects of narration, which necessarily obliterates the ordinariness of the ordinary" (18). Thus, while the stranger constitutes the "mysterious dark matter" (14) of modern social life, the necessity of the weak social ties required by strangers remains at odds with the dense networks of connection that novels inevitably forge. In his reading of Dickens's early sketch "Omnibus," McWeeny suggests that the sketch form—and the space of the omnibus itself—offer a scale that balances the tension between, on the one hand, the "kaleidoscopic variety and ceaseless change" that characterizes the society of strangers, and, on the other, a "reliable sameness" that enables the sketch to generate the "illusion of repetitive everydayness" (17). According to McWeeny, then, while the logic of plot relentlessly enfolds characters within meaningful social relations, the novel form nevertheless needed to cultivate weak forms of attachment in order to endow a world of anonymity with everyday familiarity. In this light, if the coincidence at the conclusion of *Martin Chuzzlewit* asserts a narrative logic of incorporation, the continued anonymity of Mark's friends reveals the distortions required to reconcile the society of strangers with a vision of social interconnection. Their partial incorporation—they are known but never named—acknowledges the representational impossibility of disaggregating the anonymous mass of strangers into discrete individual connections.

This chapter's recuperation of Dickensian coincidence draws on McWeeny's identification of the key "figurational challenges" (3) that shape the realist novel's depiction of modern social life, but it argues that Dickens's realism exposes and historicizes the conditions that structure the anonymous experience nurtured by the metropolis. Rather than "depicting ordinary life as ordinary," Dickens leverages the improbability of coincidence to reveal the asymmetries of scale that structure market subjectivity: Chance encounters juxtapose the individual's embedded experience of autonomy and anonymity with a broader perspective of the dense webs of social interconnection that bring that subjective position into being but cannot be experienced directly. While *Chuzzlewit* has typically been regarded as a failure,[1] its supposed aesthetic flaws are, in fact, integral to its thematic exploration of selfishness. The novel does not merely depict selfishness through a tableau of memorable characters such as Pecksniff, Mrs. Camp, and Jonas Chuzzlewit; it historicizes selfishness and reveals its material conditions of possibility by establishing the illegibility of social connections within the new economic order. The labyrinthine nature of social space in the novel is exemplified by Mrs. Todgers's boarding house, which "Nobody had ever found [. . .] on a verbal direction, though given within a minute's walk of it" (131). The improbability of coincidental encounters—the fact that, instead of an anonymous mass, characters repeatedly confront individuals known to them—foregrounds the individual's limited capacity to grasp the social totality that gives shape to their experience. As Raymond Williams has argued of Dickens, "In the experience of the city, so much that was important, and even decisive, could not be simply known or simply communicated, but had [. . .] to be revealed, to be forced into consciousness" (165). The surprise and astonishment generated by coincidental encounters—in characters and readers alike—not only figure the cogni-

---

1. Critical assessment of the novel has generally followed that of Dickens's friend and biographer John Forster, who judged the novel "defective" in "construction and conduct," with "character and description constituting the chief part of its strength" (335).

tive limitations that are the structural condition of selfishness but also burst characters' bubbles of presumed self-containment. The networks of interconnection generated through coincidence are not simply asserted but "forced into consciousness" experientially.

Identifying improbability as integral to Dickens's realist method has significant implications beyond *Martin Chuzzlewit*, as it defines the parameters by which narrative can give form to a society whose expanding scope resulted in a qualitative shift in scale. Alongside McWeeny, Paul Fyfe has emphasized how Dickens's novelistic method developed through both his awareness of the aleatory, contingent nature of urban experience and his effort to make that environment knowable. Both McWeeny and Fyfe focus on the sketch as a unique narrative vehicle for exploring the new experiences of chaos and estrangement in the metropolis. Fyfe argues that Dickens's early sketches reflect "the material practices of knowing London in the 1830s," which required transforming the experience of the haphazard environment of the city into a social text that could be ordered (74). Because of its "generic privilege of improbability" (96), the sketch becomes a tool for generating an "urban supercollider" (98) capable of exploring the dialectics of chaos and order, accident and design in the burgeoning metropolis. While accounts of realism have typically assumed that novels must avoid the "accidental and strange conjunctions" (90) Fyfe identifies as central to Dickens's early sketches, *Chuzzlewit* demonstrates how, even within the elongated form of the serial novel, coincidence remains a narrative tool for bringing views of "the panoramic and the particular" together (75). Dickens claimed in *Chuzzlewit*'s preface that he had "endeavoured in the progress of this Tale, to resist the temptation of the current Monthly Number, and to keep a steadier eye upon the general purpose and design" (5). These pretensions to formal coherence appear disingenuous (if not downright Pecksniffian) in light of Dickens's rash decision to send young Martin[2] off to America at the end of the novel's fifth monthly number in the hopes of boosting its disappointing sales. Rather than confirming the formal disorganization of the novel, however, its staggering number of coincidences—at least twenty-two, by my count[3]—show Dickens harnessing the methods he first developed

---

2. For the sake of clarity, I refer to the younger Martin Chuzzlewit as Martin and to his grandfather as Mr. Chuzzlewit.

3. Encounters in the novel that can be categorized as coincidental include the following: Pecksniff encounters Mr. Chuzzlewit at the Blue Dragon (chapter 3); Tom Pinch encounters Mark Tapley on the road to Salisbury (chapter 5); the Pecksniffs find themselves in the same carriage to London with Jonas and Anthony Chuzzlewit (chapter 8); Jonas runs into Pecksniff in the streets of London (chapter 11); Martin encounters Tigg in the pawnbroker's shop in London (chapter 13); Mark passes Martin in the streets of London (chapter 13); Mark sees Mr. Chuzzlewit in London (chapter 13); Martin encounters General Fladdock at the Norris's after

in sketch form for more ambitious representational ends. *Martin Chuzzlewit* illustrates that the "generic privilege of improbability" associated with the sketch was not something Dickens had to overcome or abandon to focus on "the general purpose and design" of his serial novels.

By demonstrating how improbability enables Dickens to figure the relation between market subjectivity and its material conditions, this chapter also provides new ways of understanding Dickens's development as a novelist. It positions *Chuzzlewit* as a fulcrum in Dickens's career, where his strategic use of coincidence enables his growing concern with the "design" of his novels to facilitate his emerging belief in their "purpose" of social reform. Whereas McWeeny and Fyfe have shown how the sketch form offered Dickens a means of grappling with the aleatory and kaleidoscopic nature of the metropolis, other critics have emphasized Dickens's increasing attention to underlying social structures as his career progressed. In particular, Anna Gibson, Jonathan Grossman, and Caroline Levine have all used the idea of networks to show how Dickens mobilizes the affordances of serial form to represent systems of interconnection with increasing sophistication. In her book *Forms*, for instance, Levine suggests that *Bleak House* (1852–53) represents society as composed of dynamically unfolding networks whose totality cannot be grasped, extending Gibson's argument that the "network form" of *Our Mutual Friend* (1864–65) conceives of social life as an open-ended system of evolving connections. This chapter argues that, at a pivotal moment in his career, Dickens not only turns to coincidence in *Martin Chuzzlewit* to negotiate the formal tension between episodic sketch and novelistic whole, but he also embraces it as he comes to recognize how the networked nature of social existence could be grasped *through* these accidental collisions. Dickens's use of coincidence to

---

having seen him on "The Screw" (chapter 17); Poll Sweedlepipe and young Bailey run into each other on the streets in Holborn (chapter 26); Pecksniff overhears Tom and Mary talking in the church (chapter 28); Mrs. Gamp encounters Mr. and Mrs. Mould on the street (chapter 29); Mark meets the nameless woman from *The Screw* and her husband in Eden (chapter 33); Mark and Martin reencounter Mrs. Hominy on their trip back to New York (chapter 34); Mark and Martin see Pecksniff pass while sitting in a tavern upon their return to England (chapter 35); Tom arrives in London and "after roaming up and down for hours, looking at some scores of lodgings" (543) takes rooms in what is later revealed to be Nadgett's house (chapter 36); Tom gets lost in London and runs into Charity Pecksniff by the Monument (chapter 37); Tom and Nadgett pass each other on the street in London (chapter 38); Tom and Ruth encounter Nadgett on the wharves (chapter 40); Tom finds that the man he is delivering Nadgett's note to is Jonas (chapter 40); Tom and Ruth, on their way to Mrs. Todgers's, encounter Charity and Moddle looking into a shop window (chapter 46); Martin, by chance, discovers that Tom's employer is his grandfather (chapter 50); Mark encounters his neighbors from Eden on the streets of London (chapter 54).

apprehend the material conditions of selfishness thus establishes the aesthetic foundations of his later "network form."

Dickens's intent to engage with his contemporary reality in *Martin Chuzzlewit* and to reorient his readers' relationship to that reality is evident in the motto he contemplated for the novel: "The scene, your homes. Yourselves the actors, here" (Stone 31). Anticipating and even outstripping the more explicit reforming impulse of his later works, *Martin Chuzzlewit* wields improbability to capture the growing discrepancy between the situated, individual experience of the metropolis, and an abstract, totalizing view of the social body. If, as J. Hillis Miller has suggested, characters in the novel exist in a "state of isolation" or a "warm cocoon" (*Dickens* 104, 99), then coincidences reveal this self-containment to be a subjective illusion that is a consequence of the sheer complexity and scale of modern social existence. The first section of this chapter turns to Fredric Jameson's idea of "cognitive mapping" to explore the constraints on the individual's capacity to grasp the conditions of their existence within the capitalist economy. It shows how coincidence, through its improbable assertion of connection, becomes a narrative mechanism capable of figuring the gulf between subjective experience and a macroscopic view of the social body. The second section traces the pervasive language of "strangers" and "neighbors" in the novel to show how social relations are no longer predicated upon proximity since the metropolis exists through the obliteration of what Raymond Williams deemed "knowable communities." While London features centrally in *Martin Chuzzlewit,* the novel opens in Wiltshire and travels to the undeveloped regions of the American West; however, its vocabulary of strangers and neighbors posits the metropolitan environment as the condition of social experience more broadly. The chapter concludes by situating *Chuzzlewit*'s thematic treatment of coincidence within the broader context of Dickens's development as a novelist. By reclaiming the parts of the novel deemed most "defective" as instruments of its realism (J. Forster 335), this chapter argues that improbability provides a formal logic to link Dickens's growing concern with the design of his novels to his emerging reformist impulse.

I. MAPPING THE METROPOLIS: THE "EXHIBITION" OF SELFISHNESS THROUGH COINCIDENCE

If much of the critical discomfort with the status of coincidence in realist fiction stems from the fact that it brings together characters through "unforeseen circumstances" (Dannenberg 99), a historicist approach to realism has the capacity to appreciate that unexpectedness as a specific feature of the reality being represented. In chapter 8 of *Martin Chuzzlewit*, Dickens resorts to the very plot mechanism that Sinclair Lewis later critiques: Pecksniff and his daughters (Charity and Mercy) are quite literally "produced in the stage-coach at the same time" with Anthony and Jonas Chuzzlewit as they all travel to London (Lewis 70). Like the constructed contingencies that Scott devises, this moment has a clear functional purpose within the plot, yet it also exploits the chanciness of the encounter to explore issues of thematic significance. On the one hand, the chance encounter initiates the courtship plot between Jonas and Pecksniff's daughters that unfolds during their ensuing stay in London—it brings about "something very nasty and entertaining," indeed. On the other hand, the scene of recognition that follows the encounter—which extends over several pages—explores the dynamics of connection and disconnection in the display of selfishness. As Pecksniff and his daughters enter the heavy coach bound for London, they find the outside of it crowded with passengers chilled by the weather. Pecksniff's response to the scene highlights his sense of detachment from his fellow travelers. With particular relish, he explains to his daughters that "'it is always satisfactory to feel, in keen weather, that many other people are not as warm as you are,'" and that this is a "'quite natural, and a very beautiful arrangement; not confined to coaches, but extending itself into many social ramifications'" (120). Far from being distressed by the suffering of others, the arch-hypocrite justifies it on the grounds that it engenders the noblest human sentiments in his breast, nourishing his "'sense of gratitude.'" When the coach next stops, Anthony and Jonas unexpectedly embark, making similar use of the beleaguered passengers for different but equally selfish ends. The unavailability of seats on the outside of the coach enables Anthony to negotiate seats inside at a discount. "'That was lucky!' whispered the old man [. . .]. 'We couldn't have gone outside. I should have died of the rheumatism!'" (122). Whereas Pecksniff exploits the suffering of the strangers to cultivate his facade of virtue, Anthony and Jonas capitalize upon it for financial gain. In both instances, selfishness manifests itself through a particular dissociative stance toward the strangers on the coach. Because the three men believe themselves to be disconnected from those physically proximate to them, they can act is if there is no moral bond or obligation between them. Yet even though the coach appears to generate the anonymity that makes this kind of cultivated detachment possible, the coincidence that unexpectedly brings these relatives together reveals their inability to assess their relation to those around them. As Pecksniff is forced to admit upon recognizing the Chuzzlewits, "'I thought [. . .] that I addressed a stranger. I find that I address a relative'" (123).

This moment exemplifies what Jonathan Grossman claims Dickens learned from viewing the various forms of passenger transport, both national and international: "The density and extensivity of people's interconnections exceeds their capacity to grasp them, producing a bewildering incompleteness in the understanding people have of what's going on around them" (195). It also displays, and interrogates, the category of the stranger that McWeeny has argued becomes "the distinctive figure both of and for modernity, both a condensation of modernity's anonymous settings and the bearer of new forms of collective social experience" (3). In the process, the scene reveals why coincidence offers a particularly apt mechanism for the representation and historicization of selfishness in the novel. The unexpectedness of the encounter foregrounds the discrepancy between the subjective experiences of Pecksniff and the Chuzzlewits (their feelings of disconnection from their fellow travelers) and the structural underpinnings of that experience (the connections that exist in spite of their anonymity). The seemingly contradictory juxtaposition of connection and disconnection reflects the conditions of the emerging urban landscape of the nineteenth century discussed by Raymond Williams in *The Country and the City*. The absence of legible connections between individuals demonstrates the disappearance of "knowable communities," with coincidence able to give narrative form to this experience of the "essentially opaque" structure of communal existence (165). At the same time, the unexpectedness of the encounter registers the paradoxical experience of the metropolis whereby individuals appear to be at once grouped into an anonymous collectivity but simultaneously atomized. The collision between the Pecksniffs and the Chuzzlewits is certainly "rigged," but the coincidence captures the individual's subjective experience of the social world as illegible while also intimating the webs of connection that exist despite this opacity.

Martin Chuzzlewit "exhibit[s] the commonest of all vices" by establishing it as a product of this new social environment. At the beginning of chapter 38, Dickens uses coincidence to defamiliarize the "everyday fact of life in the city" that is a "routine grazing of shoulders, [and] exchanging of glances" (McWeeny 4), as Tom Pinch and Mr. Nadgett bump elbows in the street without knowing that their lives and fates are connected through their shared relationship with Jonas Chuzzlewit. I will discuss this moment in more detail below, but here I want to draw attention to how the narrator articulates the economic and social foundations of this new form of subjectivity: "As there are a vast number of people in the huge metropolis of England who rise up every morning, not knowing where their heads will rest at night, so there are a multitude who shooting arrows over houses as their daily business, never know on whom they fall" (554). Although anonymity is the condition of "daily business," the unexpected assertion of connection through coincidence problematizes that condition by unmasking the anonymous as known. Just as the narrator reveals that Pinch and Nadgett are connected at this moment without knowing it, the coincidence on the stagecoach shows that connections between Pecksniff and his fellow travelers exist even if he refuses to acknowledge them. London's population had, of course, reached a million by the beginning of the nineteenth century, and as Jesse Molesworth has suggested, the prevalence of coincidence in eighteenth-century gothic fiction can be seen as "a means of confronting or at least coming to terms with modern estrangement" (242). Yet what differentiates Dickens's use of coincidence from those that we find in the eighteenth-century novel—whether in gothic novels or those of Henry Fielding—is that Dickens explicitly links the experience of estrangement to the economic conditions that bring that experience into being.

That Dickens is rendering a historically specific and new experience of urban dislocation is corroborated by the fact that Friedrich Engels produces a suspiciously similar observation about the homeless in *The Condition of the Working Class in England* (1845). In his account of the "Great Towns," Engels observes, "They who have some kind of shelter are fortunate in comparison with the utterly homeless. In London 50,000 human beings get up every morning, not knowing where they are to lay their heads at night" (43–44). The difference between Dickens's "vast number of people" and Engels's "50,000 human beings" reflects Caroline Levine's notion of the "enormity effect" whereby Victorian novelists "refus[e] to count" and "opt instead to provoke a shock or crisis at a vastness that they explicitly claim goes beyond their own capacity to represent" ("Enormity" 61). Yet in making, as McWeeny claims, the abstract notion of society "a coherent subject of understanding," the "formalizing activity" of the novel can also reveal how that vastness shapes subjective experience (10). Steven Marcus, for instance, makes a similar connection between Engels and Dickens by way of a passage from *Nicholas Nickleby* (1838–39) in which Nicholas walks among the London crowd and fends off feelings of personal insignificance by imagining the lives of those around him: "Although a man may lose a sense of his own importance when he is a mere unit among a busy throng, all utterly regardless of him, it by no means follows that he can dispossess himself, with equal facility, of a very strong sense of the importance of his cares" (*Nickleby* 254). Marcus notes that both Dickens and Engels capture the anonymity of urban experience, "a condition which paradoxically rivets one's reflective attention upon that anonymous reduced phantom that is one's self": "From the unreality of a nameless universal identity ('a mere unit') we pass directly over to the unreality of regarding our own apparition and its desires as all of reality and the only reality" (*Engels*

150). Thus, while J. Hillis Miller asserts that "it is impossible to imagine the process by which this situation [of isolated individuals] came into existence" in the novel (*Dickens* 101), coincidences like the one on the stagecoach in chapter 8 identify the scale of urban experience as a structural precondition of selfishness.

The improbable assertion of connection amidst the vast sea of strangers provides a means of figuring both the subjective experience of the metropolis and its structural foundations. In doing so, it can be viewed as a form of what Fredric Jameson calls "cognitive mapping," a "struggle with and for representation" that defines aesthetic production within capitalist space ("Cognitive" 348). According to Jameson, "problems of figuration" emerge in the representation of space as the result of "discontinuous expansions or quantum leaps in the enlargement of capital" as it transitions from its market to monopoly stages in the nineteenth century (and eventually to the stage of late capitalism in the twentieth century). In outlining these three stages of capitalist space, Jameson argues that in the first stage—classical or market capitalism—space becomes organized according to the logic of the grid through the "reorganization of some older sacred and heterogeneous space into geometrical and Cartesian homogeneity, a space of infinite equivalence and extension" (349). This space can be represented unproblematically because the conditions of experience are still accessible to the individual consciousness. Problems of figuration, however, emerge in the passage to monopoly capitalism, as there is "a growing contradiction between lived experience and structure, or between a phenomenological description of the life of an individual and a more properly structural model of the conditions of existence of that experience." The "lived experience of the individual" no longer "coincide[s] with the true economic and social form that governs that experience." While Jameson himself is more interested in the third stage of capitalist space and in modernist (and postmodernist) responses to the problem of figuration, critics like Garrett Stewart have shown how Dickens grapples with the inherent difficulties of representing spaces such as London since, in Jameson's words, "the truth of that limited daily experience of London [. . .] is bound up with the whole colonial system of the British Empire that determines the very quality of the individual's subjective life" (349). Although *Martin Chuzzlewit* does not look toward the empire, it does anticipate Dickens's increasing attention to these problems in his next novel (*Dombey and Son*) by identifying the contradiction between the phenomenological account of the metropolis (isolation and anonymity) and the "social form that governs that experience" (dense webs of interconnection). Rather than rendering the chaotic environment of the metropolis "ordinary" through the normative force of the probable, the improbability of coincidence renders the contingency of that subjective experience—its historical specificity—by drawing attention to the conditions that bring it into being.

II. STRANGERS AND NEIGHBORS: COMPORTMENTS TOWARD COINCIDENCE

Coincidences in *Martin Chuzzlewit* reveal how the scale and structure of social space shape the individual's experience within the sea of unknown but densely interconnected strangers. They also—as the encounter on the stagecoach illustrates—represent selfishness as a particular type of response to that condition of anonymity. Space in *Martin Chuzzlewit* is represented inconsistently; at times characters navigate it with ease, while at other times it appears impossibly opaque. This difference reflects in part the divide between "the country" and "the city." In chapter 36, for instance, Tom Pinch leaves Salisbury following his dismissal by Pecksniff, and his journey by coach toward London is described in great detail. Although the "immensity and uncertainty of London" weigh upon his mind, he cannot "resist the captivating sense of rapid motion through the pleasant air [. . .] past hedges, gates, and trees; past cottages and barns, and people going home from work"—"Yoho! Yoho!" (527) In the very next chapter, however, he arrives in London and "lost his way [. . .] and in trying to find it again, he lost it more and more" (545). Coincidences however, repeatedly negate this distinction between country and city by collapsing distance in a dizzying fashion. Although unexpected, there is nothing particularly implausible about the encounter between Pecksniff and his cousins on the stagecoach. Yet the accumulation and increasing implausibility of such encounters—culminating in Mark Tapley's encounter with his neighbors from America in the streets of London—make it seem as if the world of the novel is not a Cartesian grid traversed by roads and waterways but one full of wormholes. This transition reflects the distortions of space that occur through the "quantum leap" from market to monopoly capitalism, in which the experience of a specified locale like London is underpinned by a global system. Coincidental encounters in the novel are accompanied by a ubiquitous language of "strangers" and "neighbors," a vocabulary that draws attention to the altered status of social relations in an increasingly complex and opaque social world. This vocabulary is strongly associated with the experience of the urban environment analyzed in great detail by McWeeny Wordsworth (as Raymond Williams also notes) registers this new experience of London in *The Prelude* (1850) in these very terms: "Above all, one thought / Baffled my understanding: how men lived / Even next-door neighbours, as we say, yet still / Strangers, nor knowing each other's name" (233). Through this vocabulary, the novel discloses not just the structural conditions of market subjectivity but also how selfishness emerges as a particular comportment to those conditions.

The novel's first coincidental encounter in chapter 3 introduces this vocabulary and establishes how selfishness depends upon anonymity and thus must cultivate it where it does not, in fact, exist. Selfishness requires the existence—or creation—of strangers. The novel opens with Mr. Chuzzlewit falling ill and stopping at the Blue Dragon as he tries to distance himself from his family members, whose status as potential legatees has corrupted their relationships with him. After Pecksniff, who is summoned to console the unknown traveler, recognizes his wealthy relation in a "consternation of surprise," the two men quickly contrive to address each other as if they are strangers (45). Mr. Chuzzlewit is ill-pleased to see his cousin, and Pecksniff tries to ingratiate himself by adopting an air of disinterestedness and disavowing his connection, admitting that he "'should have been, of all things, careful not to address you as a relative'" (46). Mr. Chuzzlewit agrees to continue speaking with Pecksniff only on the condition that he does so "'as to a stranger: strictly as to a stranger'" (47). This pact implies, of course, that the stranger-relation is a guarantee of the disinterest that a blood-relation is incapable of showing. Yet just as Mr. Chuzzlewit displays his selfishness by attempting to distance himself from his family, Pecksniff serves his self-interest by estranging himself from Mr. Chuzzlewit in order to become his confidant. The coincidental encounter affirms the ties between the two men, while their selfishness is defined by their efforts to sever or occlude those ties through the process of estrangement.

The terms "stranger" and "neighbor" in the novel do not designate relationships predicated upon spatial proximity but rather indicate comportments toward a social world where the capitalist organization of space has rendered distinctions of proximity immaterial. Although selfishness appears in a range of forms in the novel, its various manifestations are united by a reliance upon estrangement. Just as Pecksniff initiates his plot to become Mr. Chuzzlewit's heir by estranging himself from the old man, he furthers his scheme by renouncing Martin in chapter 12 and later by dismissing Tom Pinch with the declaration, "'We part, Mr. Pinch, at once, and are strangers from this time'" (472). Estrangement in this instance is a rhetorical performance, but it can also be achieved through disguise. Montague Tigg, for instance, adopts a new identity of Tigg Montague by altering his appearance—dying his hair "jet-black" and donning clothes "of the newest fashion and the costliest kind" (407). His disguise enables him to operate the spurious Anglo-Bengalee Disinterested Loan and Life Insurance Company which defrauds its investors, who include people like Pecksniff who know him.[4] Disinterest in the novel is always an instrument of self-interest, as it will later be for Jaggers in *Great Expectations* (1860–61). Tigg's secretive assistant, Mr. Nadgett, makes use of estrangement as he carries out a program of surveillance on Jonas. Described as belonging to "a race peculiar to the city; who are secrets as profound to one another, as they are to the rest of mankind" (426), Nadgett self-consciously deploys the category of coincidence, appearing in the same spaces as Jonas as the result of appointments with "the man who never appeared" (446). Even Mrs. Gamp can be seen to engage in estrangement as she promotes her own interests by invoking the tributes of the apocryphal Mrs. Harris. If selfishness is predicated upon the opacity of social space, it exists through a process of estrangement that capitalizes upon these material conditions by severing moral ties and occluding connections.

The novel offers a counterexample to selfishness through the character of Mark Tapley, who is characterized by a neighborliness that forges bonds of moral obligation where estrangement severs them. The coincidences involving Mark further highlight the causes and consequences of selfishness, modeling behavior to reform the selfish society. The American episodes of *Martin Chuzzlewit*—where Mark features centrally—are a detour that threatens the novel's spatial and formal coherence. Yet while Martin and Mark's journey takes them away from the metropolis, this spatial extension establishes the urban environment as the general condition of society. The transatlantic voyage aboard *The Screw* is particularly important in this regard, as Mark befriends the overwhelmed mother that he will meet again—first in the outpost of Eden and then again in London. As already noted, it is significant that this woman and her family remain nameless—anonymous—throughout the novel even though she is involved in several of its most improbable coincidences. Dickens aligns *The Screw* with the urban milieu while also detaching it as a kind of floating social laboratory:

> A dark, low, stifling cabin, surrounded by berths all filled to overflowing with men, women, and children, in various stages of sickness and misery, is not the liveliest place of assembly at any time; but when it is so crowded (as

---

4. The name of Tigg's company is not only a fine pun on the idea of "interest" but also an indication of Dickens's uneasiness with the institutional side of statistics. The law of large numbers enabled insurance companies to interact with individuals in the context of aggregate data through mechanisms like the sale of annuities, making money ("interest") through the ostensible objectivity of "disinterested" numbers. In his pitch to Jonas Chuzzlewit, Tigg refers to "'printed calculations [. . .] which will tell you pretty nearly how many people will pass up and down that thoroughfare in the course of a day'" (423). See Cohen, Hadley, and Klotz for discussions of Dickens's engagements with statistical thinking.

the steerage cabin of the 'Screw' was, every passage out), that mattresses and beds are heaped upon the floor, to the extinction of everything like comfort, cleanliness, and decency, it is liable to operate not only as a pretty strong barrier against amiability of temper, but as a positive encourager of selfish and rough humours. [. . .] Every kind of domestic suffering that is bred in poverty, illness, banishment, sorrow, and long travel in bad weather, was crammed into the little space. (242–43)

Mark and Martin comport themselves in opposing ways toward these conditions: While Mark helps the woman care for her children, Martin implores him to stop "'worrying with people who don't belong to you'" (243) and asks him to "'tell your friend, who is a nearer neighbour of ours than I could wish, to try and keep her children a little quieter tonight'" (247). Although Martin initially accepts that these people "belong to him" because of their proximity upon the ship, his neighborliness creates bonds that transcend location. Just as coincidences belie the selfish belief in autonomy, they affirm Mark's assertions of connection and moral obligation. When Martin falls ill upon their arrival in Eden, for example, Mark knocks on the nearest door in search of aid, proclaiming, "'Neighbour, [. . .] for I *am* a neighbour, though you don't know me,' only to [hear] his own name pronounced, and [find] himself clasped upon the skirts by two little boys, whose faces he had often washed, and whose suppers he had often cooked" during their voyage (485; original emphasis). The improbable reappearance of the family in Eden is certainly an "abuse" of coincidence, but Mark's assertion of connection in spite of anonymity offers a striking contrast to the dynamics of estrangement.

Again and again, the novel's coincidences explore the relationship between the structure of social space and the affect of social relation. Mark's encounter with this nameless woman and her family upon the streets of London in the final chapter collapses space entirely in an assertion of global interconnection. In the process of rescuing Mercy Pecksniff from the scene of her sister's ill-fated wedding, Mr. Chuzzlewit notices a peculiar look upon Mark's face and inquires about its cause. After Mark explains that he has encountered "'two old neighbours'" in this "'coincidence as never was equalled,'" Mr. Chuzzlewit must ask the question "'Neighbours where?'" three times before he gets the answer that he desires (775). Mark first interprets the "where" to mean *where did you just meet these old neighbors?* ("'I was a walkin' up and down not five yards from this spot [. . .] and they come upon me like their own ghosts'"). When asked again, he interprets the "where" to mean *where are these old neighbors now?* ("'Here in the city of London! Here upon these very stones!'"). Mark only provides the information Mr. Chuzzlewit desires when he sees that he wants to know *where these people were his neighbors,* which allows him to explain that they were "'Neighbours in America! Neighbours in Eden! [. .] Neighbours in the swamp, neighbours in the bush, neighbours in the fever'" (776). The confusion is a consequence of their competing understanding of the neighbor-relation. For Mr Chuzzlewit, that relation is predicated upon a specific location: One may meet this neighbor elsewhere ("'in London'" or "'upon these very stones'"), but the "'in Eden'" is the necessary condition for addressing them as a neighbor. For Mark, however, being a neighbor is not tied to a specific location but rather a comportment one adopts toward those who were once strangers: They are neighbors here in London, just as they were in Eden, because of Mark's neighborliness aboard *The Screw.*

Although Mark's neighborliness is the antithesis of selfishness, he nevertheless experiences the same atomizing effects of social space, and his desire to be "jolly with credit" reflects a peculiar form of disconnection that links it to the processes of estrangement. Just as coincidences undermine the selfish desire for disconnection, they undermine Mark's effort to "'come out strong under circumstances as would keep other men down'" (225). Mark's "whimsical restlessness" is central to the spatial and moral logic of *Martin Chuzzlewit* but has—like Mark himself—largely been overlooked by critics (117).[5] Mark explains his condition to Tom: "'My constitution is, to be jolly; and weakness is, to wish to find a credit in it'" (690). Mark is a "'roving sort of chap'" who itinerantly seeks difficult circumstances in which he can gain "credit" for being jolly since there is "no credit" in being jolly in situations where anyone might be happy. The problem he encounters, though, is that his neighborliness transforms those difficult circumstances to the point where he can no longer find "credit" in being jolly, prompting him to seek new difficulties. As Martin suffers through his illness in the swamps of Eden, he asks Mark if he could possibly hope for better circumstances than those they have found in America under which to "'come out strong'" (244). Mark replies:

> "On the first morning of my going out, what do I do? Stumble on a family I know, who are constantly assisting of us in all sorts of ways, from that time to this! That won't do, you know: that ain't what I'd a right to expect. If I

---

5. Many critical accounts of the novel do not mention Mark, and when they do, he is primarily referenced as Martin's companion in America. Sylvère Monod, in a book-length study of *Martin Chuzzlewit,* notes that Mark is "an original creation and a character in whom Dickens took much interest," but then cites several critics' displeasure with Mark as evidence that "he is not totally convincing or engaging" (115). Andrew Miller discusses how Stanley Cavell, in a discussion of Wittgenstein's private language argument in *The Claim of Reason* (1979), turns to Mark Tapley and his seasickness aboard *The Screw* to draw upon his exercise of will and his relation to those around him; see Miller, pp. 81–83.

had stumbled on a serpent, and got bit; or stumbled on a first-rate patriot, and got bowie-knifed; or stumbled on a lot of Sympathizers with inverted shirt-collars, and got made a lion of; I might have distinguished myself, and earned some credit. As it is, the great object of my voyage is knocked on the head. So it would be, *wherever I went.*" (490, emphasis added)

Mark's neighborliness means that he is always at home and never at home. Because his jolliness is "contagious," he cannot dissociate himself from his environment and therefore cannot be jolly with credit (358). While his neighborliness forges connections that are affirmed by coincidence, his desire to earn "credit" is an effort to detach himself from his surroundings. It slips into the acquisitive and monetary idiom of selfishness and in doing so links him explicitly to Pecksniff, who early in the novel earns "credit" with others as a consequence of Tom Pinch's devotion to him (33). Although Mark personifies moral behavior in the novel, the persistent irrationality of his restlessness foregrounds his deficient grasp of his relation to the world in which he lives.

The vocabulary of strangers and neighbors in the novel supports its improbable aesthetic by destabilizing the spatial foundations of social relation. In the metropolis—and by extension, the capitalist space of the mid-nineteenth century—everybody is both a stranger and a neighbor. Everyone is connected through the dynamics of the market economy, but everyone is equally anonymous through the mediation performed by that market: The arrows of our daily business fall on anonymous neighbors. If coincidence appears to violate the realist chronotope by bringing characters together in space and time in a way that exceeds our sense of the ordinary (or the probable), the novel seems to assert that this form of connection only makes explicit an ordinary structure of interconnection that is otherwise illegible. Coincidence is the figuration of the asymmetry between the structural connections that unite characters and their foreshortened perception of those connections. It thus serves a rhetorical function similar to the more explicit and famous questions posed by the omniscient narrator of *Bleak House*:

> What connexion can there be, between the place in Lincolnshire, the house in town, the Mercury in powder, and the whereabout of Jo the outlaw with the broom, who had that distant ray of light upon him when he swept the churchyard-step? What connexion can there have been between many people in the innumerable histories of the world, who, from opposite sides of great gulfs, have, nevertheless, been very curiously brought together? (256)

What is particularly important (and overlooked) about this oft-quoted moment is that the question about the "connexion" between characters is actually a question about the "connexion" between places: "the place in Lincolnshire" and "the whereabout of Jo." The critical impulse to read Dickens's use of coincidence as an indication of his belief in an underlying cosmic or providential order is not without foundation.[6] John Forster recorded Dickens's fondness for coincidence in his biography: "On the coincidences, resemblances and surprises of life Dickens liked especially to dwell, and few things moved his fancy so pleasantly. The world, he would say, was so much smaller than we thought it; we were all so connected by fate without knowing it; people supposed to be far apart were so constantly elbowing each other" (69). Rather than focus on the word "fate" and its implications in regard to providence, we might instead find Dickens's delight in coincidence to be a sophisticated response to the epistemological problems (the world being "so much smaller than we thought it") that accompany the lived experience of the Victorian world (people "constantly elbowing each other").

III. REFORMING SELFISHNESS, REFIGURING REALISM

Dickens's recognition of coincidence's capacity to bring into relation the incommensurable perspectives of embeddedness and abstraction enabled him to address the problems of scale that accompanied the development of his reformist sensibility. Dickens engages contemporary social issues from the very outset of his career, such as his confrontation with the New Poor Law of 1834 in *Oliver Twist* (1837–39). Yet it was not until his 1842 trip to the United States, according to Amanda Claybaugh, that Dickens "learned that he could present himself publicly as a reformer" and "that he could be a reformist writer" (82). While Dickens announces his intent to "exhibit the commonest of all vices" in *Martin Chuzzlewit*, it is in its successor *Dombey and Son* that Dickens positions the serial novel more explicitly as a vehicle for social reform. Steven Marcus, for instance, argues that *Dombey and Son* is the first of Dickens's novels to exhibit a "singleness of purpose" as it "undertakes a comprehensive, unified presentation of social life" (*Dickens* 297–98). This "unified presentation" manifests itself formally through the development of a narrative perspective capable of mediating the experience of the situated individual and

---

6. See Vargish, pp. 6–10, and Forsyth.

a vision of social totality. The famous passage in chapter 47 of *Dombey* that calls for a "good spirit who would take the house-tops off [. . .] and show a Christian people what dark shapes issue from amidst their homes" performs a series of mediations that links those homes to a vision of global interconnection through the logic of miasma theory (702). If the "noxious particles that rise from vitiated air, were palpable to sight," the narrator suggests, then "should we see how the same poisoned fountains that flow into our hospitals and lazar-houses, inundate the jails, and make the convict-ships swim deep, and roll across the seas" (701). In announcing the desire to "rouse" individuals "to a knowledge of their own relation" to "the world of human life," *Dombey* both acknowledges and attempts to overcome the problems of representing social totality. Yet if the formal disorganization of *Martin Chuzzlewit* might appear to be a problem to be overcome in Dickens's developmental arc, it is through the figuration performed by coincidence that Dickens seems to discover the means of harnessing serial form in service of this broader vision of interconnection. It is through the improbable that he mediates the contradictory experience and structure of a social world that is no longer organized by the spatial logic of the grid.

Although *Chuzzlewit*'s characters continue to express "surprise" (45, 73, 657) and "astonishment" (592) at their unexpected collisions with others, they are also prompted to examine the nature of their social environment and to reflect upon their feelings of autonomy. As Jonas exclaims when he finds Pecksniff spying through his window: "'It's enough to make a man stare, to see a fellow looking at him all of a sudden, who he thought was sixty or seventy miles away'" (291). Jonas's downfall comes about in part through coincidences that expose his selfish scheme: After his disguise fails him in his plot to murder Tigg, he is confronted by the presence of Lewsome, the doctor from whom he had purchased poison which he intended to use on his father and whom he "had supposed to be at the extremest corner of the earth" (732). If these encounters work to explicitly expose Jonas's guilt, Martin's experiences with coincidence offer a more sustained and robust examination of the psychology of selfishness. When Martin goes to London after being expelled from Pecksniff's home in chapter 12, he immediately encounters Tigg in a pawnshop. It is "'one of the most tremendous meetings in Ancient or Modern History,'" according to Tigg (218). This meeting allows Mr. Chuzzlewit, for whom Tigg is working at this moment, to learn of Martin's situation and thus provide him the money that will fund his voyage to America. But Dickens dwells at length on Martin's response to the encounter, and in particular his frustration at the loss of anonymity. "With a bitter sense of humiliation," Martin curses "again and again, the mischance of having encountered this man," and can only comfort himself with the (mistaken) belief that his circumstances would at least not become known "to any members of his family" (220). The coincidence, in other words, collapses the distance between Martin and his family that is the foundation of his sense of self. Martin subsequently becomes paranoid about visiting the pawnbroker's shop as "he felt on his way there as if every person whom he passed suspected whither he was going" (220). Even as he walks in the streets, he feels "an uneasy sense of being observed—even by those chance passers-by, on whom he had never looked before, and hundreds to one would never see again" (221). These feelings diminish as he sinks into ignominy and loses self-respect, but they return just as quickly when he sets off with renewed self-confidence to America. The same dynamic is repeated upon his arrival in America, as his pride is challenged when he encounters General Fladdock at the Norris's after having seen him on board *The Screw*. During the voyage, Martin tells Mark: "'I wish to conceal my circumstances and myself, and not to arrive in the new world badged and ticketed as an utterly poverty-stricken man'" (246). His selfishness is both exposed and challenged when he runs into the General, as he is forced to reveal, much to his chagrin (and to the horror of his hosts), that he made the voyage as a passenger in steerage.

Martin's feelings of paranoia and shame resonate with other memorable moments in Dickens, such as Pip's feelings of dread, once he has entered upon his expectations, that some "coincidence might at any moment connect" him with Magwitch and disinter his past (230). There is even compelling evidence to support the claim that Dickens is drawing upon his own experience as a child as he explores the structures of shame through the experiences of Martin and Pip.[7] If the novel's reliance upon coincidence consistently draws our attention to the medium (and maker) of representation, it does so in a way that furthers—rather than threatens—its capacity "to come to grips with the fact that we live in a historical world" (Shaw, *Narrating* 6). In grounding an account of Victorian realism in John Ruskin's theories of representation, Caroline Levine has argued that, perhaps from its inception, British realism has been aware of the limits of representation and the fraught relationship between the artistic object and the world. As I argued in chapter 1, Austen's navigation of aesthetic probability demonstrates a grasp of the limitations that become more formally theorized by Ruskin. "Far from prizing the illusions

---

7. Michael Slater notes that in late 1823 and early 1824—in the period leading up to his father's imprisonment for debt and his being sent to work in Warren's Blacking Factory—Dickens's errands for his family "mainly consisted of taking household items (as well as precious books from his father's library) to the pawnbroker's" (19). The autobiographical foundations of Martin's sense of shame and self-consciousness at the pawnbroker's are further corroborated by chapter 11 of *David Copperfield*, in which David expresses similar feelings at becoming "very well known" at the pawnbroker's shop as he goes there on behalf of the Micawbers (161).

of a perfect mimesis," Dickens's improbable aesthetic, like Ruskin's realism, "relentlessly insists on the inadequacies of representation [... and] never purports to describe the intrinsic emplotment of the real" (Levine, *Serious* 60). Rather than emplot events as they might seem to happen in the real world, improbable encounters map the cognitive experience of a social world whose contours can increasingly be grasped only through processes of abstraction.

A sequence of three coincidences involving Tom Pinch and Nadgett presents the most extended example of how coincidences work iteratively to dissolve the selfish belief in self-sufficiency and produce an awareness of interconnection. This sequence also dramatizes how the structure of serial production becomes the vehicle for Dickens's discovery of the "general purpose and design" of his works. The relationship between Pinch and Nadgett comes to the fore at the beginning of chapter 38 through this striking passage discussed above:

> In walking from the City with his sentimental friend, Tom Pinch had looked into the face, and brushed against the threadbare sleeve, of Mr Nadgett, man of mystery to the Anglo-Bengalee Disinterested Loan and Life Insurance Company. Mr Nadgett naturally passed away from Tom's remembrance, as he passed out of his view; for he didn't know him, and had never heard his name.
>
> As there are a vast number of people in the huge metropolis of England who rise up every morning, not knowing where their heads will rest at night, so there are a multitude who shooting arrows over houses as their daily business, never know on whom they fall. Mr Nadgett might have passed Tom Pinch ten thousand times; might even have been quite familiar with his face, his name, pursuits, and character; yet never once have dreamed that Tom had any interest in any act or mystery of his. Tom might have done the like by him, of course. But the same private man out of all the men alive, was in the mind of each at the same moment; was prominently connected, though in a different manner, with the day's adventures of both; and formed, when they passed each other in the street, the one absorbing topic of their thoughts. (554)

This passage presents the novel's most explicit reflection on the illegibility of spatial and social connections: Both Nadgett and Tom are "shooting arrows," as it were, without seeing that they are shooting at each other. The two men bump elbows in the street and are linked through their common connection to Jonas Chuzzlewit, whom they both happen to be thinking about (Nadgett because he is conducting surveillance and Tom because he has recently chanced upon Mercy in London). Yet despite all of these connections, they pass each other on the "very stones" of London without recognition—as strangers.

If the passage offers an explicit thematic reflection upon coincidence, it also presents an example of Dickens's discovery of it as a technology for realist representation. The presentation of Tom and Nadgett as strangers—"he didn't know him, and had never heard his name"—is technically incorrect. We learn subsequently that the house in which Tom and his sister take up residence two chapters prior (chapter 36) is, in fact, Nadgett's house. In that earlier passage, the landlord is not named, so to say that the two men do not know each other in chapter 38 is not an explicit contradiction (or mistake). Yet it is not likely that Dickens (or his narrator) has simply lost track of the connections between the characters here; rather, as Jonathan Arac has suggested, it seems that Dickens decided only later in the process of composition to name Nadgett as the landlord as a way to tighten the plot.[8] That decision retroactively creates this minor glitch in the logic of the narrative. On the one hand, part of the peculiarity of the passage can be accounted for by the compositional history of the novel: Having the two men run into each other at this point enables Dickens to transition between two discrete groups of characters within the same monthly number, something that he had generally avoided to this point in *Chuzzlewit*'s production.[9] In doing so, it also provides an occasion to comment on how the conditions of "daily business" shape the way that individuals in "the huge metropolis of England" relate to each other—something that has been a thematic concern from the outset of the novel in the vocabulary of "strangers" and "neighbors." On the other hand, the passage participates in a sequence of narrative events that serendipitously produces the very kind of knowledge that is the object of thematic reflection, as Dickens himself models

---

8. See Arac, pp. 67–93. I follow Arac here in suggesting that *Martin Chuzzlewit* anticipates Dickens's later novels in attempting to represent social interconnectedness within legible social space. Arac argues that, during the novel's composition, Dickens began to understand London as a place where he could analyze social reality and create "a vision of people's specific interdependence, a sociology to replace the atomism and laissez-faire of Utilitarian psychology and political economy" (69). Although Arac emphasizes the interconnection of characters and traces the genesis of these connections (such as those between Pinch and Nadgett), he does not discuss the role of coincidence as such.

9. Dickens treats the events in America and those in England in separate monthly numbers. The sixth, seventh, ninth and thirteenth monthly numbers contain Martin and Mark's journey to England, their experiences there, and their return; the eighth, tenth, eleventh, and twelfth monthly numbers continue the story of Pecksniff, Jonas, Tigg, and others in England. With Martin and Mark's return to England at the end of the thirteenth number (chapter 35) and Tom's arrival in London at the beginning of the fourteenth number (chapter 36), it is clear that some of the different plotlines need to begin to converge.

the discoveries that he produces within the diegesis. Jonas is also the common link in the third and final coincidence involving Tom Pinch and Nadgett in chapter 40, when Nadgett happens upon Tom at the wharves and asks him to deliver a note to Jonas (who is attempting to flee the country). The scene is structured around the unknowability of connections: Nadgett does not know that Tom knows Jonas; Tom is "astonish[ed] to find" (592) that Jonas is the recipient of the note (and does not know how his landlord knows Jonas); and Jonas cannot fathom how Tom is related to the Anglo-Bengalee Company. The moment is constructed with great dramatic effect: The blow that thwarts Jonas's flight is delivered by the central figure of morality in the novel, a man who has physically struck Jonas earlier. The fact that neither man can grasp the other's relation to the note only adds to this effect. Yet the sequence of coincidences involving Tom and Nadgett does not impose a connection on them but simply makes their extant connection increasingly legible. They are connected mediately through their individual relationships with Jonas; then connected economically (chapter 36); then spatially (chapter 38); and finally concretely in the plot (chapter 40). If the passage at the beginning of chapter 38 articulates a fact of modern social existence—that we are connected to an anonymous multitude without being able to determine the exact nature of those connections—the improbable aesthetic of the novel provides a mode for discovering and cognizing that structure of relations.

By revealing obscured relationships and altering characters' understanding of social space, coincidences facilitate the novel's process of moral transformation. The articulation of moral reform in terms of vision offers a means of linking the cognitive mapping performed by the novel to the optics of reform presented in *Dombey and Son*. Martin's transformation occurs in the swamps of Eden, where privation and illness induce reflection, leading to the epiphany that he has acquired selfishness from his grandfather. Having acknowledged his selfishness, Martin resolves that it "must be rooted out" by "constantly putting his purpose before his own eyes" (497). The success of this resolution is evident both in his altered perception of Tom Pinch, which convinces John Westlock that Martin has reformed, and in his meeting with his grandfather upon his return from America. Still engaged in his plot to expose Pecksniff, Mr. Chuzzlewit remains impassive to Martin's pleas for reconciliation and allows Pecksniff to castigate Martin. "In his most selfish and most careless days," the narrator tells us, this scene would have wounded Martin's pride (624). However, "changed for the better in his worst respect; *looking through an altered medium* on his former friend [. . .], resentment, sullenness, self-confidence, and pride, were all swept away" (emphasis added). Martin reacts out of compassion rather than wounded pride because he no longer sees the world through the "medium" of self. Mr. Chuzzlewit undergoes a similar alteration in vision, inspired largely by Mark Tapley's mild-mannered suggestion that he has been mistaken in his perception of Martin. The old man admits that he has been possessed by "'a kind of selfishness [. . .] which is constantly upon the watch for selfishness in others; and holding others at a distance by suspicions and distrusts, wonders why they don't approach, and don't confide, and calls that selfishness in them'" (752). The trajectory of moral development in the novel is thus to overcome the myopia of selfishness by altering the way that characters see and thus comport themselves toward the social world.

Even Mark Tapley alters his vision of his relation to others; in overcoming his "whimsical restlessness," Mark's fate offers a palliative to the atomizing effects of social space in the novel. At the end of the novel, Mark finally settles down and decides to wed Mrs. Lupin, and the couple plan to change the name of the Blue Dragon to the Jolly Tapley. He explains his decision to marry: "'Then all my hopeful wisions bein' crushed; and findin' that there ain't no credit for me nowhere; I abandons myself to despair, and says, "Let me do that as has the least credit in it, of all; marry a dear, sweet creetur, as is wery fond of me: me being, at the same time, wery fond of her: lead a happy life; and struggle no more again' the blight which settles on my prospects"'" (691). By abandoning his "'hopeful wisions'" of trying to be jolly 'with credit," Mark embraces his connections to others and to his surroundings. His ultimate fate as proprietor of the Jolly Tapley posits a community where connections are legible—his neighborliness becomes a neighborly place. After Pecksniff's final downfall and the reconciliation between Martin and Mr. Chuzzlewit, the characters plan a celebratory feast and put Mark in charge of the festivities. As Mark and Mrs. Lupin serve the guests, he "could by no means be persuaded to sit down at table; observing, that in having the honour of attending to their comforts, he felt himself, indeed, the landlord of the Jolly Tapley, and could almost delude himself into the belief that the entertainment was actually being held under the Jolly Tapley's roof" (768). Although the ideal offered by the Jolly Tapley here is only an imagined "delusion," it offers the vision of a social space that promotes interconnectedness rather than self-interest. When he encounters his anonymous American neighbors on the streets of London in the closing pages of the novel, Mark whisks them away to the Jolly Tapley, where, as he says, "'There's nothin' in the house they sha'n't have for the askin' for, except a bill'" (776). If the circumscribed, even delusional space of the Jolly Tapley offers a fitting image of the novel's gesture toward social reform, it does so because it reflects the problems of linking the experience of the individual to an understanding of a social totality that is increasingly only knowable in the abstract. In his influential essay on Dickens, George Orwell suggested that the target of Dickens's moral outrage "is not so much society as 'human nature,'" and that the message of his works might be summed up in the platitude that "if men would behave decently the world would be decent" (416–17). However, through the representation of Mark Tapley's neighborliness and the critique of selfishness, the improbable aesthetic of *Martin Chuzzlewit* demonstrates how Dickens's realism, like Scott's, works to understand how so-called human nature is shaped by "society" in its particular historical manifestations.

CHAPTER 4

Odds, Statistics, and Chance: Problems of Causality in the Trollopean Bildungsroman

> At every turn the chances would of course be very much against him;—ten to one against him, perhaps, on every point; but it was his lot in life to have to face such odds. Twelve months since it had been much more than ten to one against his getting into Parliament; and yet he was there.
>
> —*Phineas Finn*, chapter 5

IN THEMATIZING COINCIDENCE in *Martin Chuzzlewit*, Dickens confronts the gulf between the individual's embedded experience and the abstract entity of "society," which comes into being at a level of abstraction that cannot be experienced directly. As the improbable assertion of connection amidst a sea of strangers foregrounds the individual's limited capacity to perceive the webs of interconnection created by the market economy, it also furthers the novel's effort to overcome that epistemological limitation by promoting Dickens's moral vision: While the material conditions of society estrange us from seeing our interconnectedness, it is there, and so we ought to behave in the knowledge that our fates are entwined. This chapter examines how Trollope's thematic treatment of chance in *Phineas Finn* confronts the same representational challenge of reconciling individual action with the aggregate social perspective. Trollope's novel, however, asserts the increasing difficulty of this task, and does so in language that can be directly linked to the shifting foundations of probabilistic thinking. In Trollope's bildungsroman, Parliament provides the setting both for Phineas's individual advancement and for the advance of liberal progress, as the novel depicts the period leading up to the passing of the Second Reform Act. Yet the novel's obsessive reliance on the language of chance—and Phineas's improbable string of victories to retain his seat in Parliament—signify the limits of the bildungsroman to unite the causality and temporality of Phineas's individual development with the trajectory of liberal progress. Trollope's novel charts aggregate social processes, but its reliance on chance shows how they cannot be linked causally to the individual's assertion of identity through choice and action.

The chance-filled plot of *Phineas Finn* dramatizes the pressures placed upon the bildungsroman and its cultural work of reconciling "the tendency towards *individuality*, which is the necessary fruit of a culture of self-determination" and "the opposing tendency to *normality*" in a world where the individual and the aggregate (or average, or normal) come to be understood upon different terms (Moretti 16; original emphasis). As the epigraph above (from early in the novel) illustrates, Phineas's personal advance is persistently coded in the language of odds, and his repeated successes are explicitly framed as improbable. His seemingly imprudent decision to depart from his legal training and embark on a parliamentary career is fueled by a sequence of fortuitous events: Lord Tulla provides timely patronage to help Phineas secure his first seat; Lord Brentford then assists Phineas in a string of unlikely victories in subsequent elections, and does so primarily because Phineas coincidentally rescues Brentford's son-in-law Kennedy from an attack by garrotters. Given the central role luck plays in Phineas's improbable advance, John Sutherland has suggested that "*The Luck of Phineas Finn*" might be a more appropriate title since "Phineas's career is largely conceived as a gambler's lucky streak" (Introduction 17). The novel, however, does not just characterize Phineas as a gambler, but does so by deploying the specific language of probability. From the outset, Phineas's life in Parliament and London is characterized by randomness and the effort to manage it through calculable probabilities. After initially determining that the odds were "much more than ten to one against his getting into Parliament" (81), Phineas calculates the chances of parlaying his initial victory at Loughshane into lasting success as "twenty to one against him" (65). These same idioms describe the workings of Parliament more broadly. Ratler posits the results of an upcoming division as a "fair subject for a bet" (288), and late in the novel the formation of a new government is described as "the cards [being] shuffled again" (665). The same processes that characterize the world of politics also govern the procedures of courtship in London. Phineas calculates that "'the chances are ten to one that [Violet Effingham] refuses [him]'" (348), and Violet herself tells Lady Laura that she "'shall toss up'" to make her choice among suitors (131). While Phineas's political and romantic pursuits are driven by his ambition and desire for self-determination, the language of probability encodes his actions as risky because success is both unlikely and seemingly beyond his control.

In contrast to the aleatory nature of Phineas's life in London and the language of odds, the broader dynamics of social progress in the novel embody Trollope's belief in liberal progress and the steady "diminution of [. . .] inequality" (*Autobiography* 268). The steady and certain progress of society reflects the statistical constitution of society as being "endowed with autonomous laws in relation to individuals," where chance disappears through the emergence of aggregate order (Desrosières, *Politics* 79). Throughout his time in Parliament, Phineas encounters statistics, which provide insight into the social collective and long-term processes. The certainty that emerges at this level of abstraction, however, cannot be reconciled with Phineas's individual position and action—statistical averages or intervals cannot be translated into individual choices. By pitting the language of odds against the logic of statistics, Trollope's novel stages the increasing friction between subjective and objective conceptions of probability. In doing so, it exemplifies Alain Desrosières's claim that "the tension between objective and subjective probabilities can be retranslated in terms of point of view: one based on a unique, contingent choice, or on an all-encompassing and generalizable position" (50). The kind of long-run certainty associated with statistics is made available to Phineas through the stable path of the "career," which *Phineas Finn* maps onto the realm of Ireland, work at the law, and Phineas's romance with Mary Flood Jones. Phineas's rejection of this world is a sign both of his ambition and of the insufficiencies of the narrative conventions that govern that world of romance, yet the novel's reliance on the language of odds and gambling reveals the difficulty of encoding that ambition in a manner other than as unmanageable, irrational risk.

The improbable aesthetic of *Phineas Finn* thus reveals the absence of narrative structures for emplotting risk and variation at the scale of individual choice. Chance figures the disjunction between uncertainty at the level of the individual and order in the aggregate long run; it dramatizes the difficulty of causally aligning these levels within the temporal parameters of the novel of development. This disjunction results in the bifurcation of Trollope's bildungsroman: It is divided discursively into the language of odds and the language of statistics, causally into events that are aleatory and those that are certain, geographically between London and Ireland, and ultimately formally between *Phineas Finn* and its sequel *Phineas Redux* (1874). These stark divisions are codified into the competing plots of the careerist and the adventurer. The novel's oscillation between these two plots indicates the insufficiency of either to provide narrative form to a historical world that is in motion and uncertain in its development. Nicholas Dames has argued that *Phineas Finn* exemplifies the Trollopean plot of the "career," a narrative structure that created "linear, ordered sequences out of the disruptive energies unleashed by the spread of professionalism" in the nineteenth century (248). While the novel certainly presents a careerist plot, this chapter demonstrates how it also positions Phineas equally within the Trollopean plot of the adventurer. Phineas is explicitly called an "adventurer" three times in *Phineas Finn,* most memorably when Lady Baldock chides Violet for being "'talked of with an adventurer, a young man without a shilling, a person who has come from nobody knows where in the bogs of Ireland'" (417). He is also aligned with some of Trollope's more notorious adventurers—Marie Melmotte in *The Way We Live Now* (1875) and Ferdinand Lopez in *The Prime Minister* (1876)—in his use of the mantra "nothing venture, nothing have," which he voices early in *Phineas Finn* (111) and then again at the outset of *Phineas Redux* as he contemplates a return to parliamentary life (1:11–12). The alignment of Phineas with swindlers and gamblers like Melmotte and Lopez is less a sign of thematic contiguity between these novels and more an indication of its inability to anchor the movement of history in the representation of individual action and choice. The novel does not show the triumph of the career, nor does it dramatize the bankruptcy of the adventurer: Its oscillation between the two plots indicates the inadequacy of both.

Trollope's bildungsroman dramatizes the struggles to resolve the problems of variation and scale that accompany the taming of chance, highlighting the pressures exerted upon its work of reconciling individual ambition and social stability due to the changing foundations of the nation. Jesse Rosenthal has recently extended thinking about the bildungsroman beyond the basic dynamics of integration—the tension between individuality and social belonging—by arguing that the form does not so much reconcile contradictory demands as "offer a representation of the communal basis of moral intuition" (130). The decisions that constitute the protagonist's moral development, Rosenthal argues, are, in fact, the discovery "that we have always been part of a social whole" (140): "The distinction is not between being one thing and being something else. Instead, it is a choice between, on the one hand, being something unknowingly and passively and, on the other hand, asserting it as an act of will" (141). Such a dynamic is evident in the moral trajectory of *Martin Chuzzlewit* discussed in the previous chapter, as Martin's development is defined by the way he overcomes the myopia of selfishness through his recognition and confirmation of social interconnection that was illegible but nevertheless always there. Yet Rosenthal also shows, in his reading of the arc of George Eliot's career, how her final novel, *Daniel Deronda,* troubles the inductive logic that underpins this conception of a nation as being composed of a countable number of individuals.[1] While Rosenthal focuses on the questions of probability that interest me here, Jed Esty has charted the transformations to the generic conventions of the bildungsroman in the age of empire through "antidevelopmental fictions" of the late nineteenth and early twentieth centuries (18). Viewing the bildungsroman as a "generic ideal more than an empirical object" (18), Esty argues that "the displacement of socially integrative Victorian *bildungsromane* [. . .] by the plot of disillusionment and alienation" (21) follows the disintegration of nationhood by the world system. For Mikhail Bakhtin, the importance of the bildungsroman was linked to national-historical time: The individual's emergence "reflects the historical emergence of the world itself," so that the transition between historical epochs is "accomplished in and through [the individual]" (*"Bildungsroman"* 23). As Esty argues, however, the open-ended structure of national development in capitalist modernity removes the stable boundaries of nationhood that underpin the narrative of individual development.[2] By focusing on the role of chance and questions of narrative causality in Trollope's bildungsroman, this chapter shows how the challenges presented to the novel of development can be framed in terms of the problem of scale and probability.

The first section of this chapter unpacks the philosophical underpinnings of the language of chance in the novel, arguing that the characterization of events in terms of odds and the idioms of gambling draws on the classical interpretation of probability and its effort to manage uncertainty through rational decision making. Yet by figuring events as aleatory and as separate "trials," the language of odds dissolves the causal connection between events and thus undermines the developmental logic of the careerist plot. The second section of the chapter turns to Phineas's work in Parliament and his various encounters with statistics, showing how the novel engages the problem of representativeness, which was coming into being toward the end of the nineteenth century. The question of representativeness is at the core of the novel's political backdrop in the debates surrounding the Second Reform Bill and apportionment. Representativeness might also be seen as the central formal tension of the novel, as its improbable plot is unable to link two levels of generality—the individual and the aggregate. The final section of the chapter reads the novel's peculiar resolution and sequel as negations of the developmental logic that underpins the bildungsroman form. Phineas's retreat to Ireland and marriage to Mary Flood Jones are accompanied by the recognition

---

1. See Rosenthal, pp. 124–90.
2. See Esty, pp. 1–70.

that he has had his "'romance and must now put up with reality,'" yet the outset of *Phineas Redux* undermines any effort to read this ending as evidence of growth or development (658). Ultimately, the competing languages of probability in the novel embody the gulf that emerges as subjective and objective notions of probability are pulled apart. Trollope's bifurcated bildungsroman attests to the increasing impossibility of reconciling these competing points of view in novelistic form.

I. CHANCE AND THE "ADVENTURE TIME" OF LONDON IN *PHINEAS FINN*

The language of chance in *Phineas Finn* stages a confrontation between two modes of understanding probability, and its ubiquitous discourse of odds reflects the continued significance of the classical interpretation of probability for modeling rational decision making under conditions of uncertainty. Although the classical theory of probability had been eclipsed by the frequentist interpretation by the middle of the nineteenth century, this shift was "neither sudden or clear" (Daston 371), as the underlying logic and idioms of the classical interpretation remained in circulation. It is, of course, still commonplace to speak of the outcome of uncertain events in the language of odds like Phineas does when he says that the chances are ten to one that Violet refuses him. What changes between the end of the eighteenth century and the beginning of the twentieth are the assumptions about what these "chances" actually express. For games of chance, where all outcomes are a priori equally probable, this figuration of possible outcomes to all outcomes is philosophically sound (e.g., the odds of drawing any particular card from a deck are one in fifty-two, etc.). However, very few events in the world—or, rather, very few things aside from games of chance—behave in this manner: It is not as if Phineas, in proposing to Violet, is rolling an eleven-sided die and Violet will accept him if a particular number turns up. Such statements are now generally viewed as expressions of degrees of belief, in line with the subjective theory of probability that was formally articulated by Frank Ramsay and Bruno de Finetti, independently but both around 1930.[3] But as discussed in the intro-

---

3. For an overview of the subjective theory of probability as it came to be formalized by Ramsey and de Finetti, see Gillies, pp. 50–87. The basic idea is that for any uncertain event with a defined number of possible outcomes, the various odds one would assign to each possible outcome are seen as expressions of their confidence (or belief) in the likelihood of that outcome. These "betting odds"—how much one is willing to wager on each outcome—are coherent and therefore rational as long as one allocates those odds in such a way that they are

duction, within the classical theory of probability these different aspects of probability (objective frequencies versus subjective beliefs) were not conceptually distinct since associationist psychology understood the rational mind to be a kind of counting machine that calibrated belief to the frequencies of the observed world. The important point is that by the middle of the nineteenth century, probability theory had begun to recognize the difference between circumscribed, controlled arenas of causality like games of chance and the more complex causality of events in the world.[4]

By drawing on the idioms of the classical interpretation of probability and its emphasis on rational decision making, *Phineas Finn* foregrounds the irrationality of Phineas's choices by coding his various choices as improbable gambles. Although the word *chance* appears in a range of contexts in the novel, there is a general consistency in the way the term is used. The novel not only uses the language of odds and gambling but also frequently calculates the probability of a given event as a matter of chances, or a ratio of a specific outcome to all possible outcomes. Phineas calculates the chances of his continued success in Parliament as twenty to one against him and the chances of Violet's accepting him as ten to one against him. It is not just that the odds always seem to be against Phineas; he explicitly characterizes his choices as moves in a game of chance. When he first decides to embark upon a parliamentary career, for example, Phineas reflects that "he had thrown the die in consenting to stand for Loughshane, and must stand the hazard of the cast" (98–99). Contemplating a second run at Loughshane, he thinks about how he had "run the risk, and had thrown the dice" (473). The novel seems to be working within this general framework of gambling even when specific numerical odds are not provided, such as when Phineas speaks to the Earl of Brentford about whether "there might be a chance" for him with Violet (564), or when he tells his father that a position in office is "'on the cards'" so feels that he "'must run

---

not certain to lose money, regardless of the outcome. The point, though, is that those odds are technically measurements of subjective belief, not objective possibility

4. As with just about everything in this realm of ideas, these foundational ideas about causality and order were matters of contention. Adolphe Quetelet's "intellectual edifice," for instance, was "supported by the probabilistic model of an urn of constant composition of black and white balls" that had been the dominant model of causality within the classical interpretation of probability and that assumed that the world operated according to constant causes (Desrosières, *Politics* 86). In contrast, John Venn, in his treatise *The Logic of Chance* (1866, first edition), critiqued Quetelet on the grounds that "much in what he has written upon the subject [...] is erroneous and confusing as regards the foundations of the science of Probability" (24). Venn identified "how narrow is the range of cases to which any purely deductive method can apply"; in other words, he identified the logical transposition required to treat events in the world as if they behaved like games of chance (82). I discuss Venn's theories of probability in more detail in the next chapter.

[his] chance'" (182). The novel also uses *chance* in the more colloquial sense of an opportunity, such as when Phineas musters the courage for his first speech in Parliament by telling himself that he "would dash at it and take his chance" (276). In each instance, the language of chance foregrounds the unlikelihood and thus the recklessness of Phineas's choices by invoking the idioms of gaming and gambling. To "have a chance" and to "take a chance" amount to the same thing since both entail a hazard—an outcome that appears aleatory and beyond the control of the agent.

The persistent characterization of Phineas's actions as moves in a game of chance significantly alters how we interpret causality and agency in his advancement. Not only are the outcomes of events characterized as random and thus beyond his control, but events themselves are also figured as independent trials, with individual outcomes causally unrelated to subsequent ones. Agency ends with the decision to cast the die, and the outcome of one roll has no causal relation to the outcome of the next one. From the outset of the novel, everyone describes Phineas's victory at Loughshane as a matter of luck. "'He only got it by an accident,'" remarks the Earl of Brentford (281). Whenever Phineas tries to claim responsibility for his success, he is reminded that his individuality is causally unrelated to success or failure in politics. When Phineas, for instance, notes that he has been elected unanimously, Laurence Fitzgibbon declares that "those things were accidents which fell out sometimes one way and sometimes another, and were altogether independent of any merit or demerit on the part of the candidate himself" (67). And when Phineas admits to Mr. Low that he has won his seat by chance but claims that it nevertheless confers great honor, Low retorts: "'How can there be honour in what comes [. . .] by chance?'" (102–3). Phineas's subsequent victories follow a similar logic, generating the feeling that he must "play out his game" with continually mounting stakes (162). After the pocket-borough of Loughton is "anathematized, exorcised, and finally got rid of out of the world" (454), Phineas reflects upon the necessity of seeking reelection: "And now when the game was so nearly won, must it be that everything should be lost at last?" (473). Given the unpredictability of politics and electioneering, such descriptions are perhaps unsurprising, but the intrigues of matchmaking impose a similar passivity in the face of chance. This is especially true in Phineas's pursuit of Violet Effingham, a pursuit in which he and his rival Lord Chiltern are figured as "horse[s] in the race" and success is cast as a matter of chances, rather than a matter of rightful claims or even love (564). Despite her initial rebuff, Phineas asserts his right to take his chance with Violet as long as she remains unattached. When she breaks off her engagement with Chiltern, Phineas thinks that "of course he would take his chance [. . .]

even though there were no hope, he would take his chance" (443). And when rejected yet again, he persists: "'I shall [ask again];—if ever I think that there is a chance'" (468). Phineas's view of the causal independence of his proposals to Violet approaches the comically absurd. He acts as if, given sufficient time and opportunities, Violet will accept his proposal because it is always a possibility.

Although Nicholas Dames argues that Phineas's advancement exemplifies the structure of the career—"an upward movement along a vertical hierarchy of vocational achievement and consequence" (259)—the determining role of chance in that advancement indicates that it more accurately reflects the Bakhtinian chronotrope of "adventure time." According to Bakhtin, all action in adventure time unfolds between two points: the meeting of lovers and their eventual union. The time of adventure is an "extratemporal hiatus" that leaves no "trace" on the hero and has no impact on the lovers (*Dialogic* 89). Adventure time is "highly intensified but undifferentiated" and is divorced from historical time (90). It consists of self-contained adventures that are dissociated from one another, generating a temporal span that is empty but potentially infinite. Most importantly, adventure time is governed by the "specific logic" of "sheer chance" (92): "All moments of this infinite adventure-time are controlled by one force—*chance*" (94; translator's emphasis). Although the general contours of Phineas's time in London resemble this chronotope of adventure time, the world represented in the novel is far from empty or ahistorical, and critics such as John Halperin have traced how the novel presents the "tangible historical reality" of the 1860s (125). Although it would be overly simplistic to suggest that Phineas remains entirely unchanged by his experiences in London and Parliament, the "specific logic" of chance nevertheless governs Phineas's advancement from the moment he first decides to run for Parliament to the moment he returns to Killaloe and weds Mary Flood Jones. This is particularly true in the sense that he is, as Bakhtin says of the hero in adventure time, "nothing other than completely *passive*" (105; translator's emphasis).

This idea of adventure time brings the deep formal divisions of the novel into sharper focus, and these divisions reflect the tension that Esty finds in the separation of individual development from national-historical time. The bulk of narrative attention in *Phineas Finn* is devoted to Phineas's serial romantic entanglements with Lady Laura Standish, Violet Effingham and then Madame Max Goesler, but these occur against the backdrop of his romance with Mary Flood Jones. Phineas's relationship with Mary is uninteresting because it is static (she is constant and sure in her attachment), yet it is nevertheless an essential structuring principle of the novel. It is Phineas's departure from Mary and Ireland that signals his rejection of the careerist plot and his entrance into the aleatory world of London. And it is his retreat back to Ireland and his marriage to Mary at the novel's close that confirm his renunciation of that world of chance, bringing about the novel's tenuous conclusion. In the same way that Phineas's romantic entanglements occur against the backdrop of his romance with Mary, his professional advance in Parliament takes place against a specific historical context. However, the "real" historical time presented in the novel is out of sync with Phineas's biographical time. As John Sutherland has suggested, there is a peculiar asymmetry between the pace of biographical time and that of world-historical time in the novel. "The close identification of the novel's action with a narrow historical period," Sutherland writes, "raise[s] one obvious chronological problem: the hero's career starts in 1864 and finishes five years later in 1866. To explain this we must assume a double time-scale, one for Phineas, the other for his political world" ("Background" 36). Sutherland rightly suggests that reconciling this double time-scale is not a difficult task: *Phineas Finn* does not claim to accurately record a sequence of specific historical events but merely fictionalizes select historical events that occurred in the lead-up to the passing of the Reform Act of 1867. Nevertheless, the asynchrony between biographical and historical time foregrounds the strangely elongated nature of Phineas's biographical time in London—it is sequence of iterable (ad)ventures rather than Dames's "upward movement along a vertical hierarchy."

The "adventurous" nature of Phineas's time in London is thrown into relief further by the legitimately "careerist" plot that is rejected at the outset of the novel but remains in the form of a shadow plot. Whereas Phineas's life in London appears aleatory, the world of the law and Mary Flood Jones that he abandons is characterized by its predictability and imperviousness to chance. Phineas's mentor in his legal career, Mr. Low, is the representative of this rejected careerist plot, and the initial description of his attitude toward work and Phineas's ambitions is worth quoting in full:

> The tutor had more than once told his pupil that success in his profession was certainly open to him if he would only stick to his work. Mr Low was himself an ambitious man, looking forward to entering Parliament at some future time, when the exigencies of his life of labour might enable him to do so; but he was prudent, given to close calculation, and resolved to make the ground sure beneath his feet in every step that he took forward. When he first heard that Finn intended to stand for Loughshane he was stricken with dismay, and strongly dissuaded him. "The electors may probably reject him. That's his only chance now," Mr Low had said to his wife, when he found that Phineas was, as he thought, foolhardy. (83)

Whereas Phineas's various trials in the parliamentary world fail to build upon one another or generate traction, the "drudgery" (698) of work at the law embodies a "prudent" course of advancement where one proceeds on "sure" ground rather than through the dictates of chance. Whenever Phineas confronts the possibility of failure in his ventures, he reflects upon what he has left behind in entering the political game, which generates both comfort and shame. After the failure of his first speech in Parliament, for example, Phineas incriminates himself as an "imposter" and a "cheat," believing that he has received "the reward which all cheats deserve" (285). Lying in bed, he thinks of Mary and reflects: "Had he plighted his troth to Mary, and then have worked like a slave under Mr Low's auspices,—he would not have been a cheat." The close entanglement of Phineas's work at the law and his romance with Mary is important because they constitute an alternative realm, anchored in Ireland, that operates according to a radically different causal logic than the aleatory world of politics in London.

The fact that the novel's competing plots and worlds of probability are mapped across the geographical divide between Ireland and London opens the novel to interpretations focused on questions of nationality and colonialism. Phineas's Irishness is an essential facet of the divisions within the novel, and when he returns home midway through the novel, we are even told that "he felt that he had two identities—that he was, as it were, two separate persons" (354). Critics have drawn attention to the significance of this striking split. Geoffrey Baker, for instance, has emphasized the spatial and colonial dimensions of this division, concluding that "determining the place, in English society, of an outsider from Ireland" is the "implicit task" of Trollope's bildungsroman (94). According to Baker, the novel's variable coding of and ambivalence toward Phineas's Irishness shows Trollope "grappl[ing] with questions of representation that paint a complex picture of the interplay between romance (Trollope's conception of Irishness) and the real (the political histories to which the Palliser novels bear witness)" (93–94). The significance of Phineas's Irishness and the novel's exploration of the relationship between imperial core and colonial periphery is undeniable, but the language of chance also reveals that, in addition to the spatial questions analyzed by Baker, Trollope's bildungsroman is fractured by causal and temporal tensions that accompany this problem of nationality. Put simply: The narrative of Mr. Low's slow, measured and certain advance lacks narrativity. Put more complexly: The bildungsroman, as Moretti has argued, focuses on youth because it is "circumscribed" and thus "forces the a priori establishment of a formal constraint on the portrayal of modernity" (6), yet this form is incommensurable with the duration of the career. While Mr. Low is "himself an ambitious man" (83), his ambition is of an altogether different nature than Phineas's "high ambition" (64). Phineas desires to accelerate the process of climbing the "ladder of promotion" referenced repeatedly in the novel (420). *Phineas Finn* is about domesticating an outsider from Ireland, but it is also about domesticating a form of ambition whose intensity challenges available narrative models because it requires a causal structure that can account for uncertainty and risk.

Phineas Finn dramatizes the limits of plotting the temporal duration of the career within the formal constraints of the bildungsroman. The "domestication" of Phineas's ambition cannot be accomplished within the "circumscribed" time frame of youth. Its oscillation between the plot of the career and the plot of the adventurer discloses the absence of a middle ground—a set of conventions that could emplot ambition and risk in a sequence of measured and causally related steps. Neither the certain, vertical progress of the career nor the iterable, "horizontal" hazards of the adventurer are suitable to a world that is variable and contingent yet also orderly in the aggregate. The stark bifurcation of the novel spatially—into a realm of romance where outcomes are entirely certain and a realm of pure chance—reveals the challenges of developing a narrative form that might adequately grasp the relationship between individual agency and a world of uncertainty. These divisions formalize the tensions surrounding causality and temporality in the taming of chance: The destabilizing potential of chance is mitigated through the recognition that it disappears in the long run (or in the aggregation of instances). But if the law of large numbers reveals the underlying regularity of phenomena, it does so by accepting ignorance about the causes that shape individual instances. Chance in Trollope's novel thus occupies the same position that it comes to inhabit within nineteenth-century thinking about probability: it names the intersection of two incommensurable perspectives—the situated, contingent position from which events potentially appear random (the single throw of the dice), and the abstract, totalizing view where they attain order (the theoretical long run of infinite trials).

II. PARLIAMENT, POTTED PEAS, AND THE PROBLEM OF REPRESENTATIVENESS

Foregrounding the novel's formal divisions, as I have done here, has significant implications for how we interpret the trajectory of Phineas's development; it emphasizes that the novel is open to chance—to uncertainty and variation—

but it does not have recourse to narrative conventions (i.e., a plot) adequate to the shape of that progress. It is possible to read the trajectory of Phineas's *bildung* within a more conventional critical framework that interprets chance in the context of the Victorian moral discourse against gambling. In this reading, the prominence of chance in Phineas's advancement would be interpreted as a "realistic" portrayal of a type of venturing that is possible within this environment. Phineas's eventual failure is thus the probable outcome of his venturing—a corrective to an improbable rise that has continually defied the odds. Although "the chances [are] all against" a man of Phineas's position advancing in Parliament in the way that he does, such a run is, of course, always possible (89). As Phineas notes to his father when he first decides to run for office: "'I have told myself more than once, since last night, that I shall probably ruin myself. [. . .] But I am prepared to ruin myself in such a cause. [. . .] I have weighed the matter all around, and I regard the prize as being so great, that I am prepared to run any risk to obtain it'" (53). So even though Phineas persuades himself to further hazards by recalling "stories of great generals who were said to have chained Fortune to the wheels of their chariots," his regular reckonings of odds demonstrate his awareness that the chances are indeed against him (479). In this light, we would read the novel's embodiment of "the pattern Moretti traces for all English *bildungsromane* of aborted upward struggle, lessons learned, and gracious if not heroic final acceptance of failure" (Baker 95) as simply a beginner's lesson in mathematics, as well as a warning about the dangers of what the novel calls the "over-dominant spirit of speculative commerce" (357). If the chances are ten or twenty to one against Phineas, then his hazards are both imprudent and irrational since the odds are not in his favor. This reading, as noted, situates the novel within a familiar Victorian discourse against gambling, which is rooted in the idea that the logic of chance undermines the effort to ground value in merit or moral worth. As J. Jeffrey Franklin suggests, the passivity promoted by gambling is "antithetical to the values of personal development and individual striving" since "gambling replaces merit with chance, virtue with luck and taste for risk" (45–46). Whenever Phineas reflects on his success and how it has been accomplished, he encounters doubts about whether he might after all just be a "cheat" and proceeds to "calculate whether the wonderful success which he had achieved would ever be of permanent value to him" (326). From this perspective, the novel attempts to tether Phineas's ambition to a form of labor that might carry "permanent value" through a complicated interplay of romance and realism. When Lady Laura renounces her love for Phineas to embrace a life of duty as Kennedy's wife, she does so by recalling to herself the odds: "Was it not the case with nine out of every ten among mankind, with nine hundred and ninety-nine out of every thousand, that life must be a matter of business and not of romance?" (235). The formal divisions of the novel—between romance and realism, improbability and probability—might then be seen as a tenuous reconciliation of these competing values of "business."

This reading of the novel's engagement with chance is coherent, but it requires us to accept the untenable correlation between "realism" and "probability." More to the point, it would require us to disregard the novel's competing conceptualizations of probability—the perspective of the contingent choice and the scale of the aggregate. These competing notions of probability are historically grounded, and they reveal a widening division within realism itself that emerges as frequentist ideas of probability alter the way in which reality is understood and even constituted. They also remind us that Phineas inhabits a world of transition and change—a historical world—where notions of "permanent value" and "sure ground" are obsolescent. In *Phineas Finn,* this division manifests itself as asynchrony, an inability to adequately coordinate or sync Phineas's ambition with political reality. Although the characterization of Phineas's actions might make him look like an adventurer, he is, of course, categorically different from men like Augustus Melmotte and Ferdinand Lopez. These men exploit the disjunction between appearance and value that arises in the atmosphere of speculative commerce; they lack "substance" and seek to find it in pregiven social forms like "the code of the gentleman" (Kincaid 219). The problem for Phineas, on the other hand, is that his real value cannot be recognized or find appropriate social articulation. This disjunction between Phineas's individuality and social categories is simply another reflection of the novel's difficulty in moving between levels of generality. Desrosières suggests that the "magical transmutation of statistical work" entails a "transfer from one level of reality to another," as well as "a transfer from one language to another (from unemployed persons to unemployment)" that grants both levels the status of reality but enables them to exist in "autonomous ways" (*Politics* 70). In struggling to reconcile these different levels of reality, the form of *Phineas Finn* thus also explores the problem of representativeness. If representativeness is one way of formulating the central political question of the novel, it also provides a way of thinking about the formal problem of representing the individual in relation to the social whole. Phineas's "two identities" are not just "an Irishman of Killaloe" and "a man of fashion and member of Parliament in England," but also a private individual and a public subject (354). The improbability of Phineas's run of luck is a causal manifestation of the incommensurability of these two perspectives.

This division between public and private becomes increasingly clear in Phineas's parliamentary business, and in particular in his encounters with statistics. From the outset, the novel emphasizes the incompatibility of party politics and individual belief. Phineas's early, blushing admission that he has "'views of [his] own'" is met with scorn by Barrington Erle, and public office is referred to repeatedly as a form of slavery, which links it to the drudgery of work under Mr. Low (50). "A man in office must be a slave, and that slavery is distasteful,'" Phineas bitterly concludes toward the end of the novel (619). The novel's insistence that a man in Parliament is a "servant of the public" and "must abandon all idea of independent action" voices Trollope's well-known and clearly stated political views, particularly those related to government service (550). As Trollope wrote in *An Autobiography*:

> A man, to be useful in Parliament, must be able to confine himself and conform himself, to be satisfied with doing a little bit of a little thing at a time. He must patiently get up everything connected with the duty on mushrooms, and then be satisfied with himself when at last he has induced a Chancellor of the Exchequer to say that he will consider the impost at the first opportunity. He must be content to be beaten six times in order that, on a seventh, his work may be found to be of assistance to some one else. He must remember that he is one out of 650, and be content with 1-650th part of the attention of the nation. If he have grand ideas, he must keep them to himself, unless by chance he can work his way up to the top of the tree. In short, he must be a practical man. (270)

Such abnegation of personal belief, according to Trollope, is possible—or practical—only for men of fortune who can afford to put the needs of the nation in front of their own financial self-interest. So part of the problem with Phineas's ambition is that he is simply not the right person for the job.[5] But these constraints imposed by parliamentary service foreground the problem of representativeness. In the same way that Phineas, as a representative of a borough, is "1-650th part" of a governmental body that represents the nation as a whole, he is—within the form of the bildungsroman—representative of a particular segment of the population. As Ian Hacking notes, "The very thought of being representative" did not "come into being" until the end of the nineteenth-century (*Taming* 6). Only with the formal elaboration of confi-

---

5. For a reading of *Phineas Finn* in light of debates about salaried parliamentary service, see Mouton.

dence intervals at the start of the twentieth century did statistics have available the methods of representative sampling that create the possibility of representing the whole of a population through a segment of it. Quetelet's *l'homme moyen* was premised upon the idea that "the dispersion and variable character of individual characteristics appeared to be reliably subsumed within the single figure representing the whole" (Desrosières, "Part" 221). Unlike the "average," which embodies the entire population in one (fictional) figure, the representative allows the population to be reconstituted in a microcosmic segment that preserves variation.[6] The novel foregrounds the very real and pressing problems of representativeness as it explores the political debates surrounding the redistribution of the franchise amongst boroughs and the extension of the individual franchise. These political reforms aim, of course, to have the governing body better reflect and represent the complex reality of its constituent parts. Yet, as Phineas's divided identity attests, the same institutional structure cannot at the same time provide a framework to structure the individual's integration into society.

The novel's competing languages of probability thus register the temporal and causal disjunction between the representation of individual action and the movement of the social body. These disjunctions become apparent whenever Phineas grapples with abstract information and statistics during the course of his duties. Phineas's first committee work involves not a duty on mushrooms but a decision about "the use of potted peas in the army and navy" (224). However, matters in his personal life—in particular, his harassment by the moneylender Mr. Clarkson—distract him from attending to the data. After a particularly distressing encounter with Clarkson, Phineas rushes off to a meeting on the potted peas:

> He was in such a fervour of rage and misery that he could hardly think of his position, or what he had better do, till he got into the Committee room; and when there he could think of nothing else. He intended to go deeply into the question of potted peas, holding an equal balance between the assailed Government offices on the one hand, and the advocates of the potted peas on the other. The potters of the peas, who wanted to sell their article to the Crown, declared that an extensive,—perhaps we may say, an unlimited,—use of the

---

6. For the prehistory and emergence of the idea of representativeness, see Desrosières, "Part"; and Kruskal and Mosteller. Hacking discusses Balzac's *Comédie humaine* and the "representative monographs" of Frédéric Le Play as responses to and rejections of the statistical methods of Quetelet (*Taming* 136). Analyzing the behaviors and household budgets of families in particular regions of France, Le Play's monographs aimed to provide a holistic view of society by representing "representative individuals, not average men" (137).

article would save the whole army and navy from the scourges of scurvy, dyspepsia, and rheumatism, would be the best safeguard against typhus and other fevers, and would be an invaluable aid in all other maladies to which soldiers and sailors are peculiarly subject. The peas in question were grown on a large scale in Holstein, and their growth had been fostered with the special object of doing good to the British army and navy. The peas were so cheap that there would be a great saving in money [. . .]. He had resolved to give to it all his mind, and, as far as he was concerned, to reach a just decision, in which there should be no favour shown to the Government. [. . .] But, unfortunately, on this day his mind was so harassed that he could hardly understand what was going on. (229–30)

Although financial security would presumably allow Phineas to concentrate on the potted peas, this scene captures the conceptual disjunction between personal matters and national business that is repeated throughout Phineas's time in office.

Rather than resolving or reconciling Phineas's inner self and his public identity, then, his work in Parliament repeatedly stages the incommensurability of the two perspectives. When Phineas later takes up his appointment at the Colonial Office, he spends his time basking in the luxury of his apartment, comparing it with his "dingy room" (501) at Mr. Low's, and staring at a "very interesting map [. . .] showing the American colonies as they used to be" (502). As Phineas contemplates a proposed railroad from Nova Scotia to the Rocky Mountains, the map frames the different temporalities in motion. Phineas is tasked with deciding whether the Government ought to lend "five million of money" to fund the project, and the contemplation of the "big subject" gratifies him: "It required that he should look forward to great events, and exercise the wisdom of a statesman. What was the chance of these colonies being swallowed up by those other regions,—once colonies,—of which the map that hung in the corner told so eloquent a tale?" Phineas speculates on the probable futures of North America and ponders statistics, such as that "once in nine years the harbour of Halifax was blocked up by ice." His calculations are interrupted, however, by the arrival of a letter from Lady Laura informing him of Violet's engagement to Chiltern. With this, the novel immediately reverts to the idioms of gambling as Phineas reflects on the smash of his greatest hopes: "The game was played out, and all his victories were as nothing to him"; "he was playing a great game, but hitherto he had played it with so much success,—with such wonderful luck!" (503). As with the potted peas, personal matters interfere with parliamentary business, and the shifting languages of probability register the gap between the different levels of generality. The disjunction becomes most apparent as Phineas takes up the question of Irish tenant-right that will ultimately be the decisive issue in this first phase of his parliamentary career. In an effort to perform due diligence and make an informed decision, Phineas educates himself as much as possible. He "stud[ies] all the statistics which came within his reach in reference to the proposed new law for tenant-right" (630), and after deciding to support Monk's proposal, he again "stud[ies] tenant-right statistics" as he prepares his speech (676). Yet, as the text makes clear, his support of the bill has little to do with data or convictions but rather emerges from a personal desire to remove himself from politics. In all of these situations, the data that informs statistical knowledge and the imperatives of individual action exist on different planes.

This disjunction between Phineas's private identity and the public realm of politics evacuates the political significance of the resolution of Phineas's personal development. The novel's treatment of specific political issues like tenant-right and reform is, of course, influenced by Trollope's beliefs, with its general endorsement of melioration a reflection of his "advanced Conservative-Liberal" position (*Autobiography* 269). While some critics have attempted to mine the specific political ideology of the novel,[7] its reliance on chance reveals a more fundamental problem for narrative form: the need to coordinate the progress of the nation and the progress of the individual. Statistics explain the state of the social body and disclose its direction, but they simply do not speak to the scale of the individual. Formally, this disjunction manifests itself as the novel's oscillation between the plot of the "careerist" and the plot of the "adventurer," with neither plot offering a satisfactory shape for representing how Phineas's ambition might be translated into a recognizable social identity. The novel characterizes Phineas's actions as moves in a game of chance not because they are, in fact, gambles, but rather because this is the most readily available idiom for translating aggregate processes to the scale of the individual choice. Late in the novel, Monk discusses with Phineas the potential impact their doomed tenant-right bill will have. What emerges is a picture of the incremental movement of Parliament toward an inevitable end, a movement that occurs not through individual choice and action, but rather by an almost mystical dialectic of political procedure and public opinion:

> "Many who before regarded legislation on the subject as chimerical, will now fancy that it is only dangerous, or perhaps not more than difficult. And so in time it will come to be looked on as among the things possible, then among

---

7. Patrick Lonergan, for instance, reads the novel's resolution as a direct reflection of Trollope's beliefs about evolving political issues.

the things probable;—and so at last it will be ranged in the list of those few measures which the country requires as being absolutely needed. That is the way in which public opinion is made." (703)

As with all of the political issues taken up in the novel, the passing of the tenant-right bill is not a matter of "if" but "when." Monk here suggests that there is a gradual movement toward the eventual necessity of passing this bill, but that movement cannot be meaningfully rendered into concrete actions by the individual representatives. "Public opinion" appears here not as the discrete accumulation of individual beliefs and views, but rather as an abstract entity that reflects a collective will that is composed of but distinct from its constituent parts. The fact that the various parliamentary divisions and votes are always a "fair subject for a bet" reflects the fact that, even though coalitions can be formed and party loyalty expected, Members of Parliament seem to be "purblind sheep" controlled by causal forces beyond their cognition (696). Even on the night before Monk's bill comes up for vote, Bonteen can, in the presence of Phineas, "'bet [Ratler] a sovereign'" whether Phineas will vote with them against the bill (661). Thus, while the novel represents the inexorable (if uneven) march of liberal progress, it appears only at a level of abstraction distanced from the actions of individuals, as its imperatives and timescale are incompatible with the trajectory of the individual career.

III. RETREAT TO IRELAND AND RETURN IN *PHINEAS REDUX*

With Parliament providing the institutional framework for understanding the relationship between the individual and the nation, *Phineas Finn* discloses the limitations of representativeness. This tension manifests itself through a series of peculiar formal bifurcations, the most foundational of which is a disjunction between the actions of individuals and the march of history. But it also causes bifurcations in the novel's modes of characterization, spatialization, and even publication, as Phineas's development is split over the course of two novels. The representational problem embodied by *Phineas Finn* is, ultimately, a less explicit but more multifaceted version of what we find in the contemporaneous *War and Peace* (1869), as mentioned in the introduction. Tolstoy adopts radically different modes in representing the lives of individuals like Natásha, Nikolái, and Andréi and the movement of history in his infamous historical digressions. Tolstoy articulates the disjunction between these two levels in terms that resonate with Trollope's novel: "There are two sides to each man's life: his personal life, which is the more free the more abstract its interests, and his elemental, swarmlike life, where man inevitably fulfills the laws prescribed for him" (605). While these two levels exist almost entirely on their own terms in Tolstoy's novel, the competing languages of probability in *Phineas Finn* signal the effort to bring them together through the arc of Phineas's development. Although the novel adheres to the basic pattern of the bildungsroman, its deep formal divisions challenge readings that privilege the closure brought about by the novel's conclusion. Phineas must acknowledge, by novel's end, that he "'must now put up with reality'" (658), and the narrator even goes so far as to compare him to Icarus, who "had flown up towards the sun, hoping that his wings of wax would bear him steadily aloft among the gods" (712). The novel concludes, of course, with Phineas's retreat from the parliamentary stage, back to Ireland and into the waiting arms of Mary Flood Jones. This ending has led critics to read the chanciness of public life in terms of an educative arc. Both James Kincaid and Robert Polhemus note the tension between public and private identities in the novel, but they read the conclusion as a form of resolution, even if only a temporary and tenuous one. Polhemus, for instance, frames his reading in terms of how "the clash of external pressures and internal values becomes more and more difficult to resolve" (148) in Trollope's later fiction. He nevertheless sees the novel working to establish "the inseparability of public and private life" (155), so that Phineas's decisions at the novel's close can be read as his coming to know his own mind better. Kincaid, on the other hand, suggests that the Phineas novels show how "politics demands of men the same impossible balance between the public and private selves faced by women in love" (193) and reads the novels' endings in relation to luck: Whereas in *Phineas Finn,* the hero must "begin to assert himself [and . . .] by so asserting himself he casts off luck" (201), the sequel shows how he "must learn finally to rise above all chance" (211), which he does by retreating once and for all from public view.[8] Attuned to the inherent tensions within the structure of Phineas's development, these readings nevertheless work to emphasize the closure they achieve.

Rather than presenting closure to the problems of causality, however, the ending of *Phineas Finn* reiterates the incommensurability of the competing ways it conceptualizes and attempts to manage risk. The decisive moment of *Phineas Finn* is Phineas's determination to support Monk's doomed Irish tenant-right bill, a choice that is less a matter of principle—or statistical

---

8. Kincaid does note in his reading of *Phineas Redux* that "the private life is never adequately co-ordinated with the public life," but ultimately reads society as an "enemy," so that the novel becomes "less one of attaining balance than of creating a self against great odds" (210).

data—than it is an arbitrary occasion through which to assert and enact his independence. In the period leading up to Phineas's retreat from Parliament, he becomes increasingly cognizant of the divisions within his own identity. Crucially, these are couched in the same framework of competing, irreconcilable perspectives. Reflecting on the opportunity extended to him in a potential marriage to Madame Max, Phineas considers what a "blackguard he would be [. . .] were he to desert Mary and marry Madame Max Goesler"; but he also questions himself "as to the nature and quality of his own political honesty if he were to abandon Mary in order that he might maintain his parliamentary independence" (642). Phineas thinks about what his future biographer might say about his choice, and he concludes that "his biographer would say very much more about the manner in which he kept his seat in Parliament than of the manner in which he kept his engagement with Miss Mary Flood Jones." Although it is clear that Phineas ought not to live according to what the biographer might say, it is also apparent that the choice of his commitment to Mary over "parliamentary independence" is not a straightforward choice between two commensurate options. What is most significant about Phineas's withdrawal from London is the structure of the choice he makes, rather than the specific content of the political issue that prompts action. Although it is Monk's tenant-right bill that leads Phineas to acknowledge and finally accept the necessity of his retreat, it is his vote for the Irish Reform Bill that actually effects his removal from Parliament: Phineas "gave what assistance he could to the Government, and voted for the measure which deprived Loughshane for ever of its parliamentary honours" (704). The fact that Phineas's support of the Government eliminates his seat (and thus his capacity to further support or oppose that Government) reaffirms the incompatibility of individual action and the direction of the social body. The "'only comfort'" that Phineas can take in the situation is, as he says, "'that I have done the thing myself'" (705).

Phineas's assertion of agency in this moment is significant, but it is difficult to see it as the culmination of an educative process or the unproblematic validation of a coherent system of values. Phineas's retreat highlights the unsatisfying extremes that the novel fails to synthesize in the course of Phineas's advancement. From Phineas's almost begrudging embrace of his promises to Mary, to his assertion that he ought not "'mix two things together'"—the world of London and his life in Ireland—"'that will be so different,'" Trollope seems as reluctant as Phineas himself to accept the necessity of his retreat from the parliamentary stage (710). Although it may be tempting to read Phineas's appointment to a permanent office in Dublin as a form of compromise, his marriage to Mary suggests that the end of his adventures in London is, like the close of Bakhtinian adventure time, the reassertion of an identity that existed at the outset of the novel. By returning to Ireland, Phineas does remove himself from the aleatory processes that determine the shape of his life in London, processes that the novel, through its reliance on the language of chance, cannot fully reconcile with the protocols of rational decision making. But the point is not, as Kincaid would have it, that his marriage to Mary is "essential" insofar as Phineas must commit to a "sincere if temporary dedication to pastoral values," or that Phineas must eschew luck—which is only another way of saying that Phineas must retreat from contingency and seek certainty (191). The coding of Phineas's agency in London as nothing more than the rolling of the die figures that world as one of unmanageable risk, but the retreat to Ireland conversely entails the evasion of risk and uncertainty altogether—a retreat to the static world of romance. Although the novel's closing characterizes Phineas's life in London as his "romance" and his marriage to Mary as the "reality" he "must put up with" (658), this inversion is simply another manifestation of the novel's inability to stabilize its divisions. Neither option offers a viable model for reconciling Phineas's ambition with a rational reckoning of a risky, variable, and historical world.

That the idioms of gambling in *Phineas Finn* are merely a cipher for more abstract and complex causal processes is clearest, perhaps, in the novel's most philosophical reflection on chance. As Madame Max weighs the Duke of Omnium's marriage proposal, the narrator reflects on our propensity to evade responsibility in the face of difficult decisions:

> There is nothing in the world so difficult as that task of making up one's mind. Who is there that has not longed that the power and privilege of selection among alternatives should be taken away from him in some important crisis of his life, and that his conduct should be arranged for him, either this way or that, by some divine power if it were possible,—by some patriarchal power in the absence of divinity,—or by chance even, if nothing better than chance could be found to do it? But no one dares to cast the die, and to go honestly by the hazard. There must be the actual necessity of obeying the die, before even the die can be of any use. (573)

Phineas Finn is not about "rising above chance." It is about incorporating meaningful dispositions toward chance and risk into coherent social identities. That Trollope can do this only by turning to the language of odds—or, alternately, to models of probability that manage chance through aggregation—necessitates Phineas's inevitable evasion of chance and return to Ireland. In a game of unknown odds, the only rational decision is to walk away.

The outset of *Phineas Redux* confirms that the conclusion of *Phineas Finn* reinscribes, rather than resolves, the tensions that generate its formal bifurcations. The sequel must begin by undoing the tenuous closure of its predecessor. In *An Autobiography*, Trollope comments that *Phineas Finn* is "all fairly good except the ending,—as to which till I got to it I made no provision" (290). Since he "fully intended to bring [his] hero again into the world," Trollope comments that he "was wrong to marry him to a simple pretty Irish girl, who could only be felt as an encumbrance on such return," leaving him "with no alternative but to kill the simple pretty Irish girl, which was an unpleasant and awkward necessity." If the ending of *Phineas Finn* is simply a placeholder, an arbitrary necessity for a bildungsroman split over two volumes, it formalizes the division between two worlds that operate on fundamentally different principles. Chance itself figures much less prominently in the sequel, but *Phineas Redux* continues to work with competing understandings of probability. Whereas Phineas is entirely lucky in the first volume, he is the continual victim of bad luck in the second, most prominently in his arrest for the murder of his political rival Bonteen as a result of very damning—but ultimately misleading—circumstantial evidence. Once again, this turn in luck is less a commentary on the vicissitudes of gambling than a reconceptualization of the tensions seen in *Phineas Finn*. The sequel recasts the tension between competing models of probability as an epistemological duel between "empirical and emotional knowledge," or evidence and belief (Baker 127). Trollope tells readers from the outset that Phineas is innocent of the crime, so as the trial unfolds, we watch knowing that he is innocent but wondering whether he could be convicted based upon the probable appearance of guilt, which itself is founded on an improbable series of coincidences. At a pivotal moment in the trial, Phineas's lawyer, Mr. Chaffanbrass, calls the novelist Mr. Bouncer to the stand and questions him about the construction of novelistic plots. After establishing that a plot ought to be "constructed in accordance with human nature," the two men discuss a range of murders in literary works by Shakespeare, Scott, and Bulwer-Lytton to demonstrate how the dictates of fictional probability require that sufficient causality and premeditation be established (2.231). Chaffanbrass exposes a contradiction in the prosecution's case against Phineas; they claim that the murder of Bonteen shows premeditation, yet according to their timeline the supposed "cause of the murder anteceded the murder no more than ten minutes" (2.232). Bouncer's exculpatory testimony ends with his confirmation that he "would not dare so to violate probability in a novel, as to produce a murderer to the public who should contrive a secret hidden murder,—contrive it and execute it, all within a quarter of an hour" (2.233). Within the context of my argument here, we can see the competing probabilities in conflict during the trial—one based on those who know Phineas personally and believe him incapable of the murder and one based on the ostensibly unbiased observer or juror who sees the evidence pointing to his guilt—as the reinscription of the split between subjective and objective notions of probability that give rise to the language of chance and odds in *Phineas Finn*. In both novels, improbability structures our understanding of a reality that can increasingly be grasped only through disparate and potentially incommensurable points of view.

CHAPTER 5

Chance, Historicism, Hardy

> Strange conjunctions of circumstances, particularly those of
> a trivial everyday kind, are so frequent in an ordinary life,
> that we grow used to their unaccountableness, and forget the
> question whether the very long odds against such juxtaposition
> is not almost a disproof of it being a matter of chance at all.
> —*A Pair of Blue Eyes*, CHAPTER 8

IN CONSTRUCTING IMPROBABLE PLOTS, both Dickens and Trollope use chance to figure individual experience and agency in relation to the abstract scale of the social. If Dickens deploys coincidence to develop an appreciation of interconnectedness that cannot otherwise be experienced, Trollope's bildungsroman attests to the difficulty of representing these distinct scales conjointly. Reading chance as the embodiment of this disjunction of scale also offers a new way of approaching the peculiar causality of Thomas Hardy's novels. The narrator of *A Pair of Blue Eyes* (1873) draws attention to a defining paradox of Hardy's novelistic practice: "Strange conjunctions of circumstances" seem to foreground an "unaccountabl[e]" contingency while simultaneously eliciting a sense of determinism. In a similar vein, Hardy's first novel, *Desperate Remedies* (1871), stages a conversation between Cytherea Graye and her brother Owen about "'belie[f]'" in "'odd coincidences'" (154). Cytherea remarks that people hardly take notice when "'two disconnected events [. . .] fall strangely together by chance,'" but "'when three such events coincide without any apparent reason for the coincidence, it seems as if there must be invisible means at work'" since "'three things falling together in that manner are ten times as singular as two cases of coincidence which are distinct'" (154–55). If these passages draw attention to the operations of chance and coincidence, they also display the quantitative logic that was deployed in the process of chance's "taming" over the course of the nineteenth century.

The combination of contingency and determinism in Hardy's plots embodies the central conflicts within mid- to late-Victorian thinking about causality. Although the frequentist interpretation of probability recognizes randomness and variation across individual instances, it also shows how order and even lawlike regularity emerge in the long run.

This chapter situates Hardy's realist practice within late nineteenth-century thinking about causality, tracing the impact of Darwinian evolutionary theory on probabilistic thought and narrative form. It argues that Hardy's improbable plots—with their unparalleled reliance on chance and coincidence—ground a historicism that is attuned to the force of environment and circumstance despite the unavailability of a stable vantage point from which order might appear. The coupling of chance and determinism in Hardy's narrative form foregrounds the contingent circumstantial causes that mediate the abstract deterministic laws which emerge from the flux of a temporal world. This chapter is an effort to develop a poetics of causality adequate to the peculiar coupling of contingency and determinism in Hardy's novels. If chance appears "unaccountable," the absence of immediate cause discloses the "invisible means at work" in the narrative. These "invisible means," however, are not metaphysical forces but the more humble sublunary forces that constitute the characters' social milieu. Just as chance in Scott's historical fiction elicits beliefs that illustrate a character's placement within a particular cultural matrix, Hardy deploys chance and coincidence in his narratives to represent diffuse causal forces that delimit characters' agency in ways that are powerful but that—crucially—they themselves cannot see.

A brief example from *The Woodlanders* (1887) illustrates how Hardy uses chance to structure plots that represent the abstract but intransigent forces that shape his characters' agency. In chapter 12 of *The Woodlanders*, Grace Melbury and her father see a fox that is quickly followed by a hunting party in pursuit. A "gentleman-farmer" angrily reproaches them for not alerting the hunters to the location of the fox (78). The hunters pass on, but the encounter has come at a particularly pivotal juncture of Grace's and Melbury's lives. Melbury turns "quite red" at the hunter's abusive remarks to his daughter and concludes that it is own presence that has prompted this disrespectful treatment of Grace. "'The woman who looks an unquestionable lady when she's with a polished-up fellow,'" Melbury remarks, "'looks a tawdry imitation article when she's hobbing and nobbing with a homely blade.'" This encounter is a turning point in the novel. Before this event, Melbury has—despite ambivalences and equivocations—maintained his resolve to marry off Grace to Giles Winterborne as reparation for courting Mrs. Melbury away from Giles's father. However, Melbury now abandons this resolve, as the irremediable conflict between his sense of what is due to Grace's honor and his desire to make amends to Giles forces a decision. Grace, he determines, "'shall marry well'" since "'whatever a young woman's niceness, she stands for nothing alone'" (79). The respectable but rustic Giles can never offer the accompaniment that Melbury believes Grace must have. This "strange conjunction of circumstances" alters the course of Grace's and Giles's lives, and the reader must grapple with the causal relationship between this encounter and the tragic trajectory of the narrative. The aleatory nature of the event within the narrative (the pack of hunters is an anomaly within the social topography of the novel), coupled with the overwhelming sense of consequence, encourages the reader to think counterfactually—to imagine how events would have been different had this encounter not occurred. Yet the event is not the principal *cause* of what subsequently happens, as what is causally operative here—and what the narrative draws our attention to—are the conflicts and the contradictory values implicit in Melbury's desire to offer Grace to Winterborne. His desire to offer Grace as a form of reparation to Giles leads him to educate her to a point that she is left in a "peculiar situation, as it were in mid-air between two storeys of society" (195). The moment not only reminds us, as Megan Ward notes, that the woodlanders are "inextricably enmeshed in culture, even in the secluded woodland" (879); it goes further to reveal the particular contours of that enmeshment.

Hardy's use of chance has led critics to identify him as a transitional figure within the history of the novel. Leland Monk sees Hardy as "exemplify[ing] a movement from providence to perspective in the novel at the turn of the century" (157), while Paul Fyfe suggests that Hardy presents "a challenge to when, historically speaking, the eclipse of providential with provisional views about causality registers in British literature" (215). Yet these readings typically rely upon the assumptions that define the discourse of probabilism that the preceding chapters have interrogated. Despite a broad historical and methodological scope, interpretations of Hardy's reliance on chance tend to share three interrelated assumptions. First, they proceed from the premise that realism is by definition probabilistic and that Hardy's use of chance and coincidence indicates a failed realism or a deliberate antirealism. Second, they view chance and coincidence primarily from the perspective of plot—that is, as part of the causal structure or architecture of a narrative, something potentially "imposed" upon the raw material of narrative representation.[1] Third and finally, they read chance as a narrative instantiation of authorial belief or ideology. Chance in Hardy always *means* something in the way that it signifies

---

1. See Dessner, Howe, and Monk.

something beyond itself—a worldview, a "vision," or a set of philosophical propositions about the nature of the universe or human existence.[2]

In the context of the preceding chapters, however, Hardy's improbable aesthetic is neither a break with the protocols of realism nor a ground zero for thinking about evolving dispositions toward chance in the British literary tradition. Situating Hardy's narrative craft within this longer tradition of the improbable provides a fundamentally new way of understanding what has been a persistent problem for his readers and critics. "Coincidence," Bert Hornback noted in 1974, "is the central problem for almost every critic who has had reservations about Hardy's art—and this is so because coincidence is at the center of his vision and his technique" (6). Hardy's contemporaries repeatedly derided the implausibility or improbability of his plots. Peter Widdowson, as noted at the very outset of this book, suggests that "the frequency with which the words 'probable/improbable' occur in Hardy criticism (and elsewhere) encourages coinage of the term 'probabilism' for the orthodox critical discourse of realism against which Hardy is measured" (17–18). The aesthetic imperatives of modernism further reinforce these views by highlighting Hardy's undue emphasis on plot.[3] Through much of the twentieth century, scholars approaching Hardy within a humanist paradigm saw chance and coincidence in his novels either as indications of a deliberately antirealist position or as a by-product of a pessimistic worldview that sees humans engaged in battle with an indifferent universe.[4] In the past decades, scholars have extended the foundational work of Gillian Beer and George Levine to unpack the Darwinian currents of Hardy's thinking to better situate him within his contemporary intellectual milieu. Yet chance still troubles Hardy's readers and critics. J. Hillis Miller has recently reiterated that "the inordinate role played by chance, happenstance, or just plain bad luck" is one of the "idiosyncrasies" of Hardy's art, arguing that "the absurd contingenc[ies]" Hardy relies upon happen "not because of some malign 'Fate,' but just through accidental happenstance" (*Communities* 108–10). More important, Helen Small, Paul Fyfe,

---

2. See Hornback, Ireland, and Monk.

3. Virginia Woolf, writing on the occasion of Hardy's death in 1928, suggests that, in his early works, Hardy must have been "hampered by the difficulties of his technique and driven both by maladroitness and by an innate desire to pit his human figures against forces outside themselves, to shape his book by an extreme and even desperate use of coincidence" (508). Similarly, E. M. Forster argues in *Aspects of the Novel* that the "terrible machine" of plot in Hardy's novels "never catches humanity in its teeth" and that "the flaw running through Hardy's novels" is that "he has emphasized causality more strongly than his medium permits" (90).

4. See Widdowson, pp. 11–76, for the history of critical approaches to Hardy's fiction. For more recent reconsiderations of the role of chance and coincidence in Hardy, see Faulkner, Meadowsong, Small, and D. Williams.

and Daniel Williams have begun the work of understanding Hardy within the longer history of thinking about chance and probability that interests me here.

If improbability offers a more adequate framework for theorizing the means and ends of Hardy's idiosyncratic realist aesthetic, it also identifies more precisely the ways in which the form of the novel engaged the implications of Darwinian evolutionary theory. The first section of this chapter analyzes just what "determinism" means in the post-Darwinian context by examining how probability theory responded to the problems raised by evolutionary thought. John Venn is significant in this context not only because his 1866 treatise *The Logic of Chance* was the most important work on probability in the second half of the nineteenth century (and the first formal exposition of the frequentist theory of probability), but also because he shares a surname with the reddleman Diggory Venn in *The Return of the Native* (1878). As Small and Williams have suggested, this correspondence prompts us to consider how Hardy might have been engaged with the ideas Venn explores.[5] On a fundamental level, chance and probability involve thinking about variation and irregularity, and the realist turn to improbability is motivated—as I have argued—by the desire to encode difference into the representation of a shared vision of the social. Austen and Scott not only break with the fundamental assumptions of classical probability but also interrogate probabilistic representation as a way of thinking about difference—the difference between the past and future, as well as the problem (for Scott) of difference across cultures. In Dickens and Trollope, difference is fundamentally an issue of scale, as their texts insist on the difficulties of representing individual experience and the social body simultaneously. Hardy's improbable aesthetic reflects both problems of scale and those of temporality, problems that take on new form in the context of evolutionary theory. Venn's frequentist theory articulates the attenuated status of statistical "laws" in the post-Darwinian context. While mid-century thinkers like Quetelet and Henry Buckle maintained that society operated according to laws in the strict sense of the word, Venn's approach to the "logic of chance" develops a more complex understanding of the relation-

---

5. Small states that since there is no evidence that Hardy owned Venn's work, the shared name is a "coincidence," but one that should not preclude exploration of the "conjunction" between Venn's ideas and Hardy's work (76). Williams, on the other hand, proceeds on the assumption that Diggory's name suggests that Hardy "had some familiarity with [Venn's] work (or reviews thereof)" (23). While we do not know whether Hardy had read Venn's work, it seems reasonable to assume that Hardy would have been familiar with Venn and his ideas given that Venn's cousin was Leslie Stephen, whom Hardy first met in 1873 and who served as a sort of "mentor and critic" to Hardy through his work on the *Cornhill Magazine* (Tomalin 133) As Small notes, Stephen—like Venn—responded directly to the questions of free will raised by Buckle's *History of Civilization*.

ship between randomness and order. Venn's frequentist theory is grounded in the notion of the series—a sequence of events that "combines individual irregularity with aggregate regularity" (4). Although Venn's theory maintains the logical and philosophical validity of probability statements, it also explicitly acknowledges the problem of evolution as it accepts that the uniformity found in the long run "though durable is not everlasting" (13). The "laws" and order that frequentism reveal are provisional, subject to change in the (very) long run. In this context, "environment" acquires a position of importance because it shapes the way in which abstract, deterministic laws get expressed through contingent circumstances. If Trollope's bildungsroman troubles the category of "representativeness" as it attempts to mediate the level of the individual and that of the aggregate, evolutionary theory presents another challenge to the status of the "type" (or species).

Building on this discussion of Venn's probability theory, the second half of the chapter offers an extended reading of *The Return of the Native*, arguing that its improbable aesthetic cultivates a historicist perspective attuned to these problems of causality. Improbability in Dickens and Trollope constitutes a way of coordinating two perspectives on reality—that of the situated individual and that of the abstract or aggregate social body, perspectives which are increasingly figured in incommensurate terms. The form of Hardy's novel—particularly its radical modulations in narrative perspective—reflects this fragmentation and a growing awareness of the limits to representing a unified reality. Not only does focalization shuttle between a range of characters, but the third-person narrator also invokes hypothetical viewpoints: that of an "imaginative stranger" (17), a "looker-on" (18), and even that of "anyone" (346). These viewpoints frequently frame the characters and actions in ways that seem to identify underlying historical continuities. At the beginning of the novel, for instance, the Egdonites and their Guy Fawkes bonfires are linked to "Festival fires to Thor and Woden" and "jumbled Druidical rites" (20). Yet while these juxtapositions operate along the lines of Scott's "comparative historicism" by illuminating continuities across historical distance, they also function according to the logic of what Devin Griffiths calls "disanalogy"— the gaps and differences that emerge in the failure of comparisons to establish resonances (24). The narrator, in other words, attempts to frame the characters and action of the novel through these analogies and comparisons, yet in their failure to account for the specificity of the milieu under consideration, they bring the distinct elements of that environment into focus. Bolstered by other narrative mechanisms, such as free indirect discourse and a chance-filled plot, the form of *The Return of the Native* attests, in keeping with the insights of evolutionary theory, to the absence of transhistorical structures of order. The interplay of contingency and order in Hardy's novels thus defines a historicism that works to cultivate modes of perception adequate to the contours of existence within a history that unfolds non-teleologically.

I. CONTINGENCY, CAUSALITY, AND DETERMINISM AFTER DARWIN

Hardy's fascination with ideas of chance and causality epitomizes his complex engagement with the intellectual landscape of the second half of the nineteenth century. Far from being "relentlessly monological" (Lock 20), his novels present a conflicting medley of beliefs and attitudes that also characterize his intellectual milieu. This is particularly true in relation to ideas surrounding probability and to the ways in which thinking about chance related to questions of causality and determinism. Hardy's narrative strategies can be read against debates about the nature of determinism that were occurring across an array of discourses in the 1860s and 1870s. Hardy's explicit concern with these ideas is evidenced not only by early poems like "Hap" (dated 1866), but also by his literary notebooks. Some of the earliest entries include statements invoking probability that Hardy encountered in July 1865 as he read John Henry Newman's *Apologia Pro Vita Sua* (1864), including a transcription of "[Bishop] Butlers [sic] doctrine, that Probability is the guide of life" (Björk 5). While Butler's maxim must be understood within its eighteenth-century context and an epistemology attuned to the necessary limits to human certainty, it prompts consideration of how Hardy encountered such maxims within his own context. As Small notes, in the years leading up to the writing and publication of *The Return of the Native,* Hardy was "pondering more immediately over Huxley, Spencer, Comte, Mill, and, of course Darwin," thinkers who all addressed questions of social development and who engaged ideas of probability and chance in different ways (75). Hardy's narrative engagement with chance not only responds but also contributes to this complex network of ideas about chance and determinism.

As many critics have suggested, Hardy "conceive[d] of a world governed by deterministic laws, such as those of the Immanent Will, Darwinian sexual selection, materialist laws of determinism, and the principle of heredity" (Asquith 285). However, critics have been less precise in clarifying what "determinism" and "law" mean, especially when explaining how such beliefs might have informed his artistic practice. As this book has shown, the classical theory of probability was underwritten by a belief in determinism in the form of causal necessity. Laplace and his predecessors generally believed in a divine or superhuman vantage where "all events are necessary," so that probabilities were merely a measure of "the partial certainty upon which we ill-informed mortals must ground rational belief and action" (Daston 35). In this paradigm, probability disappears as science advances. As statistics—the science of the state—developed over the course of the nineteenth century, determinism became a particularly vexed topic, especially as champions (as well as skeptics) of statistics debated whether it was a science or merely a method. The extension of measurement and quantification to an expanding array of social phenomena led to the discovery that social phenomena (e.g., births and deaths, crimes and suicides, etc.) which seemed unaccountable in specific cases actually conformed to regularities in the long run. The law of large numbers—first given mathematical proof by Jakob Bernoulli in 1713 and denominated as such by Poisson in 1835—had the potential to move beyond a mere mathematical law and become a law to explain the workings of society. It was Quetelet who, in 1844, began "to turn statistical laws that were merely descriptive of large-scale regularities into laws of nature and society that dealt in underlying truths and causes" (Hacking, *Taming* 108).

The resultant specter of "statistical fatalism" (116) raised pressing questions about free will and agency, particularly in the context of mid-Victorian liberal ideology.[6] Yet those who interrogated the meaning of "statistical laws" questioned whether these laws attained the status of scientific law. In the process, a new meaning of determinism emerged between 1850 and 1870 (151). Henry Buckle's *History of Civilization in England* (1857) was the most influential—and controversial—attempt to leverage the insights of statistical observation and argue for the regularity and determinism of human affairs. Grounding his work in the ideas of Quetelet, Buckle argued for a "rigid historical determinism, in which climates and land masses determine the course of history more than the apparent free choices of political actors" (Hacking, *Taming* 126). Buckle believed he could reconcile free will and statistical fatalism, as he argued for a distinction between the laws that govern society and the laws that determine individual action.[7] As discussed in the previous chapter, statistics worked in large part by constituting "society" as an independent entity that operated according to its own autonomous laws. Buckle's work was widely read, although it also elicited forceful responses from a number of thinkers who found his effort to elevate history to a science untenable. As Small puts it, "Buckle was the talk of the town, but almost all of the talk was against him" (68). At issue, in particular, were the "character and implication" of statistical

---

6. See Hadley; Choi, pp. 3–16.

7. For more robust accounts of Buckle's theories in this context, see Hacking, *Taming*, pp. 125–32; Porter, *Rise*, pp. 60–65; and Small, pp. 65–74.

laws as he presented them (Porter, *Rise* 165). If the "laws" revealed by statistical observation came into view only through aggregation and thus, importantly, by renouncing claims on the individual, then could statistics really be said to be a "science" or to identify "laws"? While the inductive movement from individual instances to underlying structures might be viable in the natural sciences, most thinkers maintained that society operated according to different principles, challenging the status of statistics as a science and the explanatory power of its so-called laws. As Theodore Porter notes, the German statistician Gustav Rümelin maintained in 1867 that "the term 'law' should be reserved for expressing a relation of cause and effect that is elementary, constant, and recognizable in every case" (*Rise* 185). Thus, efforts by the likes of Quetelet and Buckle to extend the province and power of statistics resulted in a philosophical backlash that brought about more tempered views of probability and statistics in the 1860s and 1870s (163).

John Venn offered one such attenuated view of probability in his 1866 *The Logic of Chance,* a work that became "the most influential nineteenth-century work on the philosophy of probability" and that was motivated in part by the problems of free will raised by Buckle's *History* (Porter, *Rise* 87). Venn's *Logic* provided the first rigorous exposition of the frequentist theory of probability. His intervention was to argue that probability statements were valid only in relation to a series; it was illogical to talk about probability in relation to individual events. Series for Venn were "classes of things or 'events' which combine individual irregularity, or chaos, with aggregate regularity, or order, in the long run" (Verburgt 254). Probabilistic statements for Venn thus accepted ignorance about individual instances; his approach implicitly recognized the complexity of the individual (person and event) as well as the heterogeneity of circumstance. Venn's theorization of probability carved out the epistemological space for individual free will that was potentially threatened by Buckle's form of statistical determinism. In the process, it formalized a new understanding of probability that had been gradually emerging in the preceding decades in response to these developments in statistics. Whereas previous theorizations of probability—from Laplace through to De Morgan and Quetelet—"assumed a fixed, pre-existent probability regulating individual trials" (Porter, *Rise* 175), Venn rejected the view that statistical data "revealed the constant causes behind surface variability" (Kılıç 560). He believed that while probability theory made use of mathematics in its operations, it should be regarded as a branch of material logic (Verburgt 266). He acknowledged the irreducible subjectivity involved in the assignation of classes and formation of series, but he also invoked a process of idealization that allowed past experience to become the ground for inferences about the future. His theory maintained the rigorous distinction between "natural" series (fixed types of classes of events in the order of things) and "artificial" series (the inductive process of *creating* classes or types for the purpose of probabilistic inference). However, he also asserted the validity of "substituting" them within the domain of logic—in other words, probability theory proceeds as if artificial series behaved in the same manner as natural series.[8] Venn's theory thus acknowledged the provisional nature of probability statements and the potential for change or irregularity over the long run. As Daniel Williams puts it, Venn's frequentist approach "commits us to a view of probability—and the inferences it affords—as an experiential, material, and mutable domain" (23).

I will address the potential significance of Venn's theories for our reading of Diggory Venn below. Here, though, I want to consider, first, how the philosophical foundations of Venn's understanding of probability register the influence of Darwinian theory and, second, the consequences of this influence for understandings of historical development. Berna Eden Kılıç has shown how Venn's unpublished *Autobiography* reveals the influence of Darwin's *On the Origin of Species* on his approach to probability.[9] Venn read Darwin in 1860, and the ideas he encountered there (and in similar material) produced doubts that eventually prompted him to resign his position within the Church of England in 1862. The 1866 version of *The Logic of Chance* (a work Venn first conceived in 1858) does not explicitly reflect the influence of Darwinian thought, but in the 1876 second edition Venn invokes evolution to dismiss the idea that nature provides immutable types: "No one who gives the slightest adhesion to the Doctrine of Evolution could regard the type, in the qualified sense of the term, as possessing any real permanence and fixity" (Venn 42). Darwin's influence on the history and theory of probability can thus be seen in the altered philosophical status of the "type." Probability theory, both in its classical form and in some of its most ambitious statistical incarnations, had assumed the existence of invariable types. Quetelet's theorization of the "average man" rested upon the assumption that society was structured by an underlying ideal type (which was then expressed or articulated in a distributed pattern that took the shape of the normal curve). Venn, however, subscribed to a historicism that—taking on the insights of evolutionary theory—rejected the belief in such ideal or immutable types. To be clear, the insights of evolutionary theory did not liquidate the foundations of probabilistic or statistical inference. Rather, Venn simply acknowledged the historical and temporal dimension of inductive logic: The phenomena of the world were stable enough

---

8. See Verburgt.
9. The remainder of this paragraph draws heavily on Kılıç's work.

to permit the provisional assignation of individuals to classes or series for the purposes of probabilistic inferences, but the long run of trials may require that the boundaries of those classes or series be redrawn due to the ineluctable, if imperceptible, changes wrought by time.

The historicist dimension of Venn's approach to probability theory provides yet another example of the corrosive effect evolutionary theory had on totalizing systems of thought. It also reveals how "ecological contex[t]" (G. Levine, *Darwin* 112) attains a privileged position as a result of this epistemological disjunction between the individual instance and the iterable—and theoretically infinite—"long run" through which patterns are formed and laws expressed. In her influential account of the Darwinian tension between "plot" and "writing" in Hardy's works, Gillian Beer draws attention to the problems of scale that structure Hardy's thought and fiction. She argues that Hardy's profound commitment to the texture of experience is coupled with an awareness of the indifference of natural laws and that "the individual may be of small consequence in the long sequence of succession and generation" (*Darwin's* 239). The incommensurate nature of these different time scales is simply another way of expressing the "logic of chance" as it was understood within Darwinian theory and expressed in more formal terms by Venn. As George Levine has suggested, chance occupied a fraught position within Darwin's thinking. It was a "force" that Darwin recognized, although his science worked rigorously to "expel caprice from the universe by explaining even biological development in naturalistic terms of law and cause and effect" (*Darwin* 90). The problem here is an inflection of the debated status of "law" within statistical thinking in the period. As Levine notes, while Darwin and others such as T. H. Huxley and George Henry Lewes insisted that the work of random variation constituted a "law," the "nominalist" terms upon which they understood law was actually the "same as 'chance' in religious terms, for it implies no intention, no teleology, no meaning, and only order in an exclusively naturalistic sense" (90). In Levine's account, Darwin's concern with variation and abundance offered the realist novel a "world of 'mixed' conditions" in which imperfection and "perpetual change" are the universal condition (112). Darwinian interpretation is thus always "historical" because rather than describing teleological laws or timeless processes, it "describes particular alterations in form and function, developing from particular variations in relation to particular ecological contexts" (112).

The altered meaning of determinism within both statistical and evolutionary theory prompts us to see chance in Hardy's works not only as an aspect of a material world where laws are no longer the reflection of an immutable order but also as an invitation to consider the contingent dimensions of that world. Elsewhere,[10] I have argued that "relics" within Hardy's prose and poetry materialize the peculiar contours of this historical imagination. These physical remnants from the past—the skeletons from the Roman period that were unearthed in the building of Hardy's home Max Gate, the hair or writing of Phena that Hardy laments the absence of in "Thoughts of Phena," the D'Urberville spoon and seal that Tess's family retain—create striking juxtapositions that highlight the lingering presence and influence of the past but disclose its incongruity with the present. The structure of conjunction and disjunction that relics generate allow the past to be accessed (and recovered) in its otherness, but in the process foreground the dynamics of "chance and change" that shape human experience, often to tragic effect in Hardy's novels (*Poems* 84). Although scholars have identified the influence of the work of early anthropologists such as Sir Edward Tylor on Hardy's thinking in his use of terms like the "survival,"[11] the relic demonstrates that while Hardy was engaged with disciplines such as anthropology, history, and antiquarianism, his thinking also diverges from the philosophical foundations of these practices in its recognition of the fragmented shape of historical development. Darwin's influence is felt in Hardy's sense of the shape of history as "rather a stream than a tree" with "nothing organic in its shape, nothing systematic in its development" (F. Hardy 225). By revealing the "jerks" (T. Hardy, *Woodlanders* 279) of historical development, relics contribute to a historicism that aims to immerse readers in the "stream" of history by coupling the representation of the present's intransigency with an awareness of its contingency.

Such moments of juxtaposition within Hardy's narratives are usually the product of chance or coincidence, and they draw attention to salient features of the milieus he represents. Hardy's historicism participates in these debates about determinism by developing a narrative perspective that registers a disjunction between immediate causes and deterministic laws: It not only foregrounds local environmental causes of events that shape the contours of individual experience but also discloses the absence of an underlying logic or order to history. Chapter 2 argued that Scott's deployment of chance generates moments of juxtaposition that contribute to a "comparative historicism" that reflects the absence of "a single governing narrative, a master plot of history" (Griffiths 94). While Scott's historicism emerges in response to the recognition of such an absence, the moments of resonance that occur between distinct cultural and historical formations in his novels maintain the legibility of the historical record. Similarly, the realism of Dickens and Trollope registers a

---

10. See Grener, "Relics."
11. See Radford.

growing inability to reconcile the situated experience of the individual with a macroscopic view of the social body, yet the tension here is a matter of epistemology and representation. Dickens's craft relies upon the coherence and interconnectedness of individual lives within the social body, while Trollope's works take as given the trajectory of liberal progress. Hardy's novels, in contrast, offer a more radical claim about the potential impossibility of cognizing the shape of the "stream" of history.

II. PROBABILITY AND PERSPECTIVE IN *THE RETURN OF THE NATIVE*

The Return of the Native has perhaps the most intricately plotted causal structure of all of Hardy's novels, and critics have emphasized its heavy reliance on the mechanisms of chance and coincidence. Irving Howe, for instance, suggests that "readers untrained to a large allowance of probability in fiction are likely to be troubled" by its "repeate[d]" use of chance and coincidence (65). The novel does not just present an improbable plot but also thematizes probability, most explicitly in the famous game of dice between Wildeve and Diggory Venn at the midpoint of the novel. While the novel is notable for its distortions of probability, it is also characterized by its disorienting manipulations of narrative point of view. It focalizes events through a range of characters and even through hypothetical observers in a manner that undermines the possibility of a coherent or unified vision. Like probability, vision also becomes a central thematic concern of the novel, seen most directly through the eye troubles that beset Clym Yeobright, but present also in a range of motifs (e.g., Eustacia's telescope) that draw attention to the way in which individual perspectives are shaped by social position and spatial location. These two features of the novel's form—its improbable plot and its manipulations of perspective—work together to foreground the "concrete, material, social process[es]" that operate causally in the unfolding of the characters' lives (Widdowson 74). John Plotz has emphasized the "complementary" (123) relationship between character and environment in Hardy's works, arguing that his commitment to "perspectivalism" (127) challenges the logic of regionalism so often seen to be at the center of his novelistic project.[12] The diverse perspectives adopted in the novel—and Hardy's use of the free indirect mode—support Plotz's idea that "Hardy notices noticing, in all of its diverse forms'

---

12. There is considerable scholarship on vision and perception in Hardy's work, both novels and poetry. In addition to Plotz, see Berger; Bullen; and Paulin.

(123). However, the modulations in perspective also make visible "environmental" factors that characters themselves cannot perceive directly. Causality in the novel appears in a tenuous middle ground, beyond the intensely localized perception of individuals, but far below the level of generalization where the operations of "deterministic laws" become visible. The "strange conjunctions of circumstances" noted by the narrator of *A Pair of Blue Eyes* lead Hardy's characters to perceive causality operating either at the level of seeming chance or that of some fatalistic determinism. However, the narrative's modulations in perspective allow the "invisible means" of circumstance to become visible for readers, anchoring a historicism attuned to the interplay of these competing causal logics.

The early chapters of *The Return of the Native* exemplify the movement of narrative perspective between intensely embodied and inhumanly abstract positions. The novel's famous opening description of Egdon Heath—"A Face on which Time makes but little Impression"—quickly yields to the human drama that unfolds on the heath in the second chapter (9). The narration in the opening chapter lacks a clear perspectival position ("A Saturday afternoon in November was approaching the time of twilight"; "the heath wore the appearance of an instalment of night"; "the place became full of a watchful intentness now") (9–10). However, the narration in subsequent chapters persistently foregrounds the embodied and localized dimensions of perspective. The second chapter begins with Captain Drew's perception of Diggory and his van ahead of him on the road: "At length [Drew] discerned, a long distance in front of him, a moving spot, which appeared to be a vehicle" (13). That same chapter concludes with Diggory's distant view of a woman atop Blackbarrow. Diggory "watche[s] [Drew's] form as it diminished to a speck on the road"; then as he "looked at the barrow he became aware that its summit [. . .] was surmounted by something higher" (16–17). It is not just characters such as Drew and Venn that serve as focalizers, however, as the narrator frequently invokes a hypothetical or counterfactual perspective to provide particular interpretations of various tableaux and events. For instance, the image of Eustacia standing atop the barrow is viewed through the perspective of an "imaginative stranger," whose "first instinct" might have been "to suppose it the person of one of the Celts who built the barrow" (17). Similarly, as the third chapter shifts to a description of the Egdonites who have gathered upon the heath for their bonfire, the narrator describes these individuals by referring to an absent observer: "Had a looker-on been posted in the immediate vicinity of the barrow he would have learned that these persons were boys and men of the neighbouring hamlets" (18).

These frequent shifts in focalization have a peculiar, almost contradictory effect: They foreground the embodied, situated nature of perception while also abstracting the action from its immediate context. Hypothetical perspectives are accompanied by turns to the subjunctive that place the actors and action in a transhistorical perspective appropriate to the heath's seeming imperviousness to change. Just as the "imaginative stranger" is tempted to see Eustacia as one of those ancient Celts, the reader is invited to see the Egdonites and their bonfire through a dehistoricized, even mythic, lens: "It was as if the bonfire-makers were standing in some radiant upper storey of the world [. . .] It was as if these men and boys had suddenly dived into past ages and fetched therefrom an hour and deed which had before been familiar with this spot" (20). This characterization of the bonfires upon the heath as an act of "Promethean rebelliousness" draws on a register of universality or typification that is also used in the introduction of the novel's main characters—first Eustacia in the seventh chapter, then Clym at the outset of Book Third. Eustacia is described as the "raw material of divinity" with "Pagan eyes" (68); "in a dim light," we are told, "her general figure might have stood for that of either of the higher female deities" (69). Similarly, Clym is presented as the culmination of humankind's intellectual development. In his "face could be dimly seen the typical countenance of the future," as the "Hellenic idea of life" has been displaced by the increasing recognition of "the defects of natural laws, and [. . .] the quandary that man is in by their operation" (167).

While these acts of reframing might be read as Hardy's effort to suggest the epic quality of the lives led in Wessex, they also generate a feeling of dissonance and mismatch as they attempt to transcend the novel's specified milieu. In other words, these attempts at abstraction and typification can be seen as efforts to grasp an essential "character," but they fall short as character is revealed to be inextricable from its social "environment." To the "imaginative stranger," Eustacia appears "like an organic part" of the heath, as her image atop the barrow presents a "strangely homogenous" tableau of natural and social elements that "amounted only to unity" (17). But the subsequent action—beginning with her flight down the barrow at the approach of other members of the community—foregrounds the fundamentally social nature of the conflicts in the novel. The scene that we witness from a distance at the end of chapter 2 is picked up in chapter 6 from a nearer perspective, as Eustacia's bonfire draws Wildeve to her. Diggory Venn provides the clearest example of the mechanisms the novel utilizes to establish the entanglement of character and social environment. He is initially introduced through the lens of the anthropologist-cum-evolutionary biologist: "He was one of a class rapidly becoming extinct in Wessex, filling at present in the rural world the place which, during the last century, the dodo occupied in the world of animals" (13). His character is further developed as we learn how he is seen by the other members of the community—either as the mythic figure of the reddleman or as a man whose trade physically and socially alienates him from the genteel community. However, the presentation of the letter from Thomasin (in which she rejects his suit two years prior to the opening of the novel) reveals that, even before his turn to the reddle trade, class prejudice has shaped the community's perception of him. Thus, the characterization of the novel's main actors—Clym, Eustacia, Thomasin, Diggory, Wildeve, and Mrs. Yeobright[13]— occurs through the accumulation of various perspectives on them, and in particular through the tension between their place within the social world of the novel and the attempt to understand them through gestures of abstraction or typification. Hardy's historicism operates through this dynamic in which a plane of abstraction is conjured only to be negated or qualified by the particularities of circumstance.

The narrative discourse therefore dramatically reveals rather than explicitly names the determining power of circumstance on the characters through these modulations in perspective. The accumulation of these modulations asserts the absence of a unifying or totalizing point of view but nevertheless produce effects that accrue in meaningful ways. The juxtaposition of perspectival distances probes the extent to which characters might be abstracted from their environment or milieu. This demarcation of limits is furthered by the effects of free indirect discourse, a technique that reveals the horizon of characters' perception of their own social embeddedness. Critics have typically focused on the absence of the free indirect mode in Hardy's narrative prose, an absence particularly striking in relation to contemporaries like Trollope and Henry James. Charles Lock suggests that rather than a dialogical "discursive exchange between narrator and characters," Hardy's novels instead present us with narrators who are observers; Lock attributes this to Hardy's "obsession with seeing, with describing, with remaining on the outside" (25). In a long-overdue narratological account of the psychological dimensions of Hardy's novels, Suzanne Keen has also noted the general paucity of the free indirect mode in Hardy. According to Keen, Hardy's avoidance of the inner workings of characters' minds and stylistic preference for psycho-narration (or thought report) follow from his understanding of human psychology.

---

13. In a letter to Arthur Hopkins, who produced the illustrations for the novel as it was serialized in *Belgravia* from 1876 to 1878, Hardy lists the "order of importance" of the characters: "1 Clym Yeobright 2 Eustacia 3 Thomasin & the reddleman 4 Wildeve 5 Mrs Yeobright" (*Letters* 53).

These formal choices reflect his understanding of "individual nescience"—a state of not-knowing and "lack of awareness of their own motivations" (55). Keen sees "intermental thought" (shared or communal thinking) as central to Hardy's conception of sociality and suggests that psycho-narration embodies the "painful paradox" of individual consciousness. Characters fail to understand their own motives but are easily legible to members of their community. Thus, if free indirect discourse constitutes a "linguistic realisation [. . .] of the permeating of the border that separates inner from outer, speech from thought" (Lock 20), its negligible presence in Hardy's fiction seems to affirm the rigidity of that border and his narrator's distance from his characters.

Although the free indirect mode appears only sporadically in *The Return of the Native,* its presence at a number of critical junctures in the plot establishes a pattern that complicates these general accounts of Hardy's representation of consciousness. Rather than a stark division between (internal) nescience and (external) transparency, the novel offers more subtle gradations of insight. Characters demonstrate a keen awareness of their own motives and the complexities of social dynamics, yet the extent of their insight has significant limits. Take, for instance, this important passage at the close of Book First, as Eustacia learns that Thomasin might not desire Wildeve. The narration moves into the free indirect mode[14] following the description of Eustacia's "stupefied silence":

> *What curious feeling was this coming over her? Was it really possible that her interest in Wildeve had been so entirely the result of antagonism that the glory and the dream departed from the man with the first sound that he was no longer coveted by her rival?* She was, then, secure of him at last. Thomasin no longer required him. *What a humiliating victory! He loved her best,* she thought; *and yet—dared she to murmur such treacherous criticism ever so softly?—what was the man worth whom a woman inferior to herself does not value?* The sentiment which lurks more or less in all animate nature—that of not desiring the undesired of others—was lively as a passion in the supersubtle, epicurean heart of Eustacia. Her social superiority over him, which hitherto had scarcely ever impressed her, became unpleasantly insistent, and for the first time she felt that she had stooped in loving him. (101–2)

Eustacia here shows deep awareness of the triangulated nature of her desire for Wildeve, as well as the role class plays in her wavering desire ("what was

---

14. In the following quotations, I have italicized the segments of the text where free indirect report of characters' thoughts is present.

the man worth whom a woman inferior to herself does not value?"). The shift from the free indirect mode back into thought report performs the characteristic work of "divulg[ing] characters' states of mind through the better-informed observations of an authorial narrator *about* his characters" (Keen 56; original emphasis). But the interplay between the two modes marks the precise limits of Eustacia's discernment. Although she grasps the inherently social nature of her desire, she fails to see its broader implications—that the sentiment of "not desiring the undesired of others" permeates all of "animate nature," and Wildeve himself in particular.

It is important to remember, as Lock reminds us, that the concept of free indirect discourse was not articulated until the early decades of the twentieth century, so we should take care when considering an author's use of it—or avoidance of it, in the case of Hardy—as a matter of deliberate intent (Lock 24–25). Nevertheless, it produces consistent effects in Hardy's novel as it is deployed to explore the minds of the main characters. Contrasts between what characters can and cannot perceive are established through this combined use of the free indirect mode and thought report, cumulatively reinforcing their inability to transcend their social situation. Here are three such examples: The first describes Mrs. Yeobright's altered strategy to compel Wildeve to marry Thomasin after learning that Diggory has presented his own suit to her; the second depicts Wildeve's reaction to Eustacia's rejection of him; and the third relates Clym's reflections on the conflict between his relationship with his mother, his desire for Eustacia, and his ambition to open a school:

> [Mrs. Yeobright] knew enough of the male heart to see that with Wildeve, and indeed with the majority of men, the being able to state, at such a critical juncture, that another lover had eagerly bid for the hand that he was disposed to decline would immensely alter the situation. [. . .] Mrs. Yeobright accordingly resolved that her system of procedure should be changed. She had left home intent upon straightforwardness; she reached the inn determined to finesse. *To influence Wildeve by piquing him rather than by appealing to his generosity was obviously the wise course with such a man. She thanked God for the weapon which the reddleman had put into her hands.* (98)

> Wildeve was put upon his mettle by the situation. *To lose the two women— he who had been the well-beloved of both—was too ironical an issue to be endured. He could only decently save himself by Thomasin; and once he became her husband, Eustacia's repentance, he thought, would set in for a long*

and bitter term. It was no wonder that Wildeve, ignorant of the new man at the back of the scene, should have supposed Eustacia to be playing a part. To believe that the letter was not the result of some momentary pique, to infer that she really gave him up to Thomasin, would have required previous knowledge of her transfiguration by that man's influence. (153)

Along with that [recognition that Eustacia loved an idealized version of himself] came the widening breach between himself and his mother. Whenever any little occurrence had brought into more prominence than usual the disappointment that he was causing her it had sent him on lone and moody walks; or he was kept awake a great part of the night by the turmoil of spirit which such a recognition created. *If Mrs. Yeobright could only have been led to see what a sound and worthy purpose this purpose of his was, and how little it was being affected by his devotion to Eustacia, how differently she would regard him!* Thus as his sight grew accustomed to the first blinding halo kindled about him by love and beauty Yeobright began to perceive what a strait he was in. [. . .] Three antagonistic growths had to be kept alive: his mother's trust in him, his plan for becoming a teacher, and Eustacia's happiness. His fervid nature could not afford to relinquish one of these, though two of the three were as many as he could hope to preserve. (198–99)

If the relative infrequency of free indirect discourse in Hardy's works can be interpreted as the effort to maintain the rigid boundary between "inner and outer, speech and thought," then its appearance in *The Return* shifts that boundary. The free indirect mode makes boundaries of individual subjectivity permeable, but in the process it affirms the rigid boundaries of the social community and historical circumstance. In these moments, individuals demonstrate an uncharacteristic (at least for Hardy) awareness of their own psychological motivations and conflicts, but they cannot account for the motivations of others or grasp how the effects of their actions are determined by the interplay of intention and context. Following her encounter with Wildeve, for example, Mrs. Yeobright is unaware that "the greatest effect of her strategy on that day was, as often happens, in a quarter quite outside her view when arranging it," as she fails to grasp the nature of Wildeve's desire (that "piquing" him will send him back to Eustacia) (100). Likewise, Wildeve misinterprets Eustacia's romantic maneuvers, failing to consider the possibility of a new variable such as the arrival of Clym. And Clym himself cannot see the conditions that make the survival of his three "growths" mutually exclusive. Each character's attempt to rise above their situation and control (or manipulate) others works instead to foreground the degree to which they are entangled in a complex web of social determinants.

While these perspectival fluctuations demarcate the limitations of individual perception, the action of the novel itself is organized by spatial boundaries. The dynamic of return to and escape from the boundaries of the community is a central thematic concern in the novel. The plot of the novel, with its strong reliance on chance encounters, links the spatial and thematic dimensions of social embeddedness. This is particularly true in the case of Eustacia, who from the outset of the novel desires to escape Egdon. Whereas the free indirect mode manipulates the boundaries between inner and outer on the discursive level, chance and coincidence operate in the plot to juxtapose the dream of escape with the reality of social embeddedness. Even before Clym returns to Egdon, we are aware that Eustacia desires him primarily because he comes from the glamorous world of Paris and thus has the potential to transport her there. Their coincidental encounter on the night of his return home both heightens this desire and discloses its illusory foundations. Upon crossing paths with Clym and Mrs. Yeobright, Eustacia "could not, for a moment, believe that chance, unrequested, had brought into her presence the soul of the house she had gone to inspect" (116). While this moment enhances the mystery surrounding Clym, their incompatibility is ironically signaled through Clym's remark about "the friendliness and geniality written in the faces of the hills around." This tension is reinforced in Eustacia's dream that night: Although her dream was "amid the circumstances of [her] life [. . .] as wonderful as a dream could be," the heath nevertheless "dimly appeared behind the general brilliancy of the action" (118).

A later coincidence demonstrates how these discursive and structural elements of the narrative work in conjunction. To "battle against [the] depression" generated by Clym's eye troubles and his growing fondness for rustic life, Eustacia attends a dance in a nearby village, where she happens to meet Wildeve. The two dance, and dormant desires are awakened in Eustacia:

> How near she was to Wildeve! it was terrible to think of. She could feel his breathing, and he, of course, could feel hers. How badly she had treated him! yet, here they were treading one measure. The enchantment of the dance surprised her. A clear line of difference divided like a tangible fence her experience within this maze of motion from her experience without it. (256)

The free indirect mode and the encounter itself juxtapose two perspectives on Eustacia's experience, as readers are drawn into Eustacia's feeling of momentary escape from the social order that has thwarted her dreams. Yet while the dance was "an irresistible attack upon whatever sense of social order there was in their minds," the "clear line of difference" that "fence[s]" this moment off from her life in the community is "tangibl[y]" felt but nevertheless illusory (257).

This encounter displays the characteristic peculiarity of improbable moments in this and other Hardy novels: an "absurd contingency" of "accidental happenstance" (in Miller's words) that suggests a "disproof of it being a matter of chance at all" (in the words of Hardy's own narrator). Yet these moments foreground not "the defects of natural laws," but rather the powerful causal force exerted by the social "environment" that is the defining feature of Hardy's historicism. The causal sequence that leads to the novel's tragic denouement seems to be a string of "absurd contingenc[ies]": Mrs. Yeobright charges Christian Cantle to deliver fifty guineas each to Clym and Thomasin; Christian encounters Wildeve and loses all hundred in a game of dice; Diggory wins the hundred back but mistakenly delivers them all to Thomasin; Mrs. Yeobright perceives the mistake, but on the way to Clym and Eustacia's house she encounters Eustacia alone on the heath; the unfortunate timing and wording of her query offends Eustacia by implying she has maintained contact with Wildeve; Mrs. Yeobright attempts to amend the consequent rupture by visiting Clym and Eustacia at home, but she arrives when Wildeve himself is visiting (and Clym is asleep on the floor); Eustacia, hiding Wildeve, believes that Clym has answered the door; Mrs. Yeobright leaves and interprets Eustacia's face at the window as a sign of Clym's rejection, leading to her death on the heath; in the aftermath, Charley attempts to cheer Eustacia with a bonfire that unintentionally summons Wildeve; Eustacia plans an escape facilitated by Wildeve, but in the attempt realizes its futility, leading to her suicide and Wildeve's death in Shadwater Weir.

Yet the claim that the novel is simply a string of contingencies is true only at the level of abstraction that is plot summary. What operates throughout—what is moving the plot from one chance event to the next—are the characters' reactions to these events, responses that are thoroughly conditioned by their complex class identifications. The misunderstanding between Mrs. Yeobright and Eustacia on the heath, for instance, is in fact the expression of their respective class identities What might have been a seemingly straightforward question—"Did you receive the fifty guineas?"—becomes exceptionally complicated in the context of its asking. Mrs. Yeobright refers to it as a "gift from Thomasin's husband" (238), and in doing so elicits the shame and ire of Eustacia, triggering the conversation that results in their break. The dialogue between the two women generates a similar effect to the free indirect mode by providing the reader with multiple perspectives on the encounter. This structure of "perspectivalism" is also present in the climactic chapter that sees the group of characters converge on the "closed door" of Clym and Eustacia's cottage on the fateful day of Mrs. Yeobright's death. We look out the window with Eustacia, but we also see, with Mrs. Yeobright, Eustacia's face looking out. The "awkward conjuncture" becomes the occasion for the expression of the inherent tensions within the community as its genteel members attempt to control, change, or escape it.

The one glaring challenge to this account of causality in the novel is the iconic scene of gambling on the heath, where Wildeve wins the hundred guineas from Christian through an improbable run of luck in dice, only to immediately lose them to Diggory in a run equally unlucky (and improbable). Although the "game fluctuate[s]" in the initial throws between Wildeve and Christian, "the average was in Wildeve's favour" (224). As Christian's losses mount, both men are excited and enthralled by the game, an experience repeated though inverted in the sequel between Wildeve and Diggory where "Fortune [. . .] unmistakably fall[s] in love with the reddleman" (228). Gillian Beer has argued that scenes of gambling such as this, particularly in the late nineteenth-century novel, figure what she calls the "reader's wager"—the way that narratives mobilize the play between uncertainty and the teleological structure of novelistic plot. More specifically, Helen Small suggests that in this scene, Hardy is "making deliberate play with the logic of probability": Although the scene does not violate the laws of chance in a strict sense (since such runs of luck are logically possible), "the inevitable non-neutrality of plot puts the scene outside the reader's sense of what is probable" (80). However, if this surreal sequence foregrounds the "non-neutral" and conventional dimensions of novelistic plot, it also suggests the incommensurability of these competing "logics" of probability. For John Venn, remember, the "aggregate regularity" that forms the foundation for any science of probability emerges only in the very long run and through a process of "idealization" that allows complex events in the world to be treated as if they behaved in the controlled way that games of chance do. As the random single throw of the dice expands into a sequence that begins to form a series, the scene conjures the imaginary position of abstraction where order reappears and lawlike behavior might be observed. The conclusion of the game—which ends when the dice literally break in half—intimates that plot operates on a different order of causality. The dice do, of course, play a part in the dramatic "game" unfolding between the characters. The scene begins with Wildeve's "revengeful intention [. . .] to teach Mrs. Yeobright a lesson" (223). It ends with Diggory trying to restore events to their previous course, though in directing all hundred guineas to Thomasin he commits "an error which afterwards helped to cause more misfortune than treble the loss in money value could have done" (232). However, the causality governing the throws of the "magical machines" is inscrutable (221)—the absence of causality at this level directs attention toward the causality embodied by the characters who operate as agents in the scene.

Intentionally or coincidentally, then, Diggory and his name evoke the idealized position of observation at which the contingencies of circumstance disappear as probabilistic regularities begin to stabilize. Yet in evoking that idealized position of abstraction, Hardy's historicism asserts its irrelevance to the causal structures that are meaningful in shaping the action of the novel. Although Diggory himself might be seen to inhabit such a position in the world of the novel, his "isolated and weird character" reflects the incompatibility of such a position with the diegetic worlds of realist fiction (*Return* 427). Small, for instance, suggests that Diggory might be considered "a Vennian (that is, John Vennian) statistical observer," insofar as he is a detached and seemingly omnipresent figure through much of the action (79). However, as she concedes, this position is "specious": Even though Venn observes the actions of others (most notably Wildeve), he is, of course, one of the main actors and is "an instigator of plot" (80). Although Diggory perhaps maintains a privileged position of perception in relation to his fellow characters, the exposure of the limits of his knowledge reinforces the inability of characters to transcend the circumstances of their milieu. Indeed, in becoming a "ghost of [him] self" in the novel's final book—abandoning the reddle trade and marrying Thomasin—Diggory's character foregrounds the power of circumstance and dramatizes the impermeable barriers of the community.[15]

Whereas Scott's historicism works through the juxtaposition and comparison of different cultural formations, Hardy's historicism mobilizes the power of "disanalogy" that Devin Griffiths discusses in relation to George Eliot's work. Rather than bringing two "positive" contents together so that common structures harmonically reveal themselves, Hardy's novel attempts to grasp the contours of the lives on Egdon Heath through a range of perspectives and lenses, many of which reveal those contours in the failure of comparison. This occurs, as we have seen, on the discursive level, as the narrator invokes the hypothetical position of a neutral observer—an "imaginative stranger," a "looker-on," and so on—to offer interpretations that subsequent action

---

15. The infamous footnote Hardy appended to the 1912 edition of the novel confirms this internal logic of the narrative. Hardy claims that "the original conception of the story" was that Diggory was "to have retained his isolated and weird character to the last, and to have disappeared mysteriously from the heath, nobody knowing wither,' and that "certain circumstances of serial publication" led to the change The issue of the boundaries of Hardy's communities has been central to interpretations of his historicism. See Barrell; R. Williams, pp. 197–214.

reveals to be misguided in their presuppositions. This attempt to step outside of history and culture also becomes a thematic motif, as characters repeatedly attempt to rise above their milieu through imaginative acts of transcendence. On the night of his engagement to Eustacia, for example, Clym views a lunar eclipse from the heath and ponders an "escape from the chafing of social necessities" on the heath by imaginatively transporting himself to the moon "till he almost felt himself to be voyaging bodily through its wild scenes [. . .] mounting to the edges of its craters" (193). Likewise, as she rests on the heath while attempting to return home on the day of her death, Mrs. Yeobright looks down upon a colony of ants as if "observing a city street from the top of a tower" and ponders that social world's history: "She remembered that this bustle of ants had been in progress for years at the same spot—doubtless those of the old times where the ancestors of these which walked there now" (282). While she momentarily inhabits this privileged vantage, she is recalled to her own position through the flight of a heron, who is free of "all contact with the earthly ball to which she was pinioned." Even Clym's "curious microscopic" experience as a furze-cutter dramatizes this illusion of escape. Clym's identity dissolves into his immediate surroundings, as "creeping and winged things [. . .] seemed to enroll him in their band" (247). The nature of this experience is, of course, a result of his near-blindness, yet if it provides Clym with a form of escape, it is an escape predicated upon an impossible renunciation of the social: "His closest friend might have passed by without recognizing him," and when Eustacia approaches, Clym must confess, "'I did not see you'" (247–48).

The final presentation of the various characters demonstrates the cumulative effect of the novel's improbable aesthetic. The final image of the novel—that of Clym acting as an "itinerant open-air preacher" atop Blackbarrow—presents a complex irony through its invocation of Jesus and the Sermon on the Mount, as well as its doubling of the opening image of Eustacia atop the barrow (396). The narrative arc that culminates in Eustacia's exclusion from and Clym's tenuous reconciliation with the Egdon community tests the boundaries of the social, only to inscribe the primacy of historical circumstance. The rhetorical effect of this movement between perspectives is particularly important in the final presentation of Eustacia. The final paragraphs in which Eustacia appears alive solicit pity for her from two perspectives, that of a hypothetical observer and the dramatic soliloquy of Eustacia herself:

> Anyone who had stood by now would have pitied her, not so much on account of her exposure to weather and isolation from all of humanity except the mouldered remains inside the Barrow; but for that other form of misery which was denoted by the slightly rocking movement that her feel-

ings imparted to her person. Extreme unhappiness weighed visibly upon her. [. . .] When a woman in such a situation, neither old, deaf, crazed, nor whimsical, takes upon herself to sob and soliloquise aloud there is something grievous the matter.

"I can't go, I can't go!" she moaned. "No money: I can't go! And if I could, what comfort to me? I must drag on next year as I have dragged on this year, and the year after that as before. How I have tried and tried to be a splendid woman, and how destiny has been against me! . . . I do not deserve my lot! [. . .] O the cruelty of putting me into this imperfect, ill-conceived world! I was capable of much; but I have been injured and blighted and crushed by things beyond my control!" (346)

Although both voices tell us to pity Eustacia, our view of her is considerably more complicated than either perspective offers. The reader views Eustacia neither as a hypothetical "anyone" nor as she views herself. The two voices instead play off one another. Eustacia's soliloquy undermines the pity the narrator arouses for her, as her unqualified attribution of her problems to "things beyond my control" is at odds with our awareness that many things certainly have been within her control. In the same way that we know that Eustacia's suffering does not result from Susan Nunsuch's voodoo doll, we recognize that Eustacia's plight is not the product of intangible forces designed to torture her. Through discursive features such as the free indirect mode and "strange conjunctions of circumstance," the novel foregrounds the entanglement of character and social environment. The determining force of circumstance materializes through a range of perspectives that attempt to transcend it.

CODA

The Difference of Scale

IN MAKING A CASE for the importance of improbability to theories of realism, this book has shown that while realism might be defined as a set of conventions that reflect our idea of the real in the very act of producing it, nineteenth-century realism is also characterized by a skeptical strain that interrogates the givenness of the real. It is precisely through disrupting the seamless presentation of the everyday that realism both acknowledges structures of difference within the world and cultivates modes of cognition adequate to its contingency and historicity. If this book was motivated, in the first instance, by the desire to make sense of the realist novel's persistent engagement with ideas of probability and its fondness for the improbable, it became a project that required new ways of understanding novelistic representations of chance. Hardy's works once again offer a useful touchstone for making the stakes of this book clear. Critics from Hardy's own moment to the present have noted his flagrant use of chance and coincidence, yet the persistent tendency to read chance in Hardy as a response to the "residual providentialism" (Monk 157) of late nineteenth-century thought seems to miss something crucial—not only about how Hardy's novels work but also about chance more broadly. It is not, of course, that Hardy's use of chance does not reflect the impact of Darwinian and other late-Victorian intellectual currents. Nor is it that the representation of chance does not, in itself, entail philosophical beliefs or assumptions: Any invocation or deployment of chance carries with it a set of assumptions or propositions about the nature of causality that lead us eventually to questions of order, providential or otherwise. Rather, it is the inclination to read chance in explicitly ideological terms that proves unsatisfactory, since it oversimplifies the philosophical import of narrative form and overlooks the more complex dynamics of narrative representation. While the preceding chapters have joined work by scholars such as Paul Fyfe, Maurice Lee, and Michael Tondre to enrich our understanding of nineteenth-century literary engagements with chance, I want to end here by emphasizing why realism and its engagements with chance remain valuable tools for confronting the problem of scale.

Although the history of thinking about probability and chance follows an uneven trajectory, there are moments that demarcate definitive shifts in that history. Charles Sanders Peirce's 1892 essay "The Doctrine of Necessity Examined"—one of the first modern articulations of the idea of "absolute chance"—was made possible by the intellectual and institutional developments that accompanied the rise of statistics and resulted in the taming of chance over the course of the nineteenth century.[1] In conferring upon chance a purported ontological status, Peirce made explicit the opposition between chance and probability, two terms which only a century prior had largely functioned synonymously. Peirce's own views on probability grew out of the frequentist theory of John Venn which, as discussed in chapter 5, not only restricted probability statements to the "long run" of the series, but also incorporated an evolutionary awareness that the fundamental parameters of the material world are changeable. It is not just that we have moved beyond the assumption that the world behaves in a deterministic manner; even the idea that there are immutable natural laws comes under scrutiny. While the far-reaching philosophical and scientific implications of these ideas are beyond the scope of this book, the emergence of this idea of absolute chance transformed ideas about causality in ways that are difficult to unthink. Once the idea of absolute chance is entertained, in other words, thinking about causality seems to acquire an all-or-nothing character: Either the determinate causes of events can be identified, or those events seem to be without cause. This type of thinking appears particularly prevalent in discussions of narrative causality. Despite the fact that Peirce's cosmology of chance "effectively reversed the Aristotelian distinction between substance and accident" (Puskar 115), his notion of absolute chance seems to resonate with the Aristotelian account of narrative causality:

---

1. As Jason Puskar writes: "Peirce's claims for absolute chance mark an important turning point in the intellectual history of chance" (109). See Hacking, pp. 200–215, and Puskar, pp. 108–18.

Aristotle excluded chance from the well-ordered plot because it undermines narrative's capacity to produce knowledge of causal effects in human affairs. In working through nineteenth-century ideas of probability and chance, this book has emphasized the need to think about causality in distributive terms in order to recover the more nuanced attitudes toward causality that eventually make the notion of absolute chance possible. In doing so, it has shown how thinking about causality in terms of distributions enriches our understanding of how narrative causality works, particularly in realist novels: It is the absence of immediate, determinate cause that makes chance such a productive instrument for representing more diffuse causal networks. Approaching narrative causality on these terms also draws attention to—and helps us to reconcile— one of the more paradoxical aspects of the nineteenth-century novel: Its realism is at once defined by attention to the particular, the material, and the concrete, while at the same time it is characterized by a totalizing ambition. Chance, as the preceding chapters have argued, helps us to understand how writers negotiated the asymmetries of scale that define these divergent poles of realist representation.

The arc of this book has traced how the reckoning with chance over the course of the nineteenth century had a palpable effect on the form of the novel, gradually pulling these poles apart. If Austen and Scott incorporate the improbable into their realist aesthetic to acknowledge forms of difference, for the Victorian novelists examined in the second part of this book, the improbable becomes a means of grappling with the problem of scale. While coincidence provided Dickens with a means of grasping and mediating the divergent perspectives of the embedded individual and the social whole, for Trollope and Hardy chance points to the increasing difficulty of accommodating both views within novelistic representation. The perspectivalism that defines Hardy's realism is not just a distinctive facet of his novels; it signals the end of a commitment to scale that had characterized the realist mode developed and handed down by Scott. This dispersion of a totalizing vision into incommensurable perspectives has, for example, been identified by critics such as John Plotz as the "repudiation of the foundational metonymies that undergird the logic of cultural portability" that characterized the Victorian novel (124). Or, as Emily Steinlight has recently described it, the "subjectivism" that becomes a "programmatic" feature of modernism "dismiss[es] the very possibility of a coherent social world that plot can order or disorder" (210). Although Steinlight argues that the inward turn of the modernist novel retains a "sociopolitical content" (215) insofar as its "intensified psychologism" (212) becomes a "means of managing the human aggregate," it operates according to the logic of a group psychology that erases historical and cultural difference. Thus, as the increasing prominence of chance in twentieth-century narrative reflects a broader cultural confrontation with ideas of indeterminism, it also constitutes a movement away from a scale of representation that makes a particular type of historical imagination possible. The nineteenth-century novel's turn to the improbable, then, might be seen not only as a means of negotiating the incommensurate scales of the particular and the collective, but also as the enabling possibility of its historicist aspirations.

Although the totalizing impulse of realist scale was viewed with skepticism and suspicion by the critical regimes that held sway in the latter decades of the twentieth century,[2] scale has returned in recent years as a defining concept for a number of fields and methodologies within the humanities. I touched upon two of these areas in the introduction: first, in ecologically or environmentally oriented criticism attempting to come to terms with anthropogenic climate change, which Amitav Ghosh suggests occurs at a scale that seems to exceed the conventions of realist representation; and second, in digital methodologies that make use of computational and quantitative analysis to address developments in literary history at a scale not available to close reading. Although the fields of the environmental and digital humanities may appear to have divergent commitments or interests, Benjamin Morgan has suggested that these varying critical reflections upon and debates about scale find common ground in their invitation to "reflect anew on philosophical questions about how historical consciousness may oscillate among multiple, divergent scales of time" (44). As they expand the dimensions of the literary and historical imagination, these methodological developments aim to address questions and problems that emerge at scale, but in doing so threaten to lose sight of the individual. In the case of ecological thought, the scope of climate change—in its origins, effects, and even its very ontology—requires a response that exceeds the scale of individual action. Although thinking at the scale of the species or collective behavior might be necessary to address the crises that we have created, the political and social transformations that follow will need to be translated into the scale of individual experience as well. In the context of quantitative methods, debates continue to focus on how the insights gained from large-scale analysis might be brought into conversation with the predominant modes of interpretation that operate at the scale of the individual text.[3] If these develop-

---

2. See Shaw, *Narrating*, especially pp. 8–37, for a succinct overview of the ways realist totality has been viewed within competing theoretical paradigms.

3. As James English and Ted Underwood suggest in their introduction to a 2016 special issue of *Modern Language Quarterly* titled "Scale and Value: New and Digital Approaches to

ments mark a return to the kind of large-scale thinking that accompanied the rise of statistical thinking and the changes to probabilistic thought that form the backdrop of this book, they do so with a full recognition of the discontinuities of scale that trouble the ability to reconcile micro- and macroscopic perspectives.

In the end, what this book's account of realism offers these "crises of largeness"[4] facing literary studies and humanistic thought more broadly is a reminder that the modes of representation developed by the nineteenth-century novel remain viable tools for thinking through problems of scale. In arguing that realism as a mode remains defined by its historicist ambitions, I have shown how improbability supports two of the fundamental aspects of this representational project: the ability to grasp historical change or difference, and the capacity to accommodate complex causal relationships. It is these features of realism that highlight how the nineteenth-century novel and its techniques might help us to grapple with the problems—representational, imaginative, political—that exist at the scale of climate change. While Ghosh and other critics such as Ursula K. Heise have suggested that the conventions of science fiction might be better equipped to engage with the scale of climate change, it has been—and no doubt will continue to be—increasingly incorporated into the thought of contemporary literary fiction that remains in dialogue with the conventions of nineteenth-century realism. Not only does Richard Powers's 2018 novel *The Overstory* offer an illustration of the ways in which contemporary fiction is extending its scale of representation to address climate change; it also illustrates how narrative mechanisms of chance and coincidence continue to provide novelists with tools to situate the experience of the individual within much broader, even inhuman scales. The novel follows and interweaves the lives of its nine main characters from their childhoods, to their chance convergence in environmental protests of the early 1990s, and finally to the fallout of those actions into the present. As it does so, it imagines those lives not only amidst longer generations but also against arboreal and evolutionary time scales. Although the novel does not foreground or thematize chance in the same way as the novels in this study, it nevertheless uses these differential scales to draw attention to the historical dimensions of the political and social questions it aims to address—it historicizes ecologi-

---

Literary History," "Quantitative methods stand to contribute most to literary studies when they complement those older practices, filling in scales of description or kinds of interpretive insight that a selection of case studies might miss" (287).

4. English and Underwood borrow this phrase from Eric Hayot to describe the implications of quantitative methodologies on the disciplinary landscape (279).

cal consciousness. If *The Overstory*'s ecological content is engaged with the concerns and crises of the present day, its form nevertheless operates on the incommensurable scales that come to define nineteenth-century realist representation. In tracing these continuities between nineteenth-century realism and the present, we might not only identify the legacies and transformations of realist representation, but also discover modes of rethinking individuality and collectivity to help make possible futures that might seem, in the present, at best improbable.

WORKS CITED

Allison, Sarah. *Reductive Reading: A Syntax of Victorian Moralizing.* Johns Hopkins UP, 2018.

Arac, Jonathan. *Commissioned Spirits.* Rutgers UP, 1979.

Aravamudan, Srinivas. *Enlightenment Orientalism: Resisting the Rise of the Novel.* U of Chicago P, 2012.

Aristotle. *The Poetics.* Translated by Malcolm Heath, Penguin, 1996.

Asquith, Mark. "Hardy's Philosophy." *Thomas Hardy in Context,* edited by Phillip Mallett, Cambridge UP, 2013, pp. 285–95.

Austen, Jane. *Emma.* 1815. Edited by Fiona Stafford, Penguin, 2003.

———. *Jane Austen's Letters.* Edited by Deidre Le Faye, Oxford UP, 2011.

———. *Juvenilia.* Edited by Peter Sabor, Cambridge UP, 2006.

———. *Later Manuscripts.* Edited by Janet Todd and Linda Bree, Cambridge UP, 2008.

———. *Mansfield Park.* 1814. Edited by Kathryn Sutherland, Penguin, 2003.

———. *Northanger Abbey.* 1818. Edited by Marilyn Butler, Penguin, 2003.

———. *Persuasion.* 1818. Edited by Gillian Beer, Penguin, 2003

———. *Pride and Prejudice.* 1813. Edited by Vivian Jones, Penguin, 2003.

———. *Sense and Sensibility.* 1811. Edited by Ros Ballaster, Penguin, 2003.

Babb, Genie. "Victorian Roots and Branches: 'The Statistical Century' as Foundation to the Digital Humanities." *Literature Compass,* vol. 15, no. 9, 2018.

Baker, Geoffrey. *Realism's Empire: Empiricism and Enchantment in the Nineteenth-Century Novel.* The Ohio State UP, 2009.

Bakhtin, Mikhail. "The *Bildungsroman* and Its Significance in the History of Realism (Toward a Historical Typology of the Novel)." *Speech Genres and Other Late Essays*. Translated by Vern McGee, U of Texas P, 1987, pp. 10–59.

———. *The Dialogic Imagination*. Edited by Michael Holquist, U of Texas P, 2004.

Barrell, John. "Geographies of Hardy's Wessex." *Journal of Historical Geography*, vol. 8, no. 4, 1982, pp. 347–61.

Baucom, Ian. *Spectres of the Atlantic: Finance Capital, Slavery, and the Philosophy of History*. Duke UP, 2005.

Beer, Gillian. *Darwin's Plots: Evolutionary Narrative in Darwin, George Eliot and Nineteenth-Century Fiction*. Routledge & Kegan Paul, 1983.

———. "The Reader's Wager: Lots, Sorts, and Futures." *Essays in Criticism*, vol. 40, no. 2, 1990, pp. 99–123.

Berger, Sheila. *Thomas Hardy and Visual Structures: Framing, Disruption, Process*. New York UP, 1990.

Biederwell, Bruce. "Death and Disappearance in *The Bride of Lammermoor*." *Critical Essays on Sir Walter Scott*, edited by Harry E. Shaw, G. K. Hall & Co., 1996.

Björk, Lennart, ed. *The Literary Notebooks of Thomas Hardy: Volume 1*. Macmillan, 1985.

Booth, Wayne. *The Rhetoric of Fiction*. 1961. U of Chicago P, 1983.

Brown, David. *Walter Scott and the Historical Imagination*. Routledge & Kegan Paul, 1979.

Buckle, Henry. *History of Civilization in England*. 1857. 3 Volumes, Longmans, Green, and Co., 1885.

Bullen, J. B. *The Expressive Eye: Fiction and Perception in the Work of Thomas Hardy*. Oxford UP, 1986.

Butler, Marilyn. *Jane Austen and the War of Ideas*. Oxford UP, 1975.

Campe, Rüdiger. *The Game of Probability: Literature and Calculation from Pascal to Kleist*. 2002. Translated by Ellwood H. Wiggins Jr., Stanford UP, 2012.

Carroll, David. *George Eliot: The Critical Heritage*. Routledge & Kegan Paul, 1971.

Cavell, Stanley. *The Claim of Reason: Wittgenstein, Skepticism, Morality, and Tragedy*. 1979. Oxford UP, 1999.

Chandler, James. *England in 1819: The Politics of Literary Culture and the Case of Romantic Historicism*. U of Chicago P, 1998.

Choi, Tina Young. *Anonymous Connections: The Body and Narratives of the Social in Victorian Britain*. U of Michigan P, 2015.

Claybaugh, Amanda. *The Novel of Purpose: Literature and Social Reform in the Anglo-American World*. Cornell UP, 2007.

Cohen, I. B. *The Triumph of Numbers*. W. W. Norton & Company, 2005.

Coleridge, Samuel Taylor. *Coleridge's Miscellaneous Criticism*. Edited by Thomas Middleton Raysor, Harvard UP, 1936.

Culler, Jonathan. "Omniscience." *Narrative*, vol. 12, no. 1, 2004, pp. 22–34.

Currie, Mark. *The Unexpected: Narrative Temporality and the Philosophy of Surprise*. Edinburgh UP, 2013.

Dames, Nicholas. "Trollope and the Career: Vocational Trajectories and the Management of Ambition." *Victorian Studies*, vol. 45, no. 2, 2003, pp. 247–78.

Dannenberg, Hilary. *Coincidence and Counterfactuality: Plotting Time and Space in Narrative Fiction*. U of Nebraska P, 2008.

Daston, Lorraine. *Classical Probability in the Enlightenment*. Princeton UP, 1988.

Desrosières, Alain. "The Part in Relation to the Whole: How to Generalise? The Prehistory of Representative Sampling." *The Social Survey in Historical Perspective 1880–1940*, edited by Martin Bulmer et al., Cambridge UP, 1991 pp. 217–43.

———. *The Politics of Large Numbers: A History of Statistical Reasoning*. 1993. Translated by Camile Naish, Harvard UP, 1998.

Dessner, Lawrence. "Space Time, and Coincidence in Hardy." *Studies in the Novel*, vol. 24, no. 2, 1992, pp. 154–72.

Dickens, Charles. *Bleak House*. 1852–53 Edited by Nicola Bradbury, Penguin, 2003.

———. *David Copperfield*. 1849–50. Edited by Jeremy Tambling, Penguin, 1996.

———. *Dombey and Son*. 1846–48. Edited by Andrew Sanders, Penguin, 2002.

———. *Great Expectations*. 1860–61. Edited by Charlotte Mitchell, Penguin, 2003.

———. *Martin Chuzzlewit*. 1843–44. Edited by Patricia Ingham, Penguin, 1999.

———. *Nicholas Nickleby*. 1838–39. Edited by Michael Slater, Penguin, 1986.

———. *Our Mutual Friend*. 1864–65. Edited by Adrian Poole, Penguin, 1997.

Duncan, Ian. *Modern Romance and Transformations of the Novel: The Gothic, Scott, Dickens*. Cambridge UP, 1992.

———. *Scott's Shadow: The Novel in Romantic Edinburgh*. Princeton UP, 2007.

Eliot, George. *Daniel Deronda*. 1876. Edited by Terence Cave, Penguin, 1995.

———. *The Mill on the Floss*. 1860. Edited by Gordon S. Haight, Oxford UP, 2015.

Engels, Fredrich. *The Condition of the Working Class in England*. 1845. Edited by David McLellan, Oxford UP, 1999.

English, James F., and Ted Underwood. "Shifting Scales: Between Literature and Social Science" *Modern Language Quarterly*, vol. 77, no. 3, 2016, pp. 277–95.

Esty, Jed. *Unseasonable Youth: Modernism, Colonialism, and the Fiction of Development*. Oxford UP, 2012.

Faulkner, Laura. "'That's Convenient, Not to Say Odd': Coincidence, Causality, and Hardy's Inconsistent Inconsistency." *Victorian Review*, vol. 37, 2011, pp. 92–107.

Fergus, Jan. *Jane Austen and the Didactic Novel*. Macmillan, 1983.

Ferguson, Frances. "Jane Austen, *Emma*, and the Impact of Form." *Modern Language Quarterly*, vol. 61, no. 1, Mar. 2000, pp. 157–180.

Ferris, Ina. *The Achievement of Literary Authority: Gender, History, and the Waverley Novels*. Cornell UP, 1991.

Fielding, Henry. *The History of Tom Jones*. 1749. Edited by R. P. C. Mutter, Penguin, 1985.

Fisch, Max H. Introduction. *Writings of Charles S. Peirce*, Indiana UP, http://peirce.iupui.edu/edition.html#introductionvol1.

Fludernik, Monica. *Towards a 'Natural' Narratology*. Routledge & Kegan Paul, 1996.

Forster, E. M. *Aspects of the Novel*. 1927. Edward Arnold, 1949.

Forster, John. *The Life of Charles Dickens. Volume 1*. Scribner's, 1902.

Forsyth, Neil. "Wonderful Chains: Dickens and Coincidence." *Modern Philology*, vol. 83, no. 2, 1985, pp. 151–65.

Franklin, J. Jeffrey. *Serious Play: The Cultural Form of the Nineteenth-Century Realist Novel*. U of Pennsylvania P, 1999.

Franklin, James. *The Science of Conjecture*. Johns Hopkins UP, 2001.

Frede, Dorothea. "Necessity, Chance, and 'What Happens for the Most Part' in Aristotle's *Poetics*." *Essays on Aristotle's Poetics*, edited by Amélie Oksenberg Rorty, Princeton UP, 1992, pp. 197–220.

Freedgood, Elaine. *Victorian Writing about Risk: Imagining a Safe England in a Dangerous World*. Cambridge UP, 2000.

Freud, Sigmund. *The Uncanny*. 1919. Translated by David McLintock, Penguin, 2003.

Fyfe, Paul. *By Accident or Design: Writing the Victorian Metropolis*. Oxford UP, 2015.

Gallagher, Catherine. "The Rise of Fictionality." *The Novel*, edited by Franco Moretti, vol. 1, Princeton UP, 2006, pp. 336–63.

Galperin, William. *The Historical Austen*. U of Pennsylvania P, 2004.

Gamer, Michael. *Romanticism and the Gothic: Genre, Reception, and Canon Formation*. Cambridge UP, 2000.

Gaskell, Elizabeth. *Mary Barton*. 1848. Edited by Shirley Foster, Oxford UP, 2006.

Ghosh, Amitav. *The Great Derangement: Climate Change and the Unthinkable*. U of Chicago P, 2016.

Gibson, Anna. "*Our Mutual Friend* and Network Form." *Novel*, vol. 48, no. 1, 2015, pp. 63–84.

Gigerenzer, Gerd et al. *The Empire of Chance: How Probability Changed Science and Everyday Life*. Cambridge UP, 1989.

Gillies, Donald. *Philosophical Theories of Probability*. Routledge & Kegan Paul, 2000.

Gissing, George. *Charles Dickens: A Critical Study*. Blackie & Son, 1898.

Grener, Adam. "Hardy's Relics." *Modern Philology*, vol. 114, no. 1, 2016, pp. 106–29.

Griffiths, Devin. *The Age of Analogy: Science and Literature between the Darwins*. Johns Hopkins UP, 2016.

Grossman, Jonathan. *Charles Dickens's Networks: Public Transportation and the Novel*. Oxford UP, 2012.

Hacking, Ian. *The Emergence of Probability: A Philosophical Study of Early Ideas about Probability, Induction and Statistical Inference*. 1975. Cambridge UP, 2006.

———. *The Taming of Chance*. 1990. Cambridge UP, 2006.

———. "Was There a Probabilistic Revolution 1800–1930?" *The Probabilistic Revolution: Ideas in History*, edited by Lorenz Krüger et al., vol. 1, MIT P, 1987.

Hadley, Elaine. "Nobody, Somebody, and Everybody." *Victorian Studies*, vol. 59, no. 1, 2016, pp. 65–86.

Hald, Anders. *A History of Probability and Statistics and Their Application before 1750*. Wiley, 1990.

Halperin, John. "Trollope's *Phineas Finn* and History." *English Studies*, vol. 59, 1978, pp. 121–37.

Hamilton, Ross. *Accident: A Philosophical and Literary History*. U of Chicago P, 2007.

Hardy, Florence. *The Early Life of Thomas Hardy 1840–1891*. Macmillan, 1928.

Hardy, Thomas. *The Collected Letters of Thomas Hardy, Vol. 1 1840–1892*. Edited by Richard Little Purdy and Michael Millgate. Oxford UP, 1978.

———. *The Complete Poems of Thomas Hardy*. Edited by James Gibson, Macmillan London, 1976.

———. *Desperate Remedies*. 1871. Edited by Mary Rimmer, Penguin, 1998.

———. *A Pair of Blue Eyes*. 1873. Edited by Pamela Dalziel, Penguin, 2005.

———. *The Return of the Native*. 1878. Edited by Tony Slade, Penguin, 1999.

———. *Tess of the D'Urbervilles*. 1892. Edited by Tim Dolin, Penguin, 2003.

———. *The Woodlanders*. 1887. Edited by Dale Kramer, Oxford UP, 2005.

Hegel, G. W. F. *The Science of Logic*. Translated by A. V. Miller, Humanity Books, 1969.

Heise, Ursula K. "Science Fiction and the Time Scales of the Anthropocene." *ELH*, vol. 86, no 2, 2019, pp. 275–304.

Hensley, Nathan K. *Forms of Empire: The Poetics of Victorian Sovereignty*. Oxford UP, 2016.

Hoeveler, Diane. "Vindicating *Northanger Abbey*: Mary Wollstonecraft, Jane Austen, and Gothic Feminism." *Jane Austen and the Discourses of Feminism*, edited by Devoney Looser, St. Martin's, 1995, pp. 117–36.

Hornback, Bert. *The Metaphor of Chance: Vision and Technique in the Works of Thomas Hardy*. Ohio UP, 1971.

Howe, Irving. *Thomas Hardy*. Macmillan, 1967.

Hume, David. *A Treatise of Human Nature*. Edited by L. A. Selby-Bigge, Oxford UP, 1978.

Ireland, Ken. *Thomas Hardy, Time and Narrative: A Narratological Approach to His Novels*. Palgrave Macmillan, 2014.

Jaffe, Audrey. *The Affective Life of the Average Man: The Victorian Novel and the Stock Market Graph*. The Ohio State UP, 2010.

James, Henry. *Literary Criticism*, vol. 1, Library of America, 1984.

Jameson, Fredric. *The Antinomies of Realism*. Verso, 2013.

———. "Cognitive Mapping." *Marxism and the Interpretation of Culture*, edited by Cary Nelson and Lawrence Grossberg, U of Illinois P, 1988, pp. 347–57.

Jockers, Matthew. *Macroanalysis: Digital Methods and Literary History*. U of Illinois P, 2013.

Johnson, Claudia. *Jane Austen: Women, Politics, and the Novel*. U of Chicago P, 1988.

Jordan, Julia. *Chance and the Modern British Novel from Henry Green to Iris Murdoch*. Continuum, 2010.

Kareem, Sarah Tindal. *Eighteenth-Century Fiction and the Reinvention of Wonder*. Oxford UP, 2014.

Kavanagh, Thomas. *Enlightenment and the Shadows of Chance: The Novel and the Culture of Gambling in Eighteenth-Century France*. Johns Hopkins UP, 1993.

Keen, Suzanne. *Thomas Hardy's Brains: Psychology, Neurology, and Hardy's Imagination*. The Ohio State UP, 2014.

Kelly, Stuart. *Scott-Land: The Man Who Invented a Nation*. Polygon, 2010.

Kern, Stephen. *A Cultural History of Causality: Science, Murder Novels, and Systems of Thought*. Princeton UP, 2004.

Kerr, James. *Fiction against History: Scott as Storyteller*. Cambridge UP, 1989.

Kılıç, Berna Eden. "John Venn's Evolutionary Logic of Chance." *Studies in History and Philosophy of Science*, vol. 30, no. 4, 1999, pp. 559–85.

Kincaid, James. *The Novels of Anthony Trollope*. Oxford UP, 1977.

Klotz, Michael. "Manufacturing Fictional Individuals: Victorian Social Statistics, the Novel, and *Great Expectations*." *Novel*, vol. 46, no. 2, 2013, pp. 214–33.

Krüger, Lorenz et al., eds. *The Probabilistic Revolution: Ideas in History*, Volumes 1 and 2. The MIT Press, 1987.

Kruskal, William, and Frederick Mosteller. "Representative Sampling, IV: The History of the Concept in Statistics, 1895–1939." *International Statistical Review*, vol. 48, 1980, pp. 169–95.

Kukkonen, Karin. "Bayesian Narrative: Probability, Plot and the Shape of the Fictional World." *Anglia*, vol. 132, no. 4, 2014, pp. 720–39.

Laplace, Pierre Simon. *A Philosophical Essay on Probabilities*. 1814. Translated by Frederick Emory and Frederick Truscott, Wiley, 1902.

Lee, Maurice. *Uncertain Chances: Science, Skepticism, and Belief in Nineteenth-Century America Literature*. Oxford UP, 2012.

Levine, Caroline. "The Enormity Effect: Realist Fiction, Literary Studies, and the Refusal to Count." *Genre*, vol. 50, no. 1, 2017, pp. 59–76.

———. *Forms: Whole, Rhythm, Hierarchy, Network*. Princeton UP, 2015.

———. *The Serious Pleasures of Suspense: Victorian Realism and Narrative Doubt*. U of Virginia P, 2003.

Levine, George. *Darwin and the Novelists: Patterns of Science in Victorian Fiction*. Harvard UP, 1988.

———. "Exorcising the Past: Scott's *The Bride of Lammermoor*." *Nineteenth-Century Fiction*, vol. 32, no. 4, 1978, pp. 379–98.

Lewis, Sinclair. "Manhattan at Last!" 1925. *John Dos Passos: The Critical Heritage*, edited by Barry Maine. Routledge, Chapman & Hall, 1988.

Lincoln, Andrew. *Walter Scott and Modernity*. Edinburgh UP, 2007.

Lock, Charles. "Hardy and the Critics." *Palgrave Advances in Thomas Hardy Studies*, edited by Phillip Mallett, Palgrave Macmillan, 2004, pp. 14–37.

Lonergan, Patrick. "The Representation of Phineas Finn: Anthony Trollope's Palliser Series and Victorian Ireland." *Victorian Literature and Culture*, vol. 32, no. 1, 2004, 147–58.

Loveridge, Mark. "*Northanger Abbey*; Or, Nature and Probability." *Nineteenth-Century Literature*, vol. 46, no. 1, 1991, pp. 1–29.

Lukács, Georg. *Balzac und der Französische Realismus*. Aufbau-Verlag, 1952.

———. *The Historical Novel*. 1937. Translated by Hannah and Stanley Mitchell, Merlin, 1962.

———. *Realism in Our Time*. Translated by John Mander and Necke Mander, Harper & Row, 1964.

———. *Studies in European Realism*. 1950. Grosset & Dunlap, 1964.

———. *Writer and Critic and Other Essays*. Translated by Arthur Kahn, Merlin, 1970.

Lynch, Deidre. *The Economy of Character: Novels, Market Culture, and the Business of Inner Meaning*. U of Chicago P, 1998.

Marcus, Steven. *Dickens: From Pickwick to Dombey*. Chatto & Windus, 1965.

———. *Engels, Manchester, and the Working Class*. Random House, 1974.

Maxwell-Stuart, P. G. Introduction. *Letters on Demonology and Witchcraft*. Wordsworth Editions Ltd., 2001.

McKerrow, Raymie E. "Richard Whately and the Revival of Logic in Nineteenth-Century England." *Rhetorica*, vol. 5, no. 2, 1987, pp. 163–85.

McWeeny, Gage. *The Comfort of Strangers: Social Life and Literary Form*. Oxford UP, 2016.

Meadowsong, Zena. "Thomas Hardy and the Machine: The Mechanical Deformation of Narrative Realism in *Tess of the D'Urbervilles*." *Nineteenth-Century Literature*, vol. 64, no. 2, 2009, pp. 225–48.

Miller, Andrew. *The Burdens of Perfection: On Ethics and Reading in Nineteenth-Century British Literature*. Cornell UP, 2008.

Miller, Christopher. *Surprise: The Poetics of the Unexpected from Milton to Austen*. Cornell UP, 2015.

Miller, Elizabeth Carolyn. "Fixed Capital and the Flow: Water Power, Steam Power, and *The Mill on the Floss*." *Ecological Form: System and Aesthetics in the Age of Empire*, edited by Nathan K. Hensley and Philip Steer, Fordham UP, 2018, pp. 85–100.

Miller, J. Hillis. *Charles Dickens: The World of His Novels*. Harvard UP, 1958.

———. *Communities in Fiction*. Fordham UP, 2015.

Molesworth, Jesse. *Chance and the Eighteenth-Century Novel: Realism, Probability, Magic*. Cambridge UP, 2010.

Monk, Leland. *Standard Deviations: Chance and the Modern British Novel*. Stanford UP, 1993.

Monod, Sylvère. *Martin Chuzzlewit*. George Allen, 1985.

Moretti, Franco. *The Way of the World: The* Bildungsroman *in European Culture*. 1987. Verso, 2000.

Morgan, Benjamin. "Scale in Tess in Scale." *NOVEL: A Forum on Fiction*, vol. 52, no. 1, pp. 44–63.

Morris, William Edward. "Belief, Probability, Normativity." *The Blackwell Guide to Hume's Treatise*, edited by Saul Traiger, Blackwell, 2006, pp. 77–94.

Mouton, Michelle. "Should Phineas Finn Be Salaried? Payment for M.P.s, Coverture, and the Merits of Public Service." *Victorians Institute Journal*, vol. 34, 2006, pp. 145–73.

Newsom, Robert. *A Likely Story: Probability and Play in Fiction*. Rutgers UP, 1988.

Orwell, George. "Charles Dickens." *The Collected Essays, Journalism and Letters of George Orwell*, edited by Sonia Orwell and Ian Angus, vol. 1, Secker & Warburg, 1968, pp. 413–60.

Patey, Douglas Lane. *Probability and Literary Form: Philosophical Theory and Literary Practice in the Augustan Age*. Cambridge UP, 1984.

Paulin, Tom. *Thomas Hardy: The Poetry of Perception*. Macmillan, 1975.

Peirce, Charles Sanders. "The Doctrine of Necessity Examined." 1892. *Chance, Love, and Logic*, edited by Morris R. Cohen, Kegan Paul, 1923, pp. 179–201.

Phelan, James. "Authors, Resources, and Audiences: Toward a Rhetorical Poetics of Narrative." *Style*, vol. 1–2, 2018, pp. 1–34.

———. *Reading People, Reading Plots: Character, Progression, and the Interpretation of Narrative*. U of Chicago P, 1989.

Pinkard, Terry. "A Reply to David Duquette." *Essays on Hegel's Logic*, edited by George di Giovanni, State U of New York P, 1990, pp. 17–25.

Piper, Andrew. *Enumerations: Data and Literary Study*. U of Chicago P, 2018.

Plotz, John. *Portable Property: Victorian Culture on the Move.* Princeton UP, 2010.

Polhemus, Robert. *The Changing World of Anthony Trollope.* U of California P, 1977.

Poovey, Mary. *A History of the Modern Fact: Problems of Knowledge in the Sciences of Wealth and Society.* U of Chicago P, 1998.

———. *Making a Social Body: British Cultural Formation, 1830–1864.* U of Chicago P, 1995.

Porter, Theodore. *The Rise of Statistical Thinking 1820–1900.* Princeton UP, 1986.

———. *Trust in Numbers: The Pursuit of Objectivity in Science and Public Life.* Princeton UP, 1995.

Powers, Richard. *The Overstory.* Vintage, 2018.

Puskar, Jason. *Accident Society: Fiction, Collectivity, and the Production of Chance.* Stanford UP, 2012.

Rabinowitz, Peter. *Before Reading: Narrative Conventions and the Politics of Interpretation.* The Ohio State UP, 1987.

Radford, Andrew. *Thomas Hardy and the Survivals of Time.* Ashgate, 2003.

Reed, John R. *Victorian Conventions.* Ohio UP, 1975.

Richardson, Brian. *Unlikely Stories: Causality and the Nature of Modern Narrative.* U of Delaware P, 1997.

Ritzema, Robert, and Carole Young. "Causal Schema and the Attribution of Supernatural Causality." *Journal of Psychology and Theology,* vol. 11, no. 1, 1983, pp. 36–43.

Robertson, Fiona. *Legitimate Histories: Scott, Gothic, and the Authorities of Fiction.* Oxford UP, 1994.

Rohrbach, Emily. *Modernity's Mist: British Romanticism and the Poetics of Anticipation.* Fordham UP, 2016.

Rosenthal, Jesse. *Good Form: The Ethical Experience of the Victorian Novel.* Princeton UP, 2017.

Ryan, Marie-Laure. "Cheap Plot Trick, Plot Holes, and Narrative Design." *Narrative,* vol. 17, no. 1, 2009, pp. 56–75.

Scott, Sir Walter. *The Bride of Lammermoor.* 1819. Edited by J. H. Alexander, Penguin, 1995.

———. *Chronicles of the Canongate.* 1827. Edited by Claire Lamont, Penguin, 2003.

———. *The Fortunes of Nigel.* 1822. Edited by Frank Jordan, Edinburgh UP, 2004.

———. "Introduction to *The Castle of Otranto.*" 1811. *Horace Walpole: The Critical Heritage,* edited by Peter Sabor, Routledge & Kegan Paul, 1987, pp. 88–99.

———. *The Journal of Sir Walter Scott.* Vol. 1, David Douglas, 1890.

———. *Letters on Demonology and Witchcraft.* 1830. Cambridge UP, 2011.

———. *Redgauntlet.* 1824. Edited by G. A. M. Wood, Penguin, 2000.

———. "Review of *Emma.*" *The Quarterly Review,* vol. 14, no. 27, 1815–1816, pp. 188–201. *Emma.* Edited by Kristin Flieger Samuelian, Broadview Press, 2007, pp. 414–22.

———. *Scott's Complete Poetical Works.* Edited by Horace Scudder, Houghton Mifflin, 1900.

———. *Waverley.* 1814. Edited by Peter Garside, Penguin, 2011.

Shaw, Harry E. *The Forms of Historical Fiction: Sir Walter Scott and His Successors.* Cornell UP, 1983.

———. "Is There a Problem with Historical Fiction (or with Scott's *Redgauntlet*)?" *Rethinking History,* vol. 9, 2005, pp. 173–95.

———. *Narrating Reality: Austen, Scott, Eliot.* Cornell UP, 1999.

Slater, Michael. *Charles Dickens.* Yale UP, 2009.

Small, Helen. "Chances Are: Henry Buckle, Thomas Hardy, and the Individual at Risk." *Literature, Science, Psychoanalysis, 1830–1970: Essays in Honour of Gillian Beer,* edited by Helen Small and Trudi Tate, Oxford UP, 2003, pp. 64–85.

Snyder, Laura J. *Reforming Philosophy: A Victorian Debate on Science and Society.* U of Chicago P, 2006.

Steinlight, Emily. *Populating the Novel: Literary Form and Politics of Surplus Life.* Cornell UP, 2018.

Stewart, Garrett. "The Foreign Offices of British Fiction." *Modern Language Quarterly,* vol. 61, no. 1, 2000, pp. 181–206.

Stigler, Stephen. *The History of Statistics: The Measurement of Uncertainty before 1900.* Harvard UP, 1986.

Stone, Harry, ed. *Dickens' Working Notes for His Novels.* U of Chicago P, 1987.

Sutherland, John. "The Background to *Phineas Finn.*" *Phineas Finn,* Penguin, 1985, pp. 35–37.

———. Introduction. *Phineas Finn,* Penguin, 1985, pp. 7–34.

Tave, Stuart. *Some Words of Jane Austen.* U of Chicago P, 1973.

Todorov, Tzvetan. *The Fantastic: A Structural Approach to a Literary Genre.* Translated by Richard Howard, Cornell UP, 1975.

Tolstoy, Leo. *War and Peace.* 1869. Translated by Richard Pevear and Larissa Volokhonsky, Alfred A. Knopf, 2007.

Tomalin, Claire. *Thomas Hardy.* Penguin, 2007.

Tondre, Michael. *The Physics of Possibility: Victorian Fiction, Science, and Gender.* U of Virginia P, 2018.

Trollope, Anthony. *An Autobiography.* 1883. Penguin, 1993.

———. *Phineas Finn.* 1869. Edited by John Sutherland, Penguin, 1985.

———. *Phineas Redux.* 1874. Penguin, 1993.

———. *The Prime Minister.* 1876. Penguin, 1993.

———. *The Way We Live Now.* 1875. Edited by John Sutherland, Oxford UP, 1999.

Vargish, Thomas. *The Providential Aesthetic in Victorian Fiction.* U of Virginia P, 1985.

Venn, John. 1866. *The Logic of Chance.* Macmillan, 1876.

Verburgt, Lukas. "John Venn's Hypothetical Infinite Frequentism and Logic." *History and Philosophy of Logic,* vol. 35, no. 3, 2014, pp. 248–71.

Waldron, Mary. *Jane Austen and the Fiction of Her Time.* Cambridge UP, 1999.

Ward, Megan. "*The Woodlanders* and the Cultivation of Realism." *SEL,* vol. 41, no. 4, 2011, pp. 865–82.

Watt, Ian. *The Rise of the Novel.* 1957. U of California P, 2001.

Whately, Richard. *Elements of Logic.* 1826. J.W. Parker & Son, 1857.

———. "*Northanger Abbey* and *Persuasion.*" *Quarterly Review,* vol. 24, Jan. 1821. *Jane Austen: The Critical Heritage,* edited by B. C. Southam, vol. 1, Routledge & Kegan Paul, 1968, pp. 87–105.

Whetstone, Ann. "The Reform of the Scottish Sherrifdoms in the Early and Eighteenth Nineteenth Centuries." *Albion,* vol. 9, no. 1, 1977, pp. 61–71.

Wickman, Matthew. "Of Probability, Romance, and the Spatial Dimensions of Eighteenth-Century Narrative." *Eighteenth-Century Fiction,* vol. 15, no. 1, 2002, pp. 59–80.

Widdowson, Peter. *Hardy in History: A Study in Literary Sociology.* Routledge & Kegan Paul, 1989.

Williams, Daniel. "Slow Fire: Serial Thinking and Hardy's Genres of Induction." *Genre,* vol. 50, no. 1, 2017, pp. 19–38.

Williams, Ioan, ed. *Sir Walter Scott on Novelists and Fiction.* Routledge & Kegan Paul, 1968.

Williams, Raymond. *The Country and the City.* Chatto & Windus, 1973.

Wiltshire, John. *The Hidden Jane Austen.* Cambridge UP, 2014.

Witmore, Michael. *Culture of Accidents: Unexpected Knowledges in Early Modern England.* Stanford UP, 2001.

Woloch, Alex. *The One vs. the Many.* Princeton UP, 2003.

Woolf, Virginia. *The Essays of Virginia Woolf, Vol. 4: 1925–1928.* Edited by Andrew McNeillie, Hogarth, 1994.

Wordsworth, William. *The Prelude.* Edited by Jonathan Wordsworth et al., Norton, 1979.

Young, Kay. *Imagining Minds: The Neuro-Aesthetics of Austen, Eliot, and Hardy.* The Ohio State UP, 2010.

Zunshine, Lisa. "Why Jane Austen Was Different, and Why We Many Need Cognitive Science to See It." *Style,* vol. 41, no. 3, 2007, pp. 275–99.

INDEX

abstraction: computational methods and, 29; Dickens, coincidence, and, 117; finance-capital view of probability (18th-century) and, 6–7; frequentism and, 19; Hardy's *Return of the Native* and, 163–64, 170–71; Jaffe on "average" and, 20n15; probability and, 8; Trollope's *Phineas Finn* and, 127, 143; Victorian metropolis and, 8–9

"adventure time," 133–34

agency: Hardy and, 150–51; in Hardy's *The Woodlanders*, 150; liberal ideology and, 25; in Scott's *Redgauntlet*, 83; in Scott's "The Two Drovers," 78–80; statistical fatalism and, 156; in Trollope's *Phineas Finn*, 132, 145–46

aggregation and the aggregate: 18th-century finance capital view of probability, 6–8; chance as tension between individual variation and aggregate order, 18–19, 21, 25; distributive causality, 22–23; frequentist model and, 18–19; Gaskell and, 25; individual, tension with, 99; Lukács on Balzac and, 84, 87; probabilism, randomness, and, 13, 15, 18; social space and proximity in Dickens's *Martin Chuzzlewit*, 111–17 statistical "laws" and, 157; Trollope's *Phineas Finn* and, 126, 136, 142, 146; Venn and, 154, 157, 170. *See also* statistics; universality

aleatory aspect of probability. *See* objective (aleatory) aspect of probability

anonymity, in Dickens, 102–3, 108–12

Arac, Jonathan, 121

Aravamudan, Srinivas, 10n5

Aristotelian theory: absolute chance and, 176–77; on contingency, 50n5; fictionality, Aristotelian foundations of, 36–37 necessary, probable, and chance as modalities, 48–49; plot and probability in, 46–50; on probability, 5–6, 38–39; "what happens for the most part," 48–49

Aristotle, 36; *Poetics*, 4n1, 5–6, 26n20, 46–49, 49n4

associationist psychology, 17, 52, 131

Austen, Jane: Aristotelian theory, Whately's review, and, 46–50; probabilistic judgment, particularity, and, 42–43, 50–60, 63n14; on probability, 38, 43–44; "probable circumstance," production of, 41–42, 43, 51, 61; Romanticism and, 42 very minor characters and closure vs. contingency, 60–67

—works: *Emma*, 45, 46, 52–56, 63–65, 67; *Love and Freindship*, 44; *Mansfield Park*, 45, 66; "The Mystery," 43; *Persuasion*, 42–43, 62–63; "Plan of a Novel," 43; *Pride and Prejudice*, 56–58, 60n11; *Sense and Sensibility*, 45, 55–56, 66–67. *See also Northanger Abbey*

averages and averageness: frequentist model and, 17–18; *l'homme moyen* (average man), 18, 22, 158; Lukácsian type vs., 27; "representative" vs., 140; Trollope's *Phineas Finn* and, 126

Baker, Geoffrey, 135

· 191 ·

Bakhtin, Mikhail, 129, 133
Balzac, Honoré de, 87; *Comédie humaine*, 140n6; *Lost Illusions*, 84–85
Baucom, Ian, 6–7
Beer, Gillian, 152, 159, 170
bell curve, 22–23
Bernoulli, Jakob, 18n13
bildungsroman generic conventions, 128–29, 135–36, 144. See also *Phineas Finn* (Trollope)
Boole, George, 46
Booth, Wayne, 79
Brown, David, 92
Buckle, Henry, 153, 156–57
Bulwer-Lytton, Edward, 2, 6, 147
Burney, Frances, 44

Campe, Rüdiger, 50n5
capitalist space, 110, 112, 116
causality: absolute chance and, 176; Aristotelian theory, 21–22; Austen and, 64–67; causal schemas, 74n3, 82; classical interpretation of probability and, 16–17; Dickens's *Martin Chuzzlewit* and, 102; distributive, 22–23, 177; Hardy and, 151, 155–61; in Hardy's *Return of the Native*, 162, 168–73; Quetelet vs. Venn on, 131n4; Scott and casual ambiguity, 75–81, 87–89; supernatural, in Scott, 94–95; Trollope's *Phineas Finn* and, 132–33
Cavell, Stanley, 115n5
chance: absolute, idea of, 176–77; as Aristotelian modality, 48–49; Hardy and, 149–52, 168–73, 175; in Hardy's *Return of the Native*, 168–73; "ordinary run of chances," 69, 98–99; as property of the world, in frequentist model, 19–20; providence and, 14n10; realism and, 14, 21–23; as rhetorical strategy, 28; in Scott's *Redgauntlet*, 80–88; in Scott's "The Two Drovers," 76–81; "taming of," 13–14, 128, 136, 149, 176; as tension between individual variation and aggregate order, 18–19, 21, 25; Trollope and, 125–26; unstable meaning of, 14–15; Venn's *The Logic of Chance*, 131n4, 153–54, 157–59; Whately's "overbalance of chances," 48–49, 50. See also coincidence; *Phineas Finn* (Trollope)

Chandler, James, 83
Choi, Tina Young, 8, 20n15, 25
classical/Enlightenment interpretation of probability: about, 15–17; Austen and, 42, 55, 58–59; determinism and, 16–17, 155–56; orderliness assumption, 98; Scott and, 70–71, 81; universality and typicality assumptions, 70–71
Claybaugh, Amanda, 117
closure: Austen's very minor characters and contingency vs., 60–67; Trollope's *Phineas Finn*, *Phineas Redux*, and, 143–48
cognitive mapping, 110–11, 122
coincidence: in Hardy's *Return of the Native*, 168–73; narratives as built on scaffolding of, 9; providence and, 14n10; Scott and, 69–70, 77–81, 89, 95; as technology for realist representation, for Dickens, 121. See also chance; *Martin Chuzzlewit* (Dickens), coincidental encounters in
Coleridge, Samuel Taylor, 69, 72, 89
computational methods, 29–30
contingency: Aristotle on, 6, 36, 50n5; Austen and, 42–43; Austen's very minor characters and closure vs., 60–67; Campe on, 50n5; causal networks and, 24–25; Dickens and, 104, 111; frequentism and, 99, 154; Hardy and, 149–53, 159–60; in Hardy's *Return of the Native*, 169–73; in Lukács and Hegel, 87n9; the novel, scale, and, 20–28; order and, 7, 8; realism and, 3–4, 12, 36; in Scott's *Redgauntlet*, 81; in Scott's "The Two Drovers," 77–78; Trollope's *Phineas Finn*, contingent choice in, 127, 136, 138

Dames, Nicholas, 127–28
Dannenberg, Hilary, 9
Darwin, Charles, 158–60
Daston, Lorraine, 6, 15, 50
de Finetti, Bruno, 130
De Morgan, Augustus, 46
description vs. narration, 83–84
desire: in Austen, 51–54, 56–58; Molesworth on plotting and, 10–11
Desrosières, Alain, 19–20, 127, 138

determinism: after Darwin, 155–61; classical interpretation of probability and, 16–17, 155–56; Hardy and, 159–61; Todorov's "pandeterminism," 80

Dickens, Charles: coincidence, fondness for, 117; Engels, capitalist space, and, 109–10; on "general purpose and design," 104–5, 120; institutional statistics and, 113n4; Orwell on, 123–24; realist method of, 103; reformist impulse and development as novelist, 117–24; social structures, attention to, 105–6

—works: *Bleak House*, 105, 116–17; *David Copperfield*, 119n7; *Dombey and Son*, 110, 117–18, 122; early sketches, 104–5; *Great Expectations*, 113; *Nicholas Nickleby*, 109; *Oliver Twist*, 117; "Omnibus," 102; *Our Mutual Friend*, 105. See also *Martin Chuzzlewit*

didacticism: in Augustan literary theory, 53; Austen and, 45–48, 61–63, 67; Whately on, 47–48

difference: Austen and, 39, 56–57, 60, 153; cultural otherness, 31, 36, 70–71, 74, 76, 80; Hardy and, 168–69; probability and, 38–39; realism and, 4–5, 36, 39, 153; of scale, 175–80; Scott and, 39, 70, 81, 89, 153; Shaw on historicism and, 36. See also particularity

disanalogy, 154, 171

"Doctrine of Necessity Examined, The" (Peirce), 176–77

Dos Passos, John: *Manhattan Transfer*, 101

Duncan, Ian, 82, 93n11

Edgeworth, Maria, 47

Eliot, George: *Daniel Deronda*, 21, 26n20 128–29; *Middlemarch*, 21; *The Mill on the Floss*, 2–3, 6, 24–25, 26

Engels, Friedrich, 109

English, James, 178n3–79n4

Enlightenment probability. *See* classical/ Enlightenment interpretation of probability

enormity effect, 109

epistemological view of probability: Austen and, 44; classical interpretation of probability and, 17; Dickens and, 117; Scott and, 70–71; speculative epistemology and actuarial historicism, 7;

statistical view vs., 4–5, 5n3; Trollope's *Phineas Redux* and, 147; uncertainty and, 16; Venn and, 157, 159. *See also* subjective aspect of probability

estrangement, in Dickens's *Martin Chuzzlewit*, 106–13

Esty, Jed, 129, 133

evolutionary theory, 158–59

fantastic, the, 79–81, 93

Fergus, Jan, 61n12

Fermat, Pierre, 15–16

Ferris, Ina, 70n1, 85n7

fictionality: Aristotelian foundations of, 36–37; Austen and, 43–44; instability of category of, 11; market economy and, 5; speculative epistemology and, 7; willing suspension of disbelief and, 11

Fielding, Henry, 37; *Tom Jones*, 41n1, 48–50

finance capital, 6–7

Fludernik, Monika, 28n22

Forster, E. M., 23, 60–61, 152n3; *Aspects of the Novel*, 75

Forster, John, 103n1, 117

Foucault-Hacking hypothesis, 15n12

Franklin, J. Jeffrey, 22n16, 23, 137

Frede, Dorothea, 48–49, 49n4

free indirect discourse, 161–62, 164–68

Freedgood, Elaine, 8

frequentist model of probability, 17–20, 99, 153–54, 157–58, 176

Freud, Sigmund, 93

Fyfe, Paul, 8, 13–15, 14n10, 104, 151–53

Gallagher, Catherine, 7, 36, 43

Galperin, William, 44, 53

gambling, in Hardy's *Return of the Native*, 169–70

gambling, in Trollope's *Phineas Finn*. *See Phineas Finn*

Gamer, Michael, 74

games of chance: classical interpretation of probability and, 15–16; Trollope's *Phineas Finn* and, 130–32, 142. *See also* chance

Gaskell, Elizabeth: *Mary Barton*, 25

Gauss, Carl Friedrich, 22–23
Ghosh, Amitav, 1–2, 5, 9, 178–79
Gibson, Anna, 105
Gillies, Donald, 5n3
Gissing, George, 101
gothic: Austen's *Northanger Abbey*, gothic romance in, 58–59, 91–92; Scott's relationship to, 71–72, 74, 89, 91–92
Graunt, John, 18n13
Griffiths, Devin, 11, 70, 154, 171
Grossman, Jonathan, 105, 108

Hacking, Ian, 4–5, 4n2, 13, 15n12, 23, 140n6
Halperin, John, 133
Hardy, Thomas: causality and, 151, 155–61, 168–73; chance and, 149–52, 168–73, 175; contingency and "strange conjunctions of circumstances" in, 149–51, 162, 173; criticism on, 151–53, 155; determinism and, 149–50, 159–61; disjunction of scale and, 149; historicism and, 154–55, 160–61, 164, 169, 171–72; "invisible means," 150; perspectivalism of, 169–70, 177; relics and, 160; Woolf and Forster on, 152n3
—works: *Desperate Remedies*, 149; "Hap," 155; *A Pair of Blue Eyes*, 149, 162; *Tess of the D'Urbervilles*, 23–24; *The Woodlanders*, 150–51. See also *Return of the Native, The*
Hegel, Georg Wilhelm Friedrich, 27n21
Heise, Ursula K., 179
Hensley, Nathan K., 7
historicism: "actuarial," 7; Hardy and, 154–55, 160–61, 162, 169, 171–72; realism as historicist, 11–12; Scott's comparative historicism, 70–73, 88, 91–92, 154; Shaw on, 23, 36; Venn and, 159
Hoeveler, Diane, 59n10
homme éclairé, l' (reasonable man), 17, 37, 59, 88
homme moyen, l' (average man), 18, 22, 158
Hornback, Bert, 152
Howe, Irving, 161
Hume, David, 51
Huxley, T. H., 159

improbability: Dickens and, 103–6; fictionality and, 11; Ghosh on, 1; Hardy and, 152–53; illusion of repetitive everydayness and, 31; Molesworth on reenchantment and, 10–11; realism and, 4, 153, 175; Scott and, 69–70; Whately on, 48. See also specific authors and works
individual: the aggregate, tension with, 99; bildungsroman and, 129; chance as tension between individual variation and aggregate order, 18–19, 21, 25; in Hardy's *Return of the Native*, 167–68; selfishness and social estrangement in Dickens's *Martin Chuzzlewit*, 106–11, 112–13; social space, proximity, strangers, and neighbors in Dickens's *Martin Chuzzlewit*, 111–17; in Trollope's *Phineas Finn*, 125–29, 136–43, 145–46. See also particularity; scale
induction: Austen and, 43, 45, 51, 55, 59, 60, 63–65; Darwinian theory and, 158–59; Eliot and, 21, 128–29; Hardy and, 157; logic and reasoning, inductive, 7, 27n21, 46, 128–29, 158–59; Venn's "series" and, 158

Jaffe, Audrey, 20n15
James, Henry, 2, 9, 164
Jameson, Fredric, 28, 110
Johnson, Claudia, 46
Johnson, Samuel, 70–71

Kareem, Sarah Tindal, 10–11
Kavanagh, Thomas, 22n16
Kazin, Alfred, 87n9
Keen, Suzanne, 164–65
Kelly, Stuart, 75
Kern, Stephen, 14n10
Kerr, James, 82, 89, 93n11, 95n12
Kılıç, Berna Eden, 158
Kincaid, James, 144, 146
Kukkonen, Karin, 10n4

Laplace, Pierre-Simon, 15, 17, 18–19, 42, 155–56
Le Play, Frédéric, 140n6
Lee, Maurice, 13–14, 13n8
Leibniz, Gottfried Wilhelm, 16, 27n21

Levine, Caroline, 105, 109, 119–20
Levine, George, 22n16, 89, 95n12, 152, 159
Lewes, George Henry, 159
Lewis, Sinclair, 101, 107
Lincoln, Andrew, 83
Lock, Charles, 164
Logic of Chance, The (Venn), 131n4, 153–54, 157–59
Lonergan, Patrick, 142n7
Loveridge, Mark, 44n2
Lukács, Georg, 26–28, 82–87
Lynch, Deidre, 7

mapping, cognitive, 110–11, 122
Marcus, Steven, 109, 117
Martin Chuzzlewit (Dickens), coincidental encounters in: anonymity and 102–3, 108–12; cognitive mapping and, 110–11; criticism of, 101; Dickens's realist method and, 103–5; list of, 104n3; network form and, 105–6; reformist impulse and moral development in, 117–24; selfishness and social estrangement, 106–11, 112–13; social space, proximity, and language of strangers and neighbors, 111–17; urban milieu and, 103–4, 108–10, 113–14
mathematical concept of probability. *See* quantitative/mathematical concept of probability
Maturin, Charles: *Fatal Revenge*, 94
McWeeny, Gage, 8, 102–4, 108–9, 111
methodology and scale, 29–30
metonymy, limits of, 25
Mill, John Stuart, 46
Miller, Andrew, 115n5
Miller, Christopher, 44
Miller, J. Hillis, 106, 152
Molesworth, Jesse, 10–11, 109
Monk, Leland, 151
Monod, Sylvère, 115n5
Moretti, Franco, 135
Morgan, Benjamin, 178

"Narrate or Describe?" (Lukács), 83–84

network form, 105–6
Newman, John Henry, 155
Newsom, Robert, 10n4, 17n12
Northanger Abbey (Austen): Aristotle's poetics and, 46–47; Dickens's *Martin Chuzzlewit* compared to, 102; *Emma* and, 53; ending of, 41–43, 51, 58–64; Loveridge on nature vs. probability in, 44n2; probability as point of engagement in, 38

objective (aleatory) aspect of probability: Austen and, 51; classical interpretation of probability and, 17; Daston on, 50; frequentist model, 17–20, 99, 153–54, 157–58, 176; historical distinction with the subjective, 5; subjective vs., 4–5, 5n3, 9, 17, 50, 127, 131; Trollope's *Phineas Finn* and, 127, 130–31; Trollope's *Phineas Redux* and, 130
odds, discourse of, 130–33. *See also Phineas Finn* (Trollope)
order: Aristotle on, 21; chance as tension between individual variation and aggregate order, 18–19, 21, 25; contingency and, 7, 8; Darwin and, 159; Dickens and, 104, 117; distributive causality and, 22–23; frequentist model and, 18–19; Hardy and, 150, 154–55, 159–60, 168–69; normative quantitative model and, 98; Quetelet vs. Venn on, 131n4; Steinlight on subjectivism and, 177; Trollope and, 127, 136; Venn's frequentism and, 154, 157–58, 170
Orwell, George, 123–24
otherness: cultural, 31, 36, 70–71, 74, 76, 80; Hardy and, 160; historical, 31, 70, 74–75, 95; probability and, 11; Scott and, 74–76, 81–82, 88–89, 95

particularity: Austen and probabilistic knowledge vs., 42–43, 50–60; Austen's minor characters and, 63–64; Eliot's *The Mill on the Floss* and, 3; Jameson on, 28; probability ideal and, 8 realist representation and, 99; Victorian social body and departicularization, 7–8. *See also* difference; scale; universality; individual
Pascal, Blaise, 15–16

Patey, Douglas Lane, 4n1, 17n12, 36–37, 42, 53
Peirce, Charles Sanders, 15n11, 46, 176–77
perspectivalism, 169–70, 177
Phelan, James, 60n11
Phineas Finn (Trollope): adventurer and careerist plots, oscillation between, 133–36, 142; asynchrony in, 134; bildungsroman generic conventions and, 128–29; chance, reliance on, 125–26; disjunctions and problem of representativeness, 136–43; odds and gambling, discourse of, 130–33, 141–42; Phineas's development and tenuous closure of, 143–48; probability, conceptions of, 126–27; Victorian moral discourse against gambling and, 137–38
Pinkard, Terry, 27n21
Piper, Andrew, 29
plotting: in Aristotelian theory and Whately, 46–50; Austen and, 41–42, 45, 46–47, 60–63; Forster on character vs., 60–61; Trollope and, 133–36
Plotz, John, 100, 161–62, 177
Poisson, Siméon Denis, 18n13
Polhemus, Robert, 144
Poovey, Mary, 7, 18, 70–71
Porter, Theodore, 18, 157
Powers, Richard: *The Overstory*, 179–80
prejudice, 51–52
probabilism: Austen and particularity vs. probabilistic knowledge, 42–43, 50–60, 63n14; genre expectations and, 28n22; Ghosh and, 1–2; Hardy criticism and, 151–52; Newsom and, 10n4; prejudice and, 51–52; Trollope's *Phineas Finn* and, 125; Whately and, 46–47
probability: "chance" as term and, 14–15; internal, 6, 32, 36–37; Scott on, 72. *See also* epistemological view of probability; objective (aleatory) aspect of probability; quantitative/mathematical concept of probability; statistics; subjective aspect of probability
probability theory, history of: 18th-century finance capital aggregation model of, 6–8; Aristotelian understanding, 5–6, 38–39; Augustan, 53; classical interpretation, 15–17; emergence of modern concept (late 17th-century), 4–5; fictionality, Aristotelian foundations of,

36–37; frequentist model, 17–20, 99, 153–54, 157–58, 176; Venn, 131n4, 157–59. *See also* Aristotelian theory; classical/Enlightenment interpretation of probability
providence: Dickens and, 117; Hardy and, 151, 175; nature of causality and, 176; Scott and, 70; theological, 22n16; writers' belief in, 14n10
Puskar, Jason, 13, 28, 176n1

quantitative/mathematical concept of probability: Aristotelian probability and, 5–6, 36, 49n4, 50n5; Austen and, 51; classical interpretation and, 15–16; Coleridge and, 69; Dickens and, 102; frequentist model, 17–20, 99, 153–54, 157–58, 176; Ghosh on, 1–2, 5; Hacking on epistemic shift of, 15n12; Hardy and, 149–50; law of large numbers, 156; as normative model in relation to narrative evaluation, 98; Scott and, 80–81; signs and, 37; Whately and, 31, 45–50. *See also* statistics
Quetelet, Adolphe, 18, 22–23, 131n4, 140, 153, 156–57

Radcliffe, Ann, 72, 93–94
Ramsay, Frank, 130
randomness: abstract view vs., 136; chance and, 14–16; Darwin and, 159; frequentism and, 150; Fyfe on, 8; inherent in the world, in frequentist model, 19–20; order and, 21, 153–54; probabilism, the aggregate, and, 13, 15, 18; Trollope's *Phineas Finn* and, 126, 132, 136; Venn and, 170
rationalism, 31, 69–70, 73, 81
realism: believability and, 11; capacity to represent levels of reality, 26–28; chance and, 14, 21–23; "the everyday" discourse and, 2–3; as historicist, 11–12; improbability and, 4, 153, 175; mimetic definition of, 28n22; of Ruskin, 119–20; scaffolding and illusion of reality, 9; skeptical strain in, 11, 175. *See also* improbability; probability; probability theory, history of
Reed, John, 14n10
reenchantment, 10–11

representativeness, problem of, in Trollope's *Phineas Finn*, 138–44

Return of the Native, The (Hardy): chance, coincidence, contingency, and causality in, 168–73; character and environment in, 161–64, 168–69; free indirect discourse in, 161–62, 164–68; historicism and, 154, 162, 164, 169, 171–72; improbable plot of, 161; manipulation of narrative perspective in, 154, 161–64; Venn's frequentist theory and, 153–54; vision as theme in, 161

Richardson, Brian, 22n16

Richardson, Samuel, 37

Robertson, Fiona, 74, 92

Rohrbach, Emily, 42, 44, 62

Romanticism, 42, 44

Rosenthal, Jesse, 21, 128–29

Rümelin, Gustav, 157

Ruskin, John, 119–20

Ryan, Marie-Laure, 75

scaffolding, 2, 4, 9, 74n3

scale: climate change and, 1, 178–79; difference of, 175–80; Hardy and, 153, 159; methodology and, 29–30, 178–79; metonymy in Eliot's *Mill* and, 22–25; the novel, contingency, and, 20–28; representational challenges of, 98–99. See also aggregation and the aggregate; particularity; individual

Scott, Sir Walter: casual ambiguity and, 72–81, 87–89; chance and "dialectics of freedom and necessity," 81–88; Coleridge on, 69, 89; comparative historicism of, 70–73, 88, 91–92, 154; the fantastic and, 79–81, 93; gothic, relationship to, 71–72, 74, 89, 91–92; introduction to Walpole's *The Castle Otranto*, 71–72; Lukács narration vs. description and, 83–84; on probability, 38, 72; on Radcliffe, 72, 93–94; realism of, 74–75; reviews by, 46, 72, 94; supernatural, gothic mode and modern incredulity, 88–95; superstition and, 69–74, 80–81, 89–95

—works: *The Bride of Lammermoor*, 88–95; *Chronicles of the Canongate*, 76, 90; *The Fortunes of Nigel*, 75–76, 85; *The Lady of the Lake*, 38; *Letters on Demonology and Witchcraft*, 80–81, 89; *The Monastery*, 75; *Old Mortality*, 84; "On the Supernatural in Fictitious Composition," 72; *Redgauntlet*, 81–88, 91–92, 92n10; "The Two Drovers," 75–81, 87–88, 89; *Waverley*, 69–70, 72–74, 80

series, notion of, 154

Shaw, Harry E.: on Austen, 56; on historicism, 23, 36; on mediation, 25n18; on probability, 5; on realism, 11–12; on Scott, 75, 93, 93n11

Shelley, Mary: *Frankenstein*, 72

signs, 37, 52–54

Slater, Michael, 119n7

Small, Helen, 152–53, 155, 156, 170

social body, Victorian: in Dickens, 106; frequentist model and, 19–20; statistical view and, 7–8; in Trollope, 100, 140, 142, 145. See also aggregation and the aggregate

statistics: computational methods, 29–30; determinism and, 156; Dickens and institutional side of, 113n4; epistemological view vs., 4–5, 5n3; frequentist model, 17–20, 39, 153–54, 157–58, 176; individual and social levels and, 20; as laws, 156–57, 159; scholarship on literary responses to, 20–21; social body and, 7–8; Trollope's *Phineas Finn* and, 127, 141

Steinlight, Emily, 7, 21n15, 177–78

Stewart, Garrett, 110

strangers, 102, 111–17

subjective aspect of probability: Austen and, 51; classical interpretation of probability and, 17; frequentist model and, 19; historical distinction with the objective, 5; objective vs., 4–5, 5n3, 9, 17, 50, 127, 131; Ramsey, de Finetti, and, 130n3 Trollope's *Phineas Finn* and, 127. See also epistemological view of probability

supernatural, the. See Scott, Sir Walter

superstition, 69–74, 80–81, 89–95

Sutherland, John, 126, 134

Tave, Stuart, 43, 58

temporality: Austen's *Persuasion*, temporal shift in, 62; Bakhtin on the bildungsroman and, 129; chronotope in Dickens's *Martin Chuzzlewit*, 116; future anterior, 62n13; Hardy and, 100, 150, 153, 159; time scales, 178–79; Trollope's *Phineas*

Finn and, 100, 125–26, 127, 133–36, 140–41; Venn on inductive logic and, 158–59

Todorov, Tzvetan, 79–80, 93

Tolstoy, Leo: *Anna Karenina*, 83–84; *War and Peace*, 25, 143–44

Tondre, Michael, 13–14

Trollope, Anthony: political views of, 139

—works: *An Autobiography*, 127, 139, 142, 147; *Phineas Redux*, 127–28, 130, 147–48; *The Prime Minister*, 128; *The Way We Live Now*, 128. See also *Phineas Finn*

Tylor, Sir Edward, 160

typicality and typification: Aristotle and, 38–39; average statistical type, 20; Baucom's "actuarial historicism" and, 7; Darwin, evolutionary theory, and, 154, 158; Enlightenment and, 70–71; Hardy's *Return of the Native* and, 163–64; Lukács on, 26–27. See also averages and averageness

"Uncanny, The" (Freud), 93

uncertainty: Austen and, 45; in Austen's *Emma*, 54; in Austen's *Northanger Abbey*, 41; in Austen's *Persuasion*, 62–63; in Hardy's *Return of the Native*, 170; in history of probability theory, 6–7, 14–17, 27n21; of London, in Dickens's *Martin Chuzzlewit*, 111; in Trollope's *Phineas Finn*, 127, 130, 136–37, 146

Underwood, Ted, 178n3–179n4

universality: appeal to, 4, 38–39, 98; Aristotle and, 6, 47–48, 49n4; Darwin and, 159; Engels on, 109–10; Enlightenment and, 70–71; Hardy's *Return of the Native* and, 163; Jameson on, 28; probabilism and, 28; Whately and, 6, 49, 50–51. See also aggregation and the aggregate; particularity

Vargish, Thomas, 14n10

Venn, John, 170, 176; *The Logic of Chance*, 131n4, 153–54, 157–59

Waldron, Mary, 61–62

Walpole, Horace: *The Castle of Otranto*, 71–72

Ward, Megan, 151

Watt, Ian, 41–42

Whately, Richard, 6, 44–50

Wickman, Matthew, 44

Widdowson, Peter, 1, 152

Williams, Daniel, 152–53, 158

Williams, Raymond, 103, 111–12

Wiltshire, John, 63n14

Woloch, Alex, 60n11

Woolf, Virginia, 152n3

Wordsworth, William: *The Prelude*, 111–12

Young, Kay, 54n8

Zola, Émile: *Nana*, 83–84

www.ingramcontent.com/pod-product-compliance
Lightning Source LLC
Chambersburg PA
CBHW020737230426
43665CB00009B/460